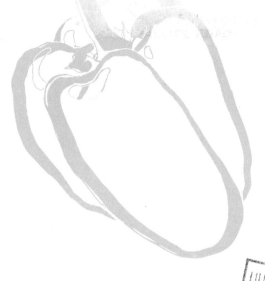

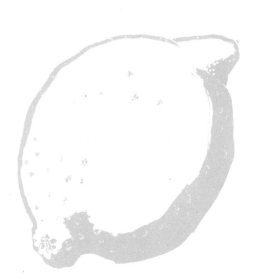

Marguerite Patten's

Century of British Cooking

Grub Street • London

Published by Grub Street
The Basement
10 Chivalry Road
London SW11 1HT

British Library Cataloguing in Publication Data

Patten, Marguerite
Marguerite Patten's Century of British Cooking
1. Cookery, British
I.Title II.Century of British cooking
641.5'941

ISBN 1902304144

Photography
Cover: Simon Smith
Food shots: Michelle Garrett

Illustrations by Bee Willey

Design by Adam Denchfield Design

The publishers wish to thank Wedgwood and Waterford Crystal for the
loan of china and glassware for photography. For information contact
Wedgwood & Sons Ltd, Barlaston, Stoke-on-Trent ST12 9ES, England.

Printed and bound in Italy by Vallardi

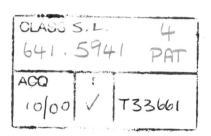

contents

1900 to 2000

Introduction

For many years I have been fascinated by the way food has changed in Britain and the fact that a large proportion of our population are happy to try the new ingredients that appear on sale in specialist shops and supermarkets. Often I have felt that the supermarkets of 1999 could be termed **'Aladdin's Caves'**, for they are full of treasures in the form of new and exciting ingredients as well as more familiar commodities.

In the past we had the reputation of being conservative in our choice of dishes and unwilling to alter our familiar routines. Undoubtedly that may have been true in the earlier part of this century but over the last decades that reputation has become completely out of date.

Think of the selection of restaurants you will find in the towns and cities of Britain. An appreciable number specialise in menus from different parts of the world and the public patronise them with great enthusiasm. Having tasted these previously unknown dishes in restaurants, keen cooks then become eager to acquire suitable recipes and make them in their own kitchens. Chefs and cooks from various countries and cultures have written authoritative books about the cuisines of their homelands and demonstrated their skills on television, so it is relatively easy to learn about foods and dishes from abroad. The popularity of foreign travel has enabled many of us to taste interesting new ingredients and cooked dishes in their own surroundings.

With the excitement of the year 2000 I felt it important to look back over the 20th century, study the events that have occurred throughout the years, and the effect they have had on our methods of selecting and cooking foods of all kinds. This is why each decade has a brief preface to sum up important changes in British life. It was difficult to make the final choice of dishes, there were so many that have made their appearance throughout the century. The recipes I have selected are those that 'hit the culinary headlines' at a particular period or are outstandingly good. Some dishes appeared suddenly and endured, others seem to have faded away. This is a pity for the best of them, like old friends, are worthy of our esteem. I hope I have given you a reminder that it is worthwhile making them once again.

We are fortunate in that our home-produced ingredients are of excellent quality, that is why many classic British dishes, made with these foods, remain favourites. The recipes given under the early decades prove this. There is no reason to forget them today, but rather to combine our own traditional fare with new ideas, that come to us from far-away places and so produce imaginative and superb meals.

I hope readers will take as much pleasure in using this book as I have in writing it. Good food and enjoyable meals play an important part in keeping us healthy.

At the end of the 19th century I have a feeling that, in many households, there could have been complaints that, while the cooking may have been good, the family dined on the same dishes week after week. In fact many people ate somewhat monotonous fare. This may have been because there was far less choice of ingredients in **1899**. Surely few people should make a complaint of monotony at the end of **1999**!

Acknowledgements

I would like to express my thanks to Anne Dolamore of Grub Street Publishing, who shares my enthusiasm for this project and has published the book. To Carole Fox who so carefully typed and checked the manuscript. To my grandson, Charles Henderson, who spent time researching events and cookery books of the First World War. To the Imperial War Museum who placed material concerning both the First and Second World Wars at my disposal.
I would like to record special thanks to my daughter Judith, granddaughter Joanna, son-in-law Michael, and indeed all my family, who have been so encouraging about my work.

Marguerite Patten

Following the recipes

The Ingredients

Spoon measures mean a level spoonful of the ingredient. In a few recipes the word level is added. This stresses that, in the particular recipe, extra care must be taken not to exceed the measure. The spoons used are the 5ml spoon for a teaspoon and the 15ml spoon for a tablespoon.

Weights and measures are given in metric followed by imperial. These give the accurate measure as compared to the imperial. Some metric weights may seem difficult to achieve, e.g. 115g is 4 oz. Many domestic scales are not as accurate as this, so all you need to do is to weigh out a generous 100 g.

In cases where you would measure out liquid in a measuring jug at home 150 ml is shown as $1/4$ pint and 300 ml as $1/2$ pint.

Where you would be purchasing a container of food, such as yoghurt, 150 ml is shown as 5 fl oz and 300 ml as 10 fl oz.

Nowadays canned foods are marked with metric measures only, so no imperial equivalent is given.

Oven Settings

Temperatures as shown in °C and °F with gas equivalent. Ovens vary slightly, so follow the instructions with the knowledge of your own cooker in mind.

All recipes have been tested in both gas and electric cookers.

Fan ovens and fan assisted ovens are now very popular. I have given the setting for these as 10°C lower than an ordinary electric oven. Check carefully with your manufacturer's manual and the knowledge of your cooker. In some cases you may find it necessary to lower the setting by 20°C not 10°C.

Cooking Times

These have been tested very carefully but check the food a few minutes early in case your oven is a little hotter than the average.

1900 to 1909

kitchen maids, cooks and servants

I have called this period the Victorian Era, for although Queen Victoria died in 1901, after reigning for 64 years, her influence on the way people lived endured for some time after her death. Her son, Edward VII, was a very different character and the way things altered under his rule is covered at the beginning of the next decade.

The war between the British and the Boers, which began in 1899, was causing great anxiety at home, for there was bitter fighting in South Africa and the British forces seemed overwhelmed at first. On February 28th 1900 there came better news, Ladysmith in Natal, which had been under siege for 118 days, was relieved by General Bullen and his forces. This victory was followed a little later by the relief of both Bloemfontein and Mafeking. The war, which caused many deaths and casualties on both sides, finally ended in 1902.

When motor vehicles first came on the roads in Britain they had to be preceded by a man walking with a red flag. In 1896 Parliament withdrew the act that had enforced this so, when the first motorbus was seen in London in 1904, it needed neither a man nor a flag.

In April 1907 Parliament withdrew the bill which was to facilitate the building of a railway tunnel under the English Channel.

In 1908 the Wright brothers stayed aloft in a plane for 2 hours and in the following year there was a flight across the English Channel by Louis Blériot.

Life in Britain from 1900 to 1909

There were enormous differences between the living standards of the rich and the poor. Many people had moved from the country into the towns and cities during the last century to find work in the various factories that opened during the Industrial Revolution. Sadly few of them found the riches they expected and they lived in slums. Those who remained in the country were poorly paid.

By 1900 a large middle class had emerged, for many men achieved executive positions in industry and in the professions. The richer middle classes lived in great luxury, hoping to achieve the style of the aristocracy. These families no longer dined at the old time of around 5 o'clock but later in the evening. Their dinners were elaborately served and had lengthy menus. The true aristocrats lived on their large country estates and in town mansions in great grandeur with an enormous staff of indoor and outdoor servants. In good households the servants enjoyed excellent conditions and in less good ones their lives were not particularly pleasant. **Mrs. Beeton's** advice from the last century on how to treat servants was still followed.

The children of the rich lived in the nursery and would be served their own special plain nursery meals.

To modern nutritionists the amount of food eaten in this era by those who could afford it was enormous. It must be remembered though that on the whole people were more energetic than they are today and they also needed more food to create warmth, for houses were so inadequately heated.

The Kitchens

Coal ranges were improving, the more modern ones had good ovens. The cook had to assess the heat in these or the gas and electric cookers of the time by feeling with her hands (this needed considerable experience) or shaking in a little flour, which reacted in the same way as the paper, described on page 13.

Some people still cooked over the top of the kitchen fire or range and took the foods they wanted baked to the local baker to be put in his oven.

Gas ovens were becoming more common, they were solid but not very attractive; the first electric cookers emerged - they looked much like the gas ones.

Ice boxes were in use in the homes of those who could afford to buy ice, delivered by the ice-man. There were simple refrigerators, described by the cookery expert of the time - Mrs. Marshall - as ice-caves. Ice cream makers, which were

turned by hand, were used a great deal by the wealthy and the ice creams often presented as ice puddings or made into elaborate shapes, such as turtle doves.

The pestle and mortar was in great use to pound foods and chefs would use a tammy cloth, in which they wrung out sauces to ensure a velvety smooth consistency.

The Foods of Britain

Excellent fresh fish, meat, poultry and game were available but often suffered from poor transport, so were far from fresh when on sale. The railways were making the transport of food better, for those who could afford to buy all the produce.

Many of the dishes served are still popular today, such as the roast joints and poultry, the chops and steaks.

A wonderful selection of vegetables were grown in **kitchen gardens**, including artichokes, asparagus, chard, seakale, and a wide range of root and green vegetables. Sadly these were almost invariably over-cooked, generally by boiling. The fact that some cooks had been trying to improve matters since the mid-1840's, but were discouraged, is illustrated by the words of Eliza Acton in her book of 1845. She stated:

'vegetables when not sufficiently cooked are known to be exceedingly unwholesome and indigestible, that the custom of serving them crisp, which means in reality, only half-boiled, should be altogether disregarded when health is considered more important than fashion'.

Parsley, thyme and sage were the most popular herbs.

In the glasshouses of the rich there were wonderful grapes, peaches and other exotic fruits. Orchards abounded with apples (Bramleys were well-known), cherries, pears, plums and quinces. Citrus fruits, such as imported oranges and lemons, were plentiful. Sadly the poor could not afford much fruit and could eat a selection of vegetables only if they were able to grow them.

Cooks made a vast selection of jams and other preserves, chutneys and pickles.
Vanilla Blancmange: Victorian blancmange was very different from those made with packets of flavoured cornflour throughout much of the 20th century. Milk was flavoured with a vanilla pod, sweetened and then set with gelatine and enriched with a generous amount of whipped cream. Often diced glacé fruits and blanched almonds were added. Other recipes thickened the milk with arrowroot or cornflour before cooking and adding the whipped cream.

Prepared Foods

There were ample supplies of tinned (now called canned) foods on sale.

Margarine was available and so was packet shredded suet.

There was a wide selection of commercial relishes, such as anchovy essence, Worcestershire sauce and catsups (ketchups).

Bird's custard powder came on the market in 1840.

Pie shops enabled people to buy ready-prepared meat pies.

Favourite Drinks

Port wine had long been enjoyed. Claret was the favourite wine of the period. Madeira also a popular fortified wine.

The after-dinner habit of ladies leaving the gentlemen to linger over their port wine for a prolonged period changed slightly as the time for serving dinner became later. It still was followed in many large households but for a less prolonged period.

The rich would serve well-chosen French wines at luncheon and dinner.

For the less sophisticated gin was considered to be the woman's drink and whisky the man's drink. Ale, stout and porter were favourites of the lower classes but ale was still drunk by many of all classes at breakfast.

Meals of 1900 to 1909

This gives an idea of the kind of foods the Victorians enjoyed. In many large households all the breakfast dishes would be arrayed over hotplates, heated with boiling water, so everyone could help themselves as they arrived into the room at different times.

Luncheon was sometimes a ladies' meal, for the men would be working or dine at their clubs or elsewhere.

Teatime was when the lady of the house would be 'At Home' and people would call, dressed in their elegant afternoon dresses and elaborate hats.

Dinner was a meal served with great ceremony; dishes were decorated and garnished very elaborately. Several courses might well be put on the table at one time.

Sometimes the gentlemen dined out in restaurants but at the beginning of the century ladies did not attend public functions only private dinner parties.

Breakfast

For those with money: porridge and a choice of egg dishes or bacon with kidneys, sausages, eggs or a cold joint or hot Kedgeree or Devilled Kidneys. Breads with preserves. Many people would eat several different main dishes.

NOTE: in farmhouse kitchens sides of home-cured bacon would be hanging and the required number of rashers sliced off just before cooking.

Tea or coffee or ale would be served.

For the poor: gruel (porridge made with barley or oats), bread and margarine; tea was the usual drink.

NOTE: quick cooking rolled oats became available towards the end of the 19th century. They were not yet widely used by the poor, for they were more expensive than ordinary oats; the rich had plenty of staff to stir oatmeal porridge.

Luncheon

For those with money: soup was rarely served at luncheon (it is reported that Queen Victoria never had soup at any meal).

Caviare or foie gras or melon	Ice cream or cold desserts
Asparagus, when in season	Seasonal fruits and/or pastries
Light meat, poultry or game dishes (probably some of each)	

For the poor: potatoes, little meat (if they could afford it); chicken (if they kept these); game (if they could catch it); home grown vegetables - not possible for town dwellers.

Teatime

For those with money: selection of tiny sandwiches; wafer-thin bread and butter; various preserves; selection of cakes. Tea to drink.

NOTE: one of the favourite cakes of the period was a Victoria Sandwich. Throughout the decades to modern times this was the light cake that good cooks strived to make to perfection. In America it is known as a Butter Sponge.

For the poor: a repetition of breakfast or if they had cooked some meat they might have bread and dripping. If they lived in the country and kept chickens a High Tea with eggs and/or bacon. Tea to drink.

Dinner

For those with money: hors d'oeuvre (similar to luncheon)

Soup	Ice Cream or other desserts
Fish dish	Savouries
Roast joint	Fresh fruits
Poultry and or Game	A selection of suitable French wines
Vegetable accompaniments	

Cookery Influences

Many homes used Mrs. Isabella Beeton's book *Household Management*, which included a vast number of recipes; it was originally published in 1861. This incredibly industrious lady died in 1865 at just 29 years but her book has been republished many times. Another important source of information was Mrs. Agnes Marshall, who not only wrote cookery books and articles but ran a successful cookery school in London. She also gave demonstrations in various towns in Britain. Mrs. Marshall died in 1905. Some people may have possessed a copy of Eliza Acton's excellent book *Modern Cookery for Private Families*, published originally in 1845 and sadly allowed to go out or print for 100 years. New editions were published in the 1960's.

In large households the cook would teach the junior kitchen staff and at home mothers instructed their daughters in the preparation of meals.

Auguste Escoffier, who had worked in luxury hotels on the continent, had already achieved fame before he came to England in 1890 to take charge of the kitchens at the Savoy Hotel, London. Later he was to create fabulous meals at the new Carlton Hotel. His recipes and advice continued for several decades and his cookery books were eagerly perused by chefs and good cooks.

Testing the Oven

The coal ranges, early gas and electric cookers had no regular settings, thermometers or thermostats. Experienced cooks would state they could 'feel' the temperature by putting their hand into the oven.

To obtain a greater heat more coal had to be added or the gas or electricity had to be turned up higher. Here is a way of testing the heat. Use fairly thick good quality writing paper, place on an oven shelf and close the door, then check the timing.

Heat required	Effect on paper	Modern settings
very low (very cool)	turns golden after 8 to 10 minutes	90 to 100°C/200 to 225°F/ Gas Mark 0 or S to ¼
low (cool) oven	turns golden in 5 minutes	140 to 150°C/275 to 300°F/ Gas Mark 1 to 2
very moderate	turns golden brown in 2 minutes	160°C/325°F/Gas Mark 3
moderate	turns golden brown in just under 1 minute	180 to 190°C/350 to 375°F/ Gas Mark 4 to 5
moderately hot	paper turns golden within seconds	190 to 200°C/375 to 400°F/ Gas Mark 5 to 6
hot	paper turns dark brown within seconds	200 to 220°C/400 to 425°F/ Gas Mark 6 to 7
very hot	paper scorches at once	220 to 230°C/425 to 450°F/ Gas Mark 7 to 8
ultra hot	do not put in paper, impossible to hold hand near oven when door is open, blast of heat so great.	230 to 240°C/450 to 475°F/ Gas Mark 8 to 9

1900 to 1909

The Recipes

Making Stock

When you see pictures of kitchens of the past often there might be a large stockpot on the coal range. This would be kept there and each day extra vegetables or bones added before reheating. This produced a stock full of flavour to enrich soups, sauces and main dishes. Obviously from a hygienic and health point of view the stockpot was a source of potential risk, allowing harmful bacteria to develop in the warmth of the kitchen. We should not however underestimate the value of first class home-made stock, it adds an excellent flavour to a variety of dishes.

Today stock can be stored in the refrigerator (even so it is wise to limit storage to a week and reheat it once or twice during that time). It can be frozen. In this case make sure all fat is removed for that causes it to deteriorate in flavour. Frozen stock should be used within 3 months.

To save freezer space boil the stock until very concentrated then pour into ice making trays. When cold freeze then pack the cubes into a container.

Today both stock cubes and prepared stock are sold and can be used in recipes. Generally these products are highly seasoned so be sparing with salt until you have tasted the dish.

Brown Stock: Beef bones and small pieces of beef give the strongest flavour and when a recipe states 'beef stock' these should be used. The bones of lamb or mutton could be substituted. Chop the bones and meat into small pieces. The colour of the stock will be darker if these are browned for a short time in the oven or in the base of a thick saucepan before adding liquid. Cover with water and simmer for at least 1 hour and preferably 2 to 3 hours. Mixed vegetables, herbs and seasoning can be added for extra flavour.

White Stock: Follow the method above but use the bones of veal, chicken or turkey with small pieces of white flesh.

Game Stock: Use the bones of venison or hare for a darker stock or pheasant and other game birds for a lighter coloured stock.

Bacon Stock: Use the bones from a bacon joint or liquid from boiling bacon.

Fish Stock: Use the bones and skin of white fish or shells of shellfish. The cooking time in this case should be about 30 minutes.

Consommé

This was the clear soup served at functions at the beginning of the century and still prized today. The soup is given interest by the variety of garnishes added. To be a perfect consommé the liquid must be well-cleared (clarified). Although meat or poultry is cooked in the liquid it intensifies the flavour if stock is used too. Peel, but do not chop, the vegetables if adding these for that could cloud the liquid. In his book *A Guide To Modern Cookery* Escoffier states that the flesh from an old animal has more flavour than that of younger ones. If you have the carcass of a chicken, add that to the beef for extra flavour.

SERVES 6

675 g/1½ lb shin or beef, diced
1.8 litres/3 pints beef stock as page 16
1 chicken carcass, chopped, optional
1 medium onion, optional
1 small carrot, optional
1 fresh bay leaf

salt and freshly ground black pepper
sherry to taste
TO CLARIFY:
1 or 2 egg whites with their shells,
  optional

Put all the ingredients, except the sherry, egg whites and shells into the saucepan. Bring the liquid to the boil, remove any scum, then cover the pan, lower the heat and simmer for 1 hour.

To clarify: strain through a very fine sieve or place several thicknesses of gauze over a sieve and pour the liquid through that. If not sufficiently clear return to the pan, without the sherry, add the unwhisked egg whites and their shells and simmer for 10 to 20 minutes. Any minute particles, that might have slipped through the sieve or gauze, cling to the whites and shells. Strain again, add the sherry and reheat.

Variations: use venison or mutton or veal instead of beef and the carcass of pheasant or other game birds or turkey. Adjust the flavour of stock used to complement the food.

Fish Consommé: use white fish instead of meat. Diced shellfish make a good garnish; the cleaned shells can be added to the liquid to colour and flavour the stock.

Garnishes for Consommé

Some of the simplest garnishes are from cooked young vegetables, either diced or cut into julienne (matchstick-shaped) strips. Croûtons of fried or toasted bread give a pleasing contrast in texture. A firm savoury egg custard, cut into tiny shapes, was a favourite of the Victorians. Cooked rice or pasta adds substance to the soup.

A modern touch: as it takes a long time to make consommé this can be prepared in a larger quantity and frozen. Use within 3 months. It is better to freeze the consommé without the sherry, this loses flavour in freezing.

Iced Consommé: lightly freeze the consommé, whisk with a fork, spoon into chilled soup cups and garnish with yoghurt, diced raw vegetables and chopped herbs.

Jellied Consommé: if the jelly does not set when cold dissolve 11 g/0.4 oz gelatine in each 1.2 litres/2 pints. If the consommé has set lightly use half the amount of gelatine. Pour into chilled soup cups. When set garnish with crème fraîche or soured cream, diced red and green peppers or sun-dried tomatoes.

Windsor Soup

The title of this soup suggests it was a favourite at Windsor Castle but I can find no record that confirms this. Over the years the word 'brown' has prefixed the name. Sadly this often describes a very indifferent dish. The true Windsor Soup, whether clear or thick and satisfying, is rich in flavour and very delicious. The bouquet garni suggested for this soup consists of parsley, thyme, rosemary and a bay leaf.

SERVES 4 TO 6

1 calf's foot	salt and freshly ground black pepper
225 g/8 oz stewing beef, diced	150 ml/¼ pint Madeira wine
few beef bones	TO GARNISH:
2.1 litres/3½ pints water	chopped parsley
bouquet garni	croûtons of diced fish, see method

Wash the calf's foot, put into the pan with the beef, bones, water, herbs and seasoning. Bring to boiling point then skim. Cover the pan and simmer gently for 2 to 2½ hours. Strain carefully. You should have approximately 1.5 litres/2½ pints of liquid. Reheat with the wine and any extra seasoning required. Garnish and serve.

A topping of diced lobster, crayfish or anchovy gives an unusual, pleasant flavour.

Iced Consommé (page 17)

Thick Windsor Soup

This, rather than the clear version, is the soup that is still known today. It is essential to retain the slightly sticky texture given by the calf's foot.

SERVES 4 TO 6

FOR THE STOCK:
1 calf's foot
few beef bones
2.1 litres/3½ pints water
bouquet garni
salt and freshly ground black pepper

FOR THE SOUP:
50 g/2 oz beef dripping or butter
1 large onion, chopped
225 g/8 oz stewing beef, diced
2 medium carrots
2 celery sticks, chopped
bouquet garni
150 ml/¼ pint Madeira wine

Put all the ingredients for the stock into a saucepan, simmer for 2 to 2½ hours then strain and measure out 1.5 litres/2½ pints.

Heat the dripping or butter, add the onion and beef and stir over a low heat for 10 minutes. Pour in the stock, bring to the boil then add the carrots, celery and extra herbs. Simmer for 2 hours, then sieve or liquidize. Return to the pan with the wine and reheat. Check the seasoning then garnish as the clear version (page 18).

Variations: it is the beef and vegetables that thicken the soup. If you like it even thicker use a little flour or cornflour or add 1 or 2 diced potatoes with the other vegetables.

Another way of adding body is to add 50 g/2 oz long grain rice when reheating the soup. Cook until the rice is tender.

Kedgeree

This was a favourite breakfast dish at the turn of the century. The word 'kedgeree' comes from the Indian 'Khichardi' or 'khicharhi' or 'Khichiri' (each of these words means a curried rice dish). Undoubtedly the original recipe was one of those brought back to Britain by people who worked in the East India Company. In the early recipes the dish was given a delicate curry flavour. Over the years this was supplanted by cayenne pepper. The following recipe does include curry flavouring. Although smoked haddock is generally chosen, other cooked fish can be used instead.

SERVES 4

115 g/4 oz long grain rice
salt
1 large smoked haddock or
    550 to 675 g/1¼ to 1½ lb
    smoked haddock fillet
pinch cayenne pepper, optional
2 eggs

50 g/2 oz butter
1 medium onion, thinly sliced then
    separated into rings
1 teaspoon curry powder,
    or amount required
3 to 4 tablespoons cream* or white sauce
* double or single

Put the rice into boiling salted water and cook until tender or follow directions on the packet. Strain well. Meanwhile poach the haddock in water flavoured with a shake of cayenne pepper. Do not over-cook the fish. When cooked remove all the skin and bones and break the fish into large flakes.

Hard-boil the eggs, shell and finely chop the whites and yolks separately.

Heat half the butter in a pan and cook the onion rings until golden brown. Put the remainder of the butter into a large saucepan, add the curry powder, then the rice, fish and cream or sauce. Stir gently over a moderate heat. When very hot add the egg whites. Spoon into a pyramid shape on a heated dish. Top with the egg yolks, which were traditionally made into the shape of a cross; add the fried onion rings.

Often a hot chutney was served with this dish.

A modern touch: the rice can be flavoured with chopped coriander during cooking.

Coriander with finely diced sun-dried tomatoes can be blended with the cooked rice and fish.

Finely grated lemon zest or chopped lemon grass or cooked peas can be mixed with the rice and fish.

Broiled Mackerel

This recipe comes form Eliza Acton's book published in the middle of the 19th century, and was still popular at the start of the 20th century. The term 'broiling' was used in those days for cooking over the fire - the equivalent of our grilling in modern days. We do not use the term much now but it crossed the Atlantic to America where it is still used today.

SERVES 4

4 small mackerel
cayenne pepper
salt

salad oil or butter, clarified
Maitre d'Hotel Butter as page 115

Wash and clean the mackerel, split and remove the intestines. Make long slits along each fish 1.25 cm/½ inch on either side of the backbone and insert a little cayenne, salt and oil or butter. (Eliza suggests doing this with a feather).

Eliza instructs the reader to 'lay over a moderate fire on a grid-iron which has been greased with suet' but today we will put the fish under a preheated grill and cook until tender. Top with pats of the Maitre d'Hotel Butter and serve.

Variation: the fish can be wrapped in foil and baked for about 25 minutes in a preheated oven, set to 190°C/375°F/ Gas Mark 5/ 170°C with a fan oven.

Asparagus

Delicious fresh asparagus was as popular with those who grew it, or could afford to buy the vegetable, as it is today. Beautiful finger bowls were an essential feature of Victorian table settings. Delicate blossoms would float on the water.

Cut away the very ends of the asparagus stalks and gently scrape the remaining lower part to remove the skin. Place into an asparagus basket with the delicate tips upright then lower into boiling salted water and cook steadily until tender. Lift out and serve hot with melted butter or Hollandaise Sauce (page 110).

A modern touch: use a large tin of water so the vegetable can be placed in a single layer. Cook as above. Many chefs of the 1990's bake asparagus in a little oil. Allow 10 to 15 minutes in a preheated oven set to 190°C/375°F/Gas Mark 5 or 180°C with a fan oven.

Devilled Kidneys (page 24)

Devilled Kidneys

While kidneys were sometimes served at dinner-time in modest households, they formed part of the extensive breakfast menu in large houses. They could be fried and served with bacon and mushrooms or as a devilled dish below.

In Victorian days it would in all probability have been mutton kidneys to produce an economical dish or a calf's kidney for greater luxury.

SERVES 4

8 to 12 lambs' kidneys or 6 mutton
   or 1 calf's kidney, skinned
pinch cayenne pepper
1 tablespoon chopped parsley
1 teaspoon chopped thyme
50 g/2 oz butter
4 shallots or 2 medium onions,
   finely chopped
1 level tablespoon plain flour
1 to 2 teaspoons curry powder

225 ml/7 $\frac{1}{2}$ fl oz chicken stock,
   see method
150 ml/$\frac{1}{4}$ pint Madeira wine
2 teaspoons lemon juice
2 to 3 teaspoons mushroom catsup or
   a savoury sauce eg. Worcestershire
salt and freshly ground black pepper
TO GARNISH:
toast

Halve lambs' but slice the larger kidney(s), remove any gristle or excess fat but leave a little to give flavour and keep the meat moist. Flavour the meat with a shake of cayenne and the herbs.

Heat the butter in a large frying pan, add the shallots or onions and cook gently for 5 minutes, add the kidney(s) and cook over a moderate heat for 5 minutes. Stir in the flour and curry powder then gradually add the stock. Use a little less than given with the lambs' kidneys as they cook more rapidly than the less tender ones. Add the wine and bring to the boil.

Lower the heat and simmer for 6 to 7 minutes for lambs' kidneys and 10 to 12 minutes for those of mutton or calf. The liquid should gradually evaporate, leaving a smooth coating around the kidneys. When tender add the lemon juice, catsup or sauce and any seasoning required. Spoon into a heated dish and serve with the toast, cut into narrow fingers (known as sippets).

Variation: substitute Worcestershire sauce for the mushroom catsup (nowadays known as ketchup).

Lamb Cutlets Reform

Mutton and lamb cutlets and chops, together with steaks of various kinds, including tournedos, were served frequently at the beginning of the century. This dish was a particular favourite. It was created by the famous chef, Alexis Soyer, who had been at the Reform Club in London in the 19th century and it has remained a classic throughout the years. Although mutton featured in the original recipe I have given lamb instead, for many people cooked this meat when in season.

SERVES 4

FOR THE SAUCE:
25 g/1 oz butter
1 tablespoon olive oil
2 small onions, finely chopped
115 g/4 oz mushrooms, thinly sliced
25 g/1 oz plain flour
300 ml/½ pint mutton or lamb stock
4 tablespoons sherry or port wine
    or Madeira
2 tablespoons finely diced cooked ham
3 tablespoons finely diced cooked
    tongue
1 hard-boiled egg white, finely chopped
1½ tablespoons redcurrant jelly
salt and freshly ground black pepper

8 lamb cutlets

FOR THE COATING:
25 g/1 oz butter, melted
1 tablespoon plain flour
85 g/3 oz soft breadcrumbs
1 tablespoon finely chopped
    cooked ham
1 tablespoon finely chopped
    cooked tongue
1 tablespoon finely chopped parsley
FOR FRYING:
50 g/2 oz butter

Prepare the sauce first so it is ready when the cutlets are cooked. Heat the butter and oil in a pan, add the onions and cook gently for 5 minutes then put in the mushrooms and cook for a further 3 minutes. Stir in the flour and then pour in the stock, bring to the boil and stir briskly until thickened. Add the rest of the sauce ingredients.

Trim the cutlets and brush with the melted butter. Season the flour, dust the cutlets with this. Mix all the other ingredients for the coating together, season lightly then press over the meat.

Heat the butter in a frying pan, add the cutlets and cook until tender. Serve with the sauce and mixed vegetables.

Stuffed Shoulder of Mutton

Roast joints of meat were one of the favourite meals during the Victorian period. Fine sheep were reared in various parts of Britain, so this recipe would be popular in both the town and country. While a variety of herbs were grown in kitchen gardens the range of flavours tended to be more restricted than those we have today. Chives, parsley, thyme and sage were the most used. Chefs and cooks who had plenty of assistance would prefer to bone the mutton themselves. For others it would be done by the butcher. The bones would be the basis for stock, with which to make the gravy.

SERVES UP TO 8

1 large shoulder of mutton, boned

FOR THE STUFFING:

225 g/8 oz lean de-rinded* bacon rashers chopped

3 tablespoons chopped parsley

2 tablespoons snipped chives

115 g/4 oz soft breadcrumbs

50 g/2 oz suet, finely chopped

2 eggs

salt and freshly ground black pepper

FOR ROASTING:

50 g/2 oz dripping

the rinds would be fried until very crisp, crumbled and saved as a garnish for soups

Preheat the oven to 180°C/350°F/Gas Mark 4/170°C with a fan oven. Open out the mutton to make a deep pocket for the stuffing. Cook the chopped bacon until crisp and mix with all the other stuffing ingredients. Insert the stuffing into the meat then tie with thin string to make a neat joint. Weigh the joint to ascertain the cooking time and place in the roasting tin. Spread the dripping over the joint.

Mutton is better roasted less rapidly so the setting above is ideal. Allow 35 minutes per 450 g/1 lb and 35 minutes over. Baste with hot fat from the roasting tin once or twice during cooking.

Serve with thickened gravy, redcurrant jelly, roast potatoes (page 27), creamed young turnips and Timbales of Spinach (page 27).

Variations: use boned leg of mutton instead of shoulder.

Use lamb instead of mutton and roast for 30 minutes per 450 g/1 lb and 30 minutes over at the setting given above. As lamb is young it can be roasted more rapidly. Preheat the oven to 200°C/400°F/Gas Mark 6/190°C with a fan oven. Allow 15 minutes per 450 g/1 lb and 15 minutes over for 'pink' lamb or 20 minutes per 450 g/1 lb and 20 minutes over for well cooked lamb.

Use veal instead of mutton and cook for the same time.

A modern touch: with today's desire to reduce fat intake do not add fat over the meat before cooking. The bacon could be omitted and replaced with 150 g/5 oz chopped uncooked tenderized apricots. Chopped coriander could be used instead of the parsley.

Accompaniments to Roast Stuffed Shoulder of Mutton

Timbales of Spinach

Wash approximately 900 g/2 lb young spinach, place in a saucepan with the water adhering to the leaves. Cook quickly for several minutes then season well. Cover the pan and cook until tender. Strain and press out any surplus liquid. Chop finely, blend with 50 g/2 oz melted butter, a shake of ground cinnamon and extra seasoning. Pack into small greased metal or ovenproof moulds and stand in a tin of hot water (a bain-marie). Place a cover over the tin. Heat in the oven with the mutton for about 10 minutes. Turn out and serve with the meat.

Creamed Young Turnips

Peel and slice turnips. Cook in salted water until just tender. Strain and mash with a little butter and cream. Season to taste. Top with chopped chervil or parsley.

Golden Roast Potatoes

Peel about 900 g/2 lb potatoes, halve large ones. Either roast around the mutton or heat 115 g/4 oz mutton or beef dripping in a meat tin. Dry the potatoes, they can be coated with a little seasoned flour but this is not essential. Turn them into the very hot dripping and cook for about 1 hour or until crisp and golden brown. Turn over several times during the cooking period.

Some Victorian recipes suggest serving the potatoes with cold butter.

A modern touch: if the potatoes are coated with a very little oil or melted fat before cooking they brown and crisp without the use of a high amount of fat.

Pulled Rabbit

The rather unusual title of this dish is because the rabbit was pulled into small pieces after cooking. Obviously it could be neatly diced if preferred. The vegetables and stock would be served as a soup while the chicken or rabbit formed the basis of a second dish or meal. Rabbits were plentiful so country people could make nutritious and satisfying meals from them.

SERVES 4 TO 6

2 to 4 bacon rashers
25 g/1 oz dripping or lard or butter
3 medium onions, neatly diced
900 ml/1 ½ pints water or chicken stock
4 medium carrots, neatly diced
1 medium turnip, neatly diced
1 small swede, neatly diced
2 leeks, thinly sliced
1 rabbit, jointed
salt and freshly ground black pepper
small bunch parsley

FOR THE HERB SAUCE:
50 g/2 oz butter
50 g/2 oz plain flour
1 to 2 teaspoons mustard powder
150 ml/¼ pint rabbit stock
450 ml/¾ pint milk
1 tablespoon chopped parsley
  or chervil
1 teaspoon chopped sage
1 tablespoon snipped chives

Remove the rind from the bacon, but leave the rashers whole. Put the bacon rinds with the fat into a saucepan and heat. Add the onions and cook gently for 5 minutes. Pour in the water or stock, bring to the boil then remove the bacon rinds and add the vegetables and rabbit together with a little seasoning and the bunch of parsley. Cover the pan and simmer gently for 1 hour, add the bacon rashers and continue cooking for a further 15 minutes, or until the rabbit is tender.

Lift the rabbit joints and bacon out of the liquid, measure out 150 ml/¼ pint of the stock for the sauce and discard the bunch of parsley. Reheat the vegetables and liquid, season well and serve as a soup.

Pull all the flesh from the rabbit bones, cut the bacon rashers into neat pieces.

Heat the butter in a saucepan, stir in the flour and mustard powder. Add the rabbit stock and milk, bring to the boil and cook until smooth and thickened. Stir in the rabbit pieces and bacon with most of the herbs. Heat gently, season well then top with the rest of the herbs. Mashed potatoes were served with this dish.

Variations: sieve the vegetables with the liquid to make a purée soup.

Vanilla Ice Cream

It may be surprising to learn that ice cream was already popular by the beginning of the 20th century. It was a favourite dessert in the homes of wealthier people, encouraged by the instructions given by Mrs. Agnes Marshall, who opened a London cookery school in 1883, and published two books on ices in 1885 and 1894. These books gave many recipes plus ideas for moulding the iced mixture into elaborate shapes for formal dinner parties. The prepared ice cream could be kept cold in an early type of refrigerator, which used ice as the refrigerant.

To make ice cream the ingredients were put into a container with ice and salt in the outer part of the appliance. By turning a handle the mixture was blended and aerated during the freezing process. The following is a typical recipe of the Victorian period.

SERVES 8

1 egg	450 ml/¾ pint milk
2 egg yolks	1 vanilla pod
85 g/3 oz caster sugar	450 ml/15 fl oz double cream

Beat the egg and egg yolks with the sugar. Warm the milk with the vanilla pod, pour over the egg mixture then transfer to the top of a double saucepan and cook over hot, but not boiling, water until thickened. Allow to become quite cold then remove the vanilla pod.

Whip the cream until it stands in soft peaks, blend with the cold custard. If placed in a container in a freezer this mixture is better frozen lightly, turned into a bowl and whisked briskly then returned to the freezer.

If using an ice cream maker there is no need to whip the cream as the mixture is aerated during freezing.

Variations: omit the custard; freeze vanilla-flavoured whipped cream.

Use the mixture as a basis for other flavours, such as chocolate, coffee and fruit. Do not exceed 450 ml/¾ pint thick purée to the quantities above.

Omit the vanilla and flavour the mixture with a liqueur such as apricot or cherry brandy or with Madeira or port wine.

A modern touch: split the vanilla pod and add the seeds.

Iced Pudding: freeze mixture lightly, spoon into a mould and freeze again.

Peach Melba

This dessert was created by Escoffier in the 1890's in honour of the great Australian soprano, Nellie Melba. At the time she was staying at the Savoy Hotel where Escoffier was in charge of the kitchens.

By the beginning of the 20th century it had become a favourite dessert in homes as well as in restaurants. It is a delicious dish if well-made. In the original recipe blanched and sliced fresh, not dried, almonds were sprinkled over the top of the raspberry purée.

SERVES 4

FOR THE RASPBERRY SAUCE:
150 ml/¼ pint water
25 to 50 g/1 to 2 oz caster sugar
few drops vanilla extract or
   a vanilla pod
225 to 300 g/8 to 10 oz raspberries

FOR THE DESSERT:
4 small or 2 large ripe peaches
4 servings of ice cream (page 29)
little whipped cream

Put the water, sugar and vanilla into a saucepan, stir until the sugar has dissolved then allow to boil briskly for 2 minutes. Place the raspberries in a bowl, add the hot syrup and leave until cold. Remove the vanilla pod. Sieve the mixture and chill well.

Lower the peaches into boiling water, leave for a few seconds then immediately put into cold water so they do not become too soft. Pull away the skin and halve the fruit.

Spoon or scoop the ice cream into serving dishes, top with the peach halves, the sauce and cream.

Variations: use the minimum of sugar in the sauce and add 2 tablespoons redcurrant jelly, stir until dissolved then pour over the raspberries.

Use half water and half sweet white wine in the sauce.

Flavour the sauce with a tablespoon of brandy or Curaçao.

A modern touch: although the dessert would be made in the same way the sauce would be termed a 'coulis'.

Defrosted frozen raspberries could be used, use the juice that slows instead of the same quantity of water in the sauce.

Making Jellies

The liking for jellies did not begin in the Victorian era but long before that. It is reported that Queen Elizabeth I was a great devotee of jellies. For some centuries gelatine was obtained by chefs and cooks boiling gelatinous substances, such as calf's foot, to obtain the setting liquids for both sweet and savoury jellies. Calf's foot is still used for making Calf's Foot Jelly or producing a gelatinous stock for aspics. Isinglass (derived from the air bladders of certain fish) or agar-agar and carragheen moss (both edible seaweeds, so suitable for vegetarians) are products that can be used instead of gelatine. Commercial gelatine is made from animal sources.

By 1900 commercial gelatine in the form of transparent leaves had become available. Many chefs and cooks prefer leaves to the more modern powdered gelatine, they consider leaves give greater clarity to a jelly. Use the same amount of leaf and powdered gelatine in recipes. Soaking gelatine in a small amount of cold liquid before adding to a hot mixture gives the best result.

The Victorians loved to serve large and unusual shaped jellies and many households had an impressive range of moulds. Many of these would be made of copper, lined inside with tin, so acid fruits would not affect the copper. As the tin lining had to be renewed from time to time a family crest might be on the moulds, to ensure the correct shapes were returned.

In order to speed the setting of jellies they would be placed in a container of ice. The ice was generally delivered by the ice-man.

Orange Jelly

This would be considered an ideal invalid or nursery dessert. In this case a small amount, such as given below, would be prepared. For a Victorian family meal where a large jelly was required the quantities would be increased but the proportions would be exactly the same.

SERVES 3 TO 4

2 oranges
450 ml/³/₄ pint water, see method
1 to 2 tablespoons sugar

11 g/0.4 oz leaf gelatine
approximately 200 ml/7 fl oz fresh
   orange juice

Wash the oranges then pare off the top zest, be careful not to use any bitter white pith. Put into the saucepan with all the water, except 3 tablespoons. Simmer gently for 10 minutes, strain and return the liquid to the saucepan with the sugar. Heat until the sugar has dissolved.

Soften the gelatine in the 3 tablespoons cold water, add to the hot liquid and stir until thoroughly dissolved. Measure this liquid, add sufficient orange juice to make 568 ml/ exactly 1 pint. Rinse one large, or several individual moulds, in cold water. Pour in the jelly and allow to set.

Variations: Orange Liqueur Jelly: for an adult jelly use less orange juice and add 2 tablespoons Curaçao instead.

Fruit Filled Jelly: to compensate for the weight of fruit use 15 g/¹/₂ oz gelatine in the recipe above. Pour enough of the liquid jelly into the mould, to give a 2.5 cm/ 1 inch layer; leave until set. Keep the rest of the jelly at room temperature. Add a layer of raspberries or other soft fruit, cover with more jelly. Continue like this, always ending with a layer of jelly.

Port Wine Jelly: heat the zest of 1 lemon in 450 ml/³/₄ pint water for 5 minutes. Strain, return the liquid to the pan with 50 g/2 oz sugar and 2 tablespoons redcurrant jelly. Stir over a low heat until the sugar and jelly have dissolved. Soften 11 g/0.4 oz of gelatine in 3 tablespoons cold port wine, stir into the hot liquid. When dissolved add sufficient port wine to give 568 ml/exactly 1 pint.

A modern touch: use the same weight of powdered gelatine. As the vitamin value of orange juice is greatly appreciated today use less water and more orange juice in the Orange Jelly. Use the orange juice without heating if possible.

Empress Rice

A milk pudding based on rice, sago, semolina or tapioca was usual nursery or family fare. For special occasions, such as luncheon or dinner parties, rice was given a more interesting flavour by the addition of eggs, sherry, jam and various fruits. The Victorians, who liked elaborately decorated food, probably arranged various prepared fruits around the edge of the dish in which the dessert was served.

SERVES 4 TO 6

40 g/1½ oz short grain (pudding) rice
750 ml/1¼ pints milk
50 g/2 oz caster sugar
1 vanilla pod or a few drops of
  vanilla extract
2 eggs
15 g/½ oz leaf gelatine
3 tablespoons sweet sherry
2 tablespoons sieved apricot jam
2 tablespoons chopped glacé cherries

1 tablespoon chopped angelica
2 tablespoons chopped preserved
  ginger, optional
150 ml/5 fl oz double cream
TO DECORATE:
little whipped cream
5 to 6 glacé cherries, halved
2 tablespoons thinly sliced
  preserved ginger
angelica leaves

Wash the rice and put into the top of a double saucepan with 450 ml/¾ pint of the milk, half the sugar and the vanilla. Cover and cook over boiling water until the rice is tender. Stir from time to time. Remove the vanilla pod. Beat the eggs with the rest of the sugar and the milk. Cook in the top of a double saucepan over simmering water until the custard is sufficiently thick to coat a wooden spoon. Blend the hot rice with the hot custard.

Soften the gelatine in the cold sherry for about 3 minutes then add to the hot rice mixture. Stir over a low heat until dissolved. Add the jam, cherries, angelica and ginger. Pour into a basin, cover and leave until lightly set. Whip the cream until it stands in soft peaks, fold into the other ingredients. Spoon into a mould and leave until firm. Turn out and decorate with the whipped cream, cherries, ginger and angelica.

Gâteau aux Pruneaux

To most cooks and chefs of the time dried prunes were not particularly exciting, for stewed prunes were regarded as food for the nursery. This particular recipe was given to me many years ago by an elderly lady, who said it was made by their cook in 1900. It certainly removes prunes from nursery fare. Of course in those days dried prunes had to be soaked for many hours before being cooked; the ready-to-eat prunes of today were unknown.

SERVES 4 TO 6

450 g/1 lb dried prunes
900 ml/1 ½ pints water
1 lemon
50 g/2 oz soft light brown sugar
150 ml/¼ pint port wine
15 g/½ oz gelatine*
2 tablespoons water

150 ml/5 fl oz double cream
50 g/2 oz blanched almonds,
   finely chopped
TO DECORATE:
little whipped cream
25 g/1 oz blanched almonds

it would have been leaf gelatine at the time

Wash the prunes then place in a basin, add the water, cover and leave to soak for some hours. Tip into a saucepan. Pare the top zest from the lemon, add to the prunes. Cover the pan tightly and simmer slowly for approximately 1 ½ hours or until very tender. Strain the prunes, discard the lemon zest but retain any juice left. Squeeze out 1 tablespoon lemon juice.

Remove the prune stones then rub the fruit through a fine sieve. Measure the thick purée and, if necessary, add just enough of the liquid to make 450 ml/¾ pint. Tip back into the saucepan with the lemon juice, sugar and port wine. Heat for a few minutes.

Soften the gelatine in the cold water, add to the hot prune mixture and stir until dissolved. Allow to become cold and stiffen very slightly. Whip the cream until it stands in soft peaks, fold into the jellied mixture with the chopped almonds. Spoon into a 1.2 litre/2 pint mould and leave to set.

Turn out and decorate with cream and the whole almonds.

Variation: use dried apricots instead of prunes.

A modern touch: use 300 g/10 oz ready-to-eat stoned prunes. Do not soak but simmer for about 45 minutes in just 450 ml/¾ pint water. Strain and proceed as above.

Tipsy Cake

The use of several different types of jam makes this dessert particularly interesting. When made on rare occasions in modern times it is generally coated with whipped cream or a custard sauce. Madeira and Marsala were two wines that were very popular in the early part of the century.

SERVES 6 TO 8

about 16 ratafia biscuits
Light Sponge, made and baked
   as page 38
4 tablespoons apricot jam
4 tablespoons raspberry jam
4 tablespoons greengage jam

FOR THE SAUCE AND TOPPING:
225 ml/7 ½ fl oz Madeira wine
   or Marsala
3 tablespoons Curaçao or brandy
1 tablespoon caster sugar
50 g/2 oz blanched almonds

Place the ratafias into a large serving bowl. Cut the sponge into 4 layers, spread the first layer with apricot jam, the second with raspberry jam and the third with greengage jam.

Mix the wines and sugar together. Arrange the first layer of sponge, jam side uppermost, over the biscuits. Moisten with a little of the wine, add the second layer of sponge, moisten and repeat with the third layer. Place the plain layer of sponge on top and spoon the rest of the wine over this. Scatter the almonds over the cake. Spoon on to plates and serve with cream or ice cream or Custard Sauce (page 96).
A modern touch: use amaretti biscuits instead of ratafias and amaretto liqueur instead of Curaçao or brandy.

Victoria Sandwich

This light cake, often referred to as a sponge, was named in honour of Queen Victoria. The classic method of gauging the amounts was to place the eggs on the scales and balance the fat, sugar and flour against them. It is assumed that an average egg weighs 50 g/2 oz. If you prefer an exact balance of ingredients return to the old method of weighing.

SERVES 6 TO 8

175 g/6 oz butter
175 g/6 oz caster sugar
3 large eggs
175 g/6 oz self-raising flour, or plain flour with 1½ teaspoons baking powder

FOR THE FILLING AND TOPPING:
3 to 4 tablespoons jam or lemon curd
little caster sugar

Preheat the oven to 180°C/350°F/Gas Mark 4/160°C with a fan oven. Grease and flour or line two 19 to 20 cm/7½ to 8 inch sandwich tins.

Cut the butter into pieces, put into a mixing bowl with the sugar. Cream until soft and light. Either beat in the eggs one at a time, or better still whisk them in a separate bowl then gradually beat into the creamed mixture. Sift the flour, or flour and baking powder, then gently fold into the other ingredients. Divide between the tins and bake for 20 minutes, or until firm to the touch. Cool for 2 or 3 minutes in the tins then turn out on to a wire cooling tray. When cold sandwich with the jam or curd and top with the sugar.

Variations: if the eggs are small add a little water or milk to make a soft dropping consistency.

Flavour the mixture with vanilla essence or use vanilla flavoured sugar (page 328) or cream 1½ teaspoons finely grated lemon or orange zest with the butter.

Chocolate Sandwich: omit 25 g/1 oz flour and substitute 25 g/1 oz cocoa. Use the same amount of baking powder as in the recipe with plain flour.

Coffee Sandwich: use small eggs and add 1 tablespoon coffee essence or ultra strong liquid coffee.

A modern touch: substitute soft margarine for the butter. This allows you to beat all the ingredients together although a lighter result is obtained by using the method above.

Use an electric mixer or food processor but take care NOT to over-beat the mixture when the flour is added, this would result in a less light texture.

Light Sponge

This type of sponge was popular, for it not only made its appearance at teatime but it was an excellent basis for the Tipsy Cake and Trifle on pages 35 and 119. These were favourite desserts for dinner party menus.

It is interesting that potato flour was frequently mixed with ordinary flour to give a particularly light texture. In modern times this is rarely used. An ordinary round cake tin is given in the recipe but the Victorians had wonderfully shaped moulds in which to make their cakes.

SERVES 6 TO 8

TO COAT THE TIN:
15 g/½ oz butter
1 to 1½ tablespoons caster sugar
FOR THE SPONGE:
5 large eggs
200 g/7 oz caster sugar
85 g/3 oz plain flour

85 g/3 oz potato flour
1 teaspoon baking powder, optional
FOR THE FILLING AND TOPPING:
jam
whipped cream
little caster sugar

Preheat the oven to 180°C/350°F/Gas Mark 4/160°C with a fan oven. Coat the inside of a 20 to 23 cm/8 to 9 inch cake tin with the softened butter and caster sugar.

Break the eggs into a bowl, add the sugar and whisk until the mixture is light and fluffy, you should be able to see the trail of the whisk. Sift the two flours and the baking powder together, if using this. The lightness given by whisking does make baking powder unnecessary but less experienced cooks liked to use this. Gently fold the flours into the whisked ingredients. Spoon into the prepared tin and bake for 50 minutes or until firm to a gentle touch. Cool in the tin for 2 to 3 minutes then turn out on to a wire cooling tray.

When cold split horizontally into two or three layers and fill with the jam and cream. Top with sugar.

Variations: cornflour was another ingredient used in cake-making to give a fine texture; often half flour and half cornflour or ⅓ cornflour and ⅔ flour.

All plain or all self-raising flour could be used.

For an even lighter texture separate the eggs, whisk the yolks and sugar and the whites separately. Fold the whisked whites into the mixture after adding the flour(s).

Various flavourings such as vanilla extract or lemon zest could be added to the eggs and sugar.

A modern touch: use an electric whisk but take care not to over-whisk the flour.

Individual Sponge Cakes

These small sponge cakes could be used instead of portions of the larger cake to make a trifle. People with less time, or less help in the kitchen, could purchase these from the bakers.

MAKES 12 TO 16

ingredients as Sponge Cake page 38

Preheat the oven to 190°C/375°F/Gas Mark 5/180°C with a fan oven. Grease and flour small oblong sponge finger tins. Half fill with the sponge mixture and bake for 10 to 12 minutes.

Variation: grease the tins and dust with caster sugar instead of flour. Top the mixture with a good sprinkling of caster sugar before baking.

Mosaic Cake

As Victorian tea-parties became more elaborate the cook would be expected to make cakes as colourful as possible. This recipe is based on the Victoria Sandwich, page 36.

SERVES 6 TO 8

ingredients as Victoria Sandwich,
 as page 36
pink colouring
green colouring

FOR THE TOPPING:
little caster sugar

Preheat the oven to 160°C/325°F/Gas Mark 3/150°C with a fan oven. Grease and flour or line an 18 to 20 cm/7 to 8 inch cake tin.

Make the Victoria Sandwich mixture, leave a third in the mixing bowl. Divide the remainder between 2 containers. Tint one part pale green and the other pale pink. Spoon the mixture into the tin, making sure the colours are evenly distributed. Bake for approximately 45 minutes, or until firm to the touch. Cool in the tin for 4 to 5 minutes then turn out on to a wire cooling tray. When cold dust with the sugar.
Variation: the cake can be iced.

Each section of the mixture can be flavoured, i.e. one part vanilla, one part with a little crème de menthe and one part with cherry brandy or use different flavouring essences. If using liqueurs, which add a liquid content to the mixture, use small eggs to compensate.

Cover the top and sides of the cake with a small amount of sieved apricot or raspberry jam. Then cover entire cake with Almond Paste (page 41), pressing firmly against the surfaces. Trim away any surplus and use to decorate the top of the cake.
A modern touch: a great deal more care is given today as to the source of colouring and flavouring ingredients.

Almond Paste

In Escoffier's book published in 1907 he states 'instead of the antiquated method of making almond pastes in the mortar, a crushing machine is now used'. If a chef, with a battery of assistants found it troublesome to crush blanched almonds, how much more difficult for the cook in a small household. Even so for some centuries cooks would work by hand to get a good almond paste with which to decorate cakes or make sweetmeals.

This is the recipe for almond paste, which was used at that time.

225 g/8 oz almonds	pinch cream of tartar
150 ml/¼ pint water	few drops ratafia* or almond essence
300 g/10 oz caster sugar	*this comes from peach or cherry stones and is considered more delicate in flavour than almond*

Blanch the almonds by putting them into boiling water for 1 minute, remove quickly and strip away the skins. Dry well then put some of the nuts into a mortar and crush with a pestle until very fine. Continue like this until all nuts are crushed.

Put the water and sugar into a saucepan, stir until the sugar has dissolved, add the cream of tartar and boil, without stirring, until the mixture reaches 116°C/240°F, i.e. when a little tested in cold water forms a soft ball. Beat until the mixture turns cloudy then stir in the ground almonds and essence. Cool and use to coat cakes.

Variation: an egg white, beaten until frothy, could be added to the ground almond mixture. In this case return the pan to a low heat and stir for 2 minutes. This gives a slightly softer almond paste.

A modern touch: today one would buy ground almonds, which produce a smoother paste.

The favourite recipe of today for what is now called marzipan is made by combining 225 g/8 oz ground almonds, a little ratafia or almond essence, 115 g/4 oz caster sugar, 115 g/4 oz sifted icing sugar and the yolks of 2 eggs. Use the whites of the eggs for a white marzipan.

There are warnings today about using uncooked eggs, for fear of salmonella, so the 'old-fashioned' almond paste is safer.

1910 to 1919

from champagne to rationing

Edward succeeded his mother, Queen Victoria, upon her death in 1901, and was crowned Edward VII the following year. Although history relates many details about Edward and his mistresses there was another side to the King. He was an excellent linguist, speaking French and German fluently, and with a good command of Italian too. He had proved himself a fine diplomat on his many visits abroad; he worried about the internal situation for his relations with the German Kaiser were not particularly friendly. Edward was a man of fashion, admired by the aristocracy and the lower classes. The middle classes tended to disapprove of him.

Edward died in May 1910, due to pneumonia and was succeded by his son, George V. Once again attitudes changed for George preferred a far less social existence although he rejoiced in the ceremony of royalty, like his father. He proved a fine monarch during the war years and became much loved by the population.

In 1912 the great liner, the Titanic, sank on her maiden voyage.

In 1914 Britain declared war on Germany. The Great War was to last for four years, with its huge loss of human life.

Emmeline Pankhurst was still striving for women to be able to vote. She suspended her militant attitude when war was declared. Her work on behalf of the war effort was rewarded in 1918 by the granting of the vote for women over 30.

One happier event was the opening of the first cinema at Harwich in Essex in 1911.

In July 1917 George V relinquished his German titles and the royal family became the House of Windsor.

November 1918, the war ended and peace returned to Europe.

1919 was the year Lady Astor entered Parliament as the first woman M.P.

Life in Britain from 1910 to 1919

At the beginning of the decade life was very good for most people, except for the poor. King Edward participated in many social events and enjoyed visiting his friends for house-parties. George V enjoyed country pursuits.

After 1914 life changed dramatically. Food gradually became more scarce but there was no official rationing until 1918. Servants started to leave their employers to join the services and go into factories. In 1916 the Prime Minister, Lloyd George, urged everyone to be economical with food and to give their servants marching orders.

By 1915 over 50,000 women were on war work and were given the right to apply to drive buses and trams. Parliament urged more women to seek war work. They had worked in the docks but in 1916 withdrew as the men refused to work with them.

The call-up of men, and work done by women in the services, factories, on the land and in other roles, meant that many poorer families were now much better off. Of course some families were poorer, as the armed services were not well-paid, and men had lost good jobs to enlist or be called-up.

The terrible loss of life throughout the war could never be forgotten. It left a great number of women without husbands or fiancés and children without fathers. This affected people of every class.

The Kitchens

During the early part of the decade gas and electric cookers improved in appearance but there were no great changes in other equipment.

The Foods of Britain

Edward and his friends were much influenced by French cuisine. This was epitomised by the cooking and books of Escoffier, the great French chef. The love of sophisticated foods continued until the war. According to Andre Simon (who in years to come was famous for his expertise on wine and food), Escoffier altered the old-fashioned attitude to ladies being seen in public eating places, for they began to accompany the men to special functions.

During the first two years of the war food traders operated much as usual. The free

play of supply and demand meant steadily rising prices but wages lagged far behind.

According to the cookery books of the time I noted differences between foods available during the first and second world wars. In World War I citrus fruits and imported nuts figured in wartime recipes, whereas these were not available during World War II.

There was great unrest as the war continued for the poorer people felt those with money were buying and hoarding food. It was reported that in London alone ½ million queued every Saturday to try and obtain basic commodities. The Government did not want to introduce rationing, for fear it would give courage to the enemy, but they had to do this in 1918 - just a few months before the war ended.

Bread, meat, butter and margarine and sugar were the foods put on ration. After this purchase of foods became easier for the mass of the population. Food rationing continued until 1921.

Throughout the war years large grocery stores accepted orders to send food parcels to those abroad in the services.

It was stated that George V and his family preferred plainer food and their tastes may well be reflected in some of the dishes given for this period.

Favourite Drinks

Champagne was a favourite drink of Edward VII and his circle of friends; French and a few German wines were served at dinners. I would imagine that people did not drink German wines after war was declared.

The amount of alcohol consumed increased a great deal during the war years, beer and spirits being the most popular. It was reported in 1915 that heavy drinking was slowing arms production and in March of that year George V offered to abstain from alcohol as an example.

Meals of 1910 to 1919

These were sharply divided into those **before** and those **after war was declared**. I have tried to reflect this influence by heading the first recipes 'Edwardian Era'.

Elaborate dinners were still as lengthy but the foods served tended to be less heavy with emphasis on souflées and other classic French dishes. Champagne was not only served as a drink but used to make sorbets. There is a recipe on page 62. This would be served half-way through the lengthy dinner to refresh the diners' appetites, so they could continue with the rest of the meal.

The ladies still enjoyed their 'At Homes' at tea-time and were beautifully dressed in the fashion of the era with sweeping skirts and tiny waists that required tight corsetting.

When foods became more scarce elaborate meals for the rich ended and so did 'At Homes'. The ladies were intent on playing their part for the war effort and dressed much more simply. Some of the dishes recommended in the many cookery books published after 1914 are reproduced in this volume.

Cookery Influences

At the beginning of this period advice would have been obtained from similar sources to those of the 1900's. The magazine *Woman's Weekly* was launched in November, 1911. I was told that the editor of that era consulted her cook as to the type of recipes to include in the magazine.

During the years 1914 onwards, as food became scarcer, a great number of wartime cookery books appeared. Many accomplished foreign chefs and high class cooks were forced to leave Britain. Even in luxurious homes women had to cook for the first time for their servants had been called up to serve in the armed forces or work in munition factories.

1910 to 1919

The Recipes

Anchovy Paste

Another name for this would have been, Potted Anchovies, for good cooks prepared a range of these smooth mixtures to serve with toast for breakfast or as a savoury filling for sandwiches. The butter covering excluded all air so the food kept for some days in a cool larder.

Canned foods were fairly plentiful at the beginning of the century and people would be able to purchase canned anchovy fillets. Fresh anchovies were far less easy to obtain.

MAKES A GOOD 175 G/6 OZ

50 g/2 oz unsalted butter
115 g/4 oz canned anchovy fillets
1 tablespoon chopped parsley
1 tablespoon lemon juice

shake black or cayenne pepper
TO COVER:
40 g/1 ½ oz unsalted butter, melted

Put the butter into a mortar. Drain the canned fillets, chop into small pieces, add to the mortar with the parsley, lemon juice and pepper. Pound with a pestle until really smooth. Put into a container and cover with melted butter.

Variations: use cooked boned anchovies, add salt as well as pepper.

Use cooked salmon or crab, lobster, shrimps and other shellfish instead of anchovies. Flavour with chopped dill or fennel leaves instead of parsley.

Use minced cooked chicken or turkey or ham or game birds instead of anchovies. Flavour with tarragon or rosemary instead of parsley.

A modern touch: put the ingredients into a food processor. Do not over-process for this produces a sticky mixture.

Potage a L'Italienne

The name of this soup may not be quite accurate, for the term 'potage' denotes a puréed soup. I have retained this title for it was the one given me by a lady who said it was a feature of her grandmother's summer meals in the early 1900's. It is a delicious and satisfying soup. The macaroni of the Edwardian era was rather large in shape, not unlike the penne of today, so would be better cut into smaller pieces after cooking and before adding to the soup.

SERVES 4 TO 6

50 g/2 oz macaroni
salt and freshly ground black pepper
1.5 litres/2½ pints Consommé
   as page 17
115 g/4 oz fresh peas

¼ small cucumber, peeled
2 medium tomatoes, skinned and diced
heart of a small lettuce, finely shredded
small wineglass of dry sherry

Put the macaroni into boiling salted water and cook until tender, strain then cut into thin rings. Heat the Consommé, season it lightly, add the peas and cook until these are almost tender. Grate the cucumber, add to the soup with the macaroni, tomatoes and lettuce. Simmer for about 6 minutes. Add the sherry, check the seasoning and then serve.

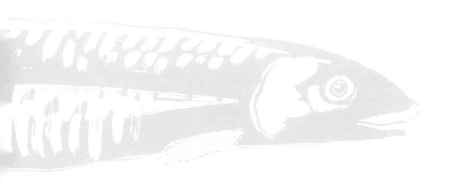

Oyster Soup

Oysters were wonderfully inexpensive during the early part of the 20th century, selling for about 1d ($\frac{1}{2}$ p) for 12, so they could be used for soups during the oyster season (when there was an 'R' in the month). The combination of meat stock, preferably made from lamb or mutton, not beef, and fish was usual and very satisfactory in this particular recipe.

SERVES 4 TO 6

FOR THE STOCK:

2 medium onions, chopped

225 g/8 oz scrag end of lamb or mutton

few lamb bones

1.8 litres/3 pints water

salt and freshly ground black pepper

50 g/2 oz butter

50 g/2 oz plain flour

24 small or 12 large oysters, which should be halved or quartered

TO GARNISH:

chopped parsley or chervil

lemon wedges

Put all the ingredients for the stock into a saucepan. Bring the liquid to the boil, remove any scum that rises to the top. Cover the pan and simmer gently for 2 hours. Strain the liquid and clarify it if possible (page 17). Return to the saucepan and boil briskly until reduced to 900 ml/1 $\frac{1}{2}$ pints or 1 litre/1 $\frac{3}{4}$ pints for a thinner soup.

Heat the butter, stir in the flour then gradually add the stock. Stir briskly until thickened and smooth. Tip in the oysters and liquid from the shells and simmer for 2 minutes only - overheating makes the oysters tough. Spoon into soup plates, top with the herbs and place the lemon wedges beside the plates.

Variation: use fish stock (page 16) instead of lamb stock.

A modern touch: due to the import of oysters these are obtainable throughout the year; they are expensive so augment with a small amount of peeled prawns and/or cooked mussels.

Oyster Cromeskies (page 52)

Oyster Cromeskies

A Cromeski (often spelt with a K) is the name given to food wrapped in bacon, then coated with batter and fried. These crisp savouries were generally served as an hors d'oeuvre.

SERVES 4

12 small or 6 large oysters
300 ml/½ pint fish stock as page 16
1 teaspoon lemon juice
6 rashers long streaky bacon
FOR COATING:
frying batter see below

FOR FRYING:
deep fat
TO GARNISH:
lemon wedges
parsley sprigs

Remove the oysters from their shells, halve large ones. Tip any liquid from the shells into the fish stock. Bring this liquid to simmering point, add the lemon juice then poach the oysters for 2 minutes only. Lift out of the stock and drain well.

Remove the rind from the bacon and stretch the rashers with the back of a knife. Cut each rasher in half then wrap around the oysters. Coat in the batter.

Meanwhile heat the fat to 180°C/355°F (or when a cube of 24-hour bread turns golden in just 1 minute) and fry the Cromeskies for approximately 4 minutes or until crisp and golden brown. Drain on absorbent paper and serve with a garnish of lemon and parsley.

Variations: use small scallops (known as queenies) instead of the oysters. Poach these for 2 minutes in the fish stock.

Fried Parsley: instead of serving fresh parsley as the garnish fry well dried sprigs in the hot fat for about 1 minute.

A modern touch: use oil, rather than fat, for frying the food.

Frying Batter: the following recipe is for a light batter. It is sufficiently liquid in consistency to give a thin coating only. Serving is dependent on the recipe. 115 g/ 4 oz plain flour, pinch salt, 4 tablespoons light ale or beer, 150 ml/¼ pint water, 1 tablespoon melted butter, 1 egg white.

Sift the flour and salt, add the ale or beer and water. Just before using stir in the melted butter and then the egg white. This should be whisked until stiff then folded into the other ingredients.

Braised Pheasant

Braising is a classic method of cooking food which is mostly applied to meat, poultry and game, although fish and vegetables are sometimes cooked in the same way. The food is first browned in hot fat, followed by slower cooking over, not in, a small amount of liquid with herbs and vegetables for flavour. The original French braising pan was known as a brasière or daubière. It was made of heavy metal, with a flat well-fitting lid. The pan was put over the heat and live charcoal placed on the lid - a somewhat dangerous method of cooking but one that ensured heat below and above the ingredients. Cooking in an oven gives the same conditions - but with safety. This dish was one way of dealing with the surfeit of game birds shot during the season. If done correctly braising gives food a very succulent texture.

SERVES 4 TO 6

2 pheasants, jointed
85 g/3 oz clarified chicken dripping
   or butter
8 shallots or 4 small onions, sliced
3 medium carrots, sliced
½ small head of celeriac or
   ½ celery heart, sliced
115 g/4 oz mushrooms, sliced
2 tomatoes, skinned and thickly sliced

1 teaspoon chopped thyme
1 teaspoon chopped tarragon
1 tablespoon chopped parsley
approximately 200 ml/7 fl oz game
   stock as page 16 or wine*
salt and freshly ground black pepper

* this can be red or white according to
  personal taste

Preheat the oven to 180°C/350°F/Gas Mark 4/160°C with a fan oven if the birds are young. For slightly older birds use the same temperature, for really old birds pre-heat to 160°C/325°F/Gas Mark 3/150°C with a fan oven. Dry the jointed birds well.

If you have the type of pan that can be used both on top of the cooker and in the oven heat half the fat in this. Add the pheasant joints and cook quickly until well browned. This gives an attractive colour and seals in the juices. Turn during cooking. When brown lift on to a dish with a perforated spoon. Heat the rest of the fat and put in the vegetables. Cook steadily for 5 minutes. Check fat left in the pan and drain away any surplus.

Add the herbs then the stock or wine; make sure the liquid only just covers the vegetables. Place the pheasant joints on top. Season lightly then put on the lid and cook for approximately 1 hour or until the pheasants are tender. Do not over-cook.

Lift the joints onto a heated dish and either serve the vegetables around or sieve or liquidize them with extra stock or wine to make a purée sauce. Older pheasants would need 1½ to 2½ hours cooking time. Since these will have some natural fat under the skin reduce the amount of fat added for browning the joints.

Variations: if the pan is unsuitable for use on top of the cooker brown the birds and vegetables in a strong frying pan then transfer to a large casserole. Make sure the lid fits tightly so the small amount of liquid will not evaporate.

Other game birds or chicken or guinea fowl or rabbit can be cooked in the same way. Partridge, quail and small young pigeons (squabs) could be left whole. Thick portions or small joints of good quality beef, venison and mutton are suitable for braising.

Adjust the selection of vegetables according to the season.

Add a little diced bacon to the vegetables or better still lard the joints of pheasant, or other foods, by inserting thin strips of fat bacon with a larding needle before cooking.

Braised Fish and Vegetables: brown thick portions of firm fish, such as turbot or halibut, or vegetables like celery hearts, fennel or whole onions in butter then cook on a layer of thinly browned shallots, diced celery and tomatoes with the fish or vegetable stock or wine. Allow about 40 minutes at 190°C/375°F/Gas Mark 5/ 180°C with a fan oven for fish and the same setting and timing as pheasant for the vegetables listed above.

Accompaniments to Braised Pheasants

Instead of serving the Braised Pheasants with a puréed vegetable sauce serve with the Game Sauce on page 320.

Medallions of Ham

Cut hot ham (boiled as bacon on page 208) into neat rounds or ovals, place on crisply fried croutons of bread of the same shape. Top with sliced fried mushrooms.

Chestnut Purée

Wash then slit the shells of about 900 g/2 lb chestnuts in the shape of a cross. Put into boiling water and simmer for 8 to 10 minutes. Cool sufficiently to handle then remove the outer shells and brown skins. Place the nuts in bacon or veal stock and simmer for 25 to 30 minutes or until tender. Drain then pound to a smooth purée. Add melted butter and seasoning to taste.

A modern touch: either process the cooked nuts until smooth or use the excellent canned unsweetened chestnut purée. Blend this with enough stock to make a softer texture. Add a little melted butter and seasoning to taste.

Artichoke Hearts

In the magnificent kitchen gardens of the wealthy globe artichokes were so abundant that the cooks could use just the bottoms (the hearts). To prepare these trim away all the leaves and the chokes, leaving just the hearts. Sprinkle with lemon juice to prevent them turning brown then cook steadily in hot butter for 20 to 25 minutes or boil in well-seasoned veal stock for the same time. Drain and top with finely chopped parsley and tarragon.

Ribbon Potatoes

Peel potatoes then cut them round and round to give long narrow ribbons. Place in cold water until ready to cook. Strain and dry well. Heat a generous amount of butter and fry the potato ribbons until golden brown. Pile into a hot dish and season with salt and cayenne pepper. Garnish with parsley.

A modern touch: fry in hot oil or a mixture of 2 parts oil and 1 part butter.

Salsify

In her book *Modern Cookery for Private Families* Eliza Acton states 'we are surprised that a vegetable as excellent as this should be so little cared for in England'. Today it is almost unknown. Salsify is often called oysterplant, for it is considered to have a flavour somewhat similar to oysters.

To prepare the long roots wash them well then scrape away the dark skin. Cut into thick slices. Place immediately into boiling salted water with a tablespoon white vinegar or lemon juice to preserve the colour and cook for 30 to 35 minutes or until tender. Strain and serve with melted butter.

Orange-flower Macaroons

The use of orange-flower water gives a delicious flavour to these biscuits. If you are fortunate enough to grow orange trees then use fresh orange blossom instead of the orange-flower water; see under Variations.

When making Almond Macaroons choose extract of almonds rather than essence to flavour the mixture. If rice paper is not available the baking trays need to be lightly greased. Wafer paper is mentioned in cookery books sold at the beginning of the century, I would imagine it was similar to rice paper.

To give the macaroons a slightly sticky texture do not over-bake and place a small bowl of water in the oven during the cooking period.

MAKES: 12 TO 18

2 egg whites from small eggs	2 teaspoons orange-flower water
175 g/6 oz ground almonds	FOR THE BASE OF THE MACAROONS:
175 g/6 oz caster sugar	rice paper

Preheat the oven to 180°C/350°F/Gas Mark 4/170°C with a fan oven. Whisk the egg whites until frothy, add the rest of the ingredients. The mixture should be soft, but firm enough to roll into balls. If too soft add a little more ground almonds or rice flour or cornflour, see under Almond Macaroons. If too dry add more orange-flower water or a few drops of water.

Arrange the rice paper on baking trays, add the macaroons, allow plenty of space for the mixture to spread during cooking. Bake for approximately 20 minutes, or until golden in colour. Cool then cut around the rice paper and remove from the trays.

Variations: use about 15 g/$^1\!/_2$ oz orange-flower petals. Cut into tiny pieces with scissors and mix with the sugar. Omit the orange-flower water.

Almond Macaroons: these were often called English Macaroons, as a contrast to the well-known *Macarons de Nancy* below. Follow the recipe above but omit the orange-flower water. The ground almonds can be reduced to 150 g/5 oz and a few drops of almond extract added together with 1 teaspoon of cornflour or rice flour. Top with whole blanched almonds then bake as the first recipe.

Chocolate Macaroons: these were a great favourite in Edwardian days. Whisk 2 egg whites until stiff, add 85 g/3 oz ground almonds, 85 g/3 oz grated plain chocolate, 25 g/1 oz ground rice and 85 g/3 oz caster sugar. Form into balls, place on rice paper and bake as the first recipe.

Coconut Macaroons: follow Almond Macaroon recipe but use half ground almonds and half desiccated coconut with the same amount of sugar; omit the rice flour or cornflour. Top the balls with halved glacé cherries before baking. Bake as the first recipe.

Macarons de Nancy: finely chop 115 g/4 oz blanched sweet almonds and 25 g/1 oz blanched bitter almonds, add 150 g/5 oz caster sugar and 1 egg yolk. Whisk the egg white stiffly, fold into the ingredients. Form into balls, place on rice paper and bake as the first recipe. If no bitter almonds are available use chopped walnuts or more sweet almonds instead.

Macaroon Fritters: sandwich 16 small Almond Macaroons with apricot jam to make 8 rounds. Make a sugar syrup with 150 ml/¼ pint water, 25g/1oz caster sugar and 1-2 tablespoons rum or kirsch. Make a frying batter (as page 52). Dip macaroons quickly into the syrup, then coat in the batter. Fry for approximately 4 minutes in fat or oil (180°C/355°F). Drain on absorbent paper and roll in caster sugar. Serve with ice cream.

Ratafias: these are very small almond macaroons. Follow the recipe above but do not use rice paper. Make about 65 very small balls. Put on greased baking trays and cook for only 10 minutes at the setting given in the first recipe. These should be very firm and they can be stored in an airtight tin for use in a Trifle or Tipsy Cake (pages 119 and 35).

A modern touch: as macaroons of all kinds are better when freshly cooked the only way to store them is in the freezer. Use within 3 or 4 weeks to prevent them becoming crumbly.

Glacé Fruit Soufflé

The British liking for savoury and sweet soufflés may well have been due to the influence of the great French chef Auguste Escoffier, who reigned in London during the early part of the 20th century. He was acknowledged to be the master of haute cuisine. Escoffier introduced many of the classic dishes of his homeland to people who enjoyed dining out in London.

SERVES 4

50 g/2 oz glacé cherries, finely chopped
25 g/1 oz glacé pineapple, finely chopped
25 g/1 oz glacé apricots, finely chopped
25 g/1 oz angelica, finely chopped
2 tablespoons kirsch
FOR THE COATING:
15 g/½ oz butter
25 g/1 oz blanched almonds, finely chopped

25 g/1 oz caster sugar
FOR THE SOUFFLÉ:
1 level tablespoon cornflour
150 ml/¼ pint milk
25 g/1 oz butter
25 g/1 oz caster sugar
2 tablespoons cream
3 eggs
2 egg whites

Preheat the oven to 190°C/375°F/Gas Mark 5/180°C with a fan oven. Put the glacé fruits and angelica into a basin with the kirsch and leave for at least 30 minutes to soften.

Grease the inside of a 15 to 18 cm/6 to 7 inch soufflé dish with the 15 g/½ oz butter then press the almonds and 25 g/1 oz sugar over this.

Blend the cornflour with the milk, pour into a saucepan, add the butter and stir over a low heat until thickened. Remove from the heat, add the sugar, cream, and half the glacé fruits and kirsch. Separate the eggs, beat the yolks into the ingredients in the saucepan. Whisk the 5 whites until stiff, beat 1 tablespoon into the soufflé mixture then fold in the remainder.

Spoon the last of the fruits and kirsch into the base of the dish, top with the soufflé mixture. Bake for 25 to 30 minutes, or until well-risen then serve at once.

A purée of raspberries or strawberries makes an excellent accompaniment.

Braised Quail (page 53)

Parmesan Soufflé

A cheese soufflé was frequently served as the savoury at the end of formal dinner parties and even in the early part of the 20th century it was recognised that Parmesan was one of the best cheeses to select for this dish. Parmesan has such a strong flavour that a relatively small amount can be used and this ensures a light mixture, so the soufflé will rise well. The early recipes do not stress the superiority of Parmigiano Reggiano so perhaps this was not imported into Britain at the time.

Do not over-bake any soufflé for this makes the mixture dry, it should be slightly soft in the centre. The soufflé mixture can be prepared, placed in the dish and covered with a large bowl to exclude all the air; this will allow it to stand for up to 1 hour before baking.

SERVES 4

25 g/1 oz butter
25 g/1 oz flour
150 ml/¼ pint milk
50 to 85 g/2 to 3 oz Parmesan cheese, finely grated

2 tablespoons double cream
3 eggs
salt and freshly ground black pepper
pinch ground nutmeg, optional
2 egg whites

Preheat the oven to 190°C/375°F/Gas Mark 5/180°C with a fan oven. Grease the inside of a 15 cm/6 inch soufflé dish.

Heat the butter in a saucepan, stir in the flour then gradually add the cold milk. Bring to the boil and stir over a low heat until thickened. Remove from the heat and stir in the cheese and cream. Separate the eggs, add the yolks to the soufflé mixture together with seasoning and nutmeg. Whisk the 5 whites until stiff, beat 1 tablespoon into the soufflé mixture to give a softer texture then fold in the remainder.

Spoon into the soufflé dish and bake for 25 to 30 minutes, or until well risen. Serve at once.

Variations: top the mixture with a little grated cheese before baking.

Use strong Cheddar or other good cooking cheese; in this case you may like to increase the quantity to 115 to 150 g/4 to 5 oz.

Use the recipe for Parmesan Soufflé with 50 g/2 oz minced cooked ham or cooked smoked haddock or cooked crab or lobster. The ultimate luxury, thinly sliced black truffles, were sometimes added.

Scotch Woodcock

At rather lavish dinners a savoury would be served at the end of the meal after the dessert. In his book *Modern Cookery*, published in 1907, Escoffier has harsh words to say on the subject of savouries. He states 'I consider their use opposed to gastronomical principles, and that they have no *raison d'être* on a good menu'. In spite of this he gives a very good recipe for the savoury which follows, my own favourite.

SERVES 4

2 large or 4 small slices of bread
home-made Anchovy Paste as page 48
25 g/1 oz butter
4 eggs

2 tablespoons cream or milk
salt and freshly ground black pepper
TO GARNISH:
canned anchovy fillets

Toast the bread, cut off the crusts, and halve the large slices. Spread with the paste. Meanwhile heat the butter in a saucepan. Beat the eggs with the cream or milk and seasoning. Scramble until lightly set, spoon on to the toast and garnish with a lattice of well-drained anchovy fillets.

Variation:

Escoffier's Scotch Woodcock: toast large slices of bread, cover with a very thick English butter sauce, combined with plenty of capers and anchovy purée.

Sprinkle with grated Parmesan, glaze quickly at the salamander (grill), speedily cut up into small rectangles and serve very hot.

Angels on Horseback: squeeze a little lemon juice over oysters, wrap in portions of bacon. Skewer with wooden toothpicks or cocktail sticks. Cook under a preheated grill until the bacon is crisp. Dust with paprika.

Devils on Horseback: use cooked stoned and well-drained prunes instead of oysters, wrap in bacon and cook as above. The prunes can be filled with pâté.

Welsh Rarebit: heat 20 g/³⁄₄ oz of butter in a saucepan, stir in 20 g/³⁄₄ oz plain flour. Add 2 tablespoons milk and 2 tablespoons beer. Stir over the heat until thickened. Remove from the heat. Add 1 teaspoon made English mustard, a shake of cayenne pepper and 175 to 225 g/6 to 8 oz grated Double Gloucester or mature Cheddar cheese. Mix well and spread over 4 small slices of buttered toast. Put under a preheated grill and cook until golden brown.

Champagne Sorbet

Sorbets were an important feature of many Edwardian meals. They were served half-way through the repast. The idea was that the cold ice refreshed the diners' appetites, so they could continue to eat the remainder of the substantial meal.

Hand-operated ice-cream freezers were very usual in wealthy households, where there was a domestic to turn the handle as the mixture froze. This would be done just before the meal and the frozen sorbet stored in the rather primitive ice-cave for a brief time.

When electric ice-cream makers for the home came on the market, in the late 1980's and 1990's, sorbets became easy to make once more.

SERVES 8

2 lemons	115 g/4 oz caster sugar
150 ml/¼ pint water	1 litre/1¾ pints champagne, preferably pink

Pare the top zest from 1 of the lemons, be very careful not to use any bitter white pith. Halve both lemons and squeeze out the juice. Pour the water into a saucepan, add the lemon zest and the sugar. Simmer for 5 minutes, stirring well until the sugar has dissolved. Strain and mix with the champagne and as much lemon juice as required. Pour into the freezer and turn the handle until the ice is frozen. Spoon into one container or individual glasses and store in the ice-cave.

Edwardian sorbet glasses were very elegant.

Variations: A good sorbet should be light and have no ice crystals in the mixture. To achieve a good result, without the help of the movement in an ice-cream maker, follow the recipe above but soften 2 level teaspoons gelatine in a little of the cold champagne then dissolve over hot water. Add to the other ingredients. Pour into a freezing container and freeze until 'mushy'. Remove from the freezer, beat hard, then fold in 2 stiffly beaten egg whites. Return to the freezer to complete freezing. Scoop into individual glasses to serve.

NOTE: there is a danger of salmonella in uncooked egg whites.

Any fruit juices or fairly liquid fruit purées can be used in the recipe above.

A modern touch: electric ice-cream makers combined with freezers, enable one to make sorbets in minutes. Follow the first recipe.

Mushroom Sauce

Many cookbooks right up to the 1960's used the measure of a gill. For most people this meant 150 ml/¼ pint. In the North of England however if you ordered 1 gill milk you expected to receive 300 ml/½ pint. Fortunately the confusing 'gill' has now been discarded. In Mrs. Peel's book she mentions 1 gill. I interpreted this as 150 ml/¼ pint and it gave the sauce a thick consistency, like a modern salsa. You can of course use more liquid. As with all cookery books of this period one is instructed to peel the mushrooms as well as discarding the stalks. Nowadays it is a matter of personal taste as to whether the mushroom skins are discarded.

SERVES 4 TO 6

15 g/½ oz fat
225 g/8 oz mushrooms, finely chopped
1 level tablespoon plain flour

150 ml/¼ pint milk
salt and freshly ground black pepper

Heat the fat in a saucepan, add the mushrooms and cook for about 5 minutes. Blend the flour with the milk, add to the pan and continue cooking for 10 minutes. By this time most of the liquid will have evaporated. Season to taste.

Variation: for a thinner sauce use 20 g/¾ oz flour and 300 ml/½ pint milk.

A modern touch: use the microwave. Cook the mushrooms with the fat for 2 minutes on full output. Blend the flour with only 4 tablespoons milk (liquids do not evaporate as much as when using a saucepan). Pour over the mushrooms, cook for 3 to 4 minutes, stir twice during this time. Season to taste. Stand for 1 minute before serving.

Trout Cream

This recipe and the one for Bread Soup come from *The Allied Forces Cook Book*. The recipes were sent in by well-wishers in aid of the forces. According to newspaper reports there was great unrest until official rationing came into force in 1918. It was felt that, while poorer people suffered greatly from lack of food, the rich people were able to buy more food and hoard it too. I think this recipe rather illustrates that point. It obviously came from someone who had access to plenty of eggs, milk and cream as well as freshly caught fish. Exact quantities of some ingredients were not given in the original recipe but I have added these after testing the recipe.

SERVES 4

1 large trout or salmon trout
50 g/2 oz butter
150 ml/¼ pint thick White Sauce
   (see below)
1 to 2 tablespoons double cream*
2 eggs
salt and freshly ground black pepper
FOR THE SAUCE:
300 ml/½ pint single cream or
   thin White Sauce (see below)

enriched with a little double cream
   or mayonnaise
2 egg whites, hard-boiled and chopped**
vinegar to taste

* *unsweetened evaporated milk could be substituted or canned cream*

** *the yolks could be chopped and used as a garnish on the fish cream*

Remove the head from the fish and clean it well, especially if freshly caught. Heat the butter and fry the fish until tender. Remove all skin and bones then pound the flesh until smooth in a mortar. Mix with the sauce, cream, eggs and seasoning. Spoon into a greased 900 ml/1½ pint basin, cover and steam for 30 minutes. When cold turn out and serve with cold sauce, made by mixing all the ingredients together.

White Sauce

This sauce has been a standby in British cooking for a very long time. It is a good basic sauce to which can be added anchovies or anchovy essence, cheese, parsley and other flavourings. The more interesting Béchamel Sauce is made by heating a small amount of diced celery, sliced carrot, chopped onion and a bay leaf (optional) in the milk for 2 or 3 minutes, covering and allowing this to stand for 30 minutes. The milk is then strained and used to make the sauce. Modern fashion dictates thinner sauce, so the proportion of milk can be increased slightly. A small amount of cream or crème fraîche can be whisked into the thickened sauce.

For a thick sauce: heat 25 g/1 oz butter or margarine in a saucepan, stir in 25 g/1 oz plain flour and continue stirring over a low heat until the 'roux' forms a dry ball. Gradually add 150 ml/¼ pint cold milk. Stir or whisk as the sauce comes to the boil and thickens. Season to taste.

For a thin sauce: follow the recipe above but use 300 ml/½ pint milk.

A modern touch: make the sauce in a basin in the microwave instead of in a saucepan. Stir several times during the cooking process. As there is less evaporation in a microwave 1 to 2 tablespoons less milk can be used.

Blending method: often this is used today. Blend the flour with the milk. Pour into the saucepan, add the butter or margarine and stir or whisk briskly as the sauce thickens. Allow to simmer for several minutes so the flour is adequately cooked. Season to taste.

Bread Soup

Although given as a First World War recipe in *The Allied Forces Cook Book* this soup is absolutely delicious if a very well-flavoured stock is used. Today many people might worry that the eggs are inadequately cooked, so see 'A modern touch'.

SERVES 6

175 g/6 oz crusts from bread
1.8 litres/3 pints very good stock
salt and freshly ground black pepper
2 eggs

50 g/2 oz mature Cheddar
   cheese, grated
1 teaspoon freshly grated nutmeg

Cut the crusts into small neat pieces. Put into a saucepan with the stock and simmer for about 10 minutes. Season well. Break the eggs into a large heated tureen, add the cheese and nutmeg. Gradually whisk or stir in the boiling soup. Taste and add additional seasoning if required. Serve hot.

A modern touch: whisk the eggs in a basin. Gradually whisk in a few tablespoons of the very hot, but not boiling, soup. Return to the pan and cook gently, stirring all the time, for 10 minutes. Add the cheese and nutmeg then serve.

Nut Rissoles

One of the outstanding points I noted in all cookery books written for use during the First World War was the emphasis on nuts. This was quite different from the Second World War when nuts, except those grown in Britain, were unobtainable.

This is another recipe from Mrs. C. S. Peel's *The Eat-Less-Meat Book*. I was extremely surprised to find pine nuts (kernels) mentioned as I thought that, while a feature of Mediterranean cookery for a very long time, they are a modern taste in Britain. These pine nuts must have been sold in a different state from those obtainable today since Mrs. Peel advises removing the skins. In the book it states it will take about 2 hours to cook the rice in a double saucepan. I found this time excessive, but rice of 1918 may have been less easy to cook. Today's rice is cooked in about 1 hour in a double saucepan.

SERVES 4

85 g/3 oz long grain rice
600 ml/1 pint milk or milk and water
   or vegetable stock
1 egg yolk
115 g/4 oz hazel nuts, skinned
   and minced
85 g/3 oz pine nuts, minced
salt and freshly ground black pepper

TO COAT:
1 egg white
50 g/2 oz crisp breadcrumbs
FOR FRYING:
50 g/2 oz fat*
TO GARNISH:
parsley

in 1918 this undoubtedly would be clarified dripping or lard. Oil could be used today.

Wash the rice and place into a double saucepan, add the liquid. Cook over steadily boiling water until the liquid is absorbed and the rice is tender. Stir several times during cooking. Beat the egg yolk and add to the cooked rice and nuts, season well and form into rissoles. Beat the white of egg slightly, dip the rissoles in this then roll in the breadcrumbs.

Heat the fat in a frying pan, add the rissoles and fry until crisp and brown on both sides. Drain well and serve on dish paper (plain doily) on a hot dish. Garnish with parsley.

Variation: bake the rissoles instead of frying them.

Scotch Woodcock (page 61)

Summer Lentil Soup

This is a recipe from the staff of the National Training College. Obviously it is called a summer soup as the peas would only be in season then. Today we could use frozen peas and make the soup throughout the year. The original recipe recommends boiling gently for 1½ hours to 2 hours. Fortunately the years have taught us to cook vegetables, even those for soup, for the shortest possible time to retain the maximum of flavour.

SERVES 4 TO 6

25 g/1 oz dripping or margarine	1.2 litres/2 pints water
1 small onion, sliced	salt and freshly ground black pepper
1 small carrot, sliced	175 g/6 oz peas, cooked
1 small turnip, sliced	TO GARNISH:
150 g/5 oz lentils	small croûtons of fried or toasted bread

Heat the dripping or margarine, add the vegetables and washed lentils and cook gently for 5 minutes. Pour in the water, add seasoning to taste. Bring to the boil then cover the pan and simmer steadily for 35 to 40 minutes, or until the vegetables and lentils are tender.

Rub all the ingredients through a sieve to give a thick smooth purée then reheat for a few minutes with the peas. Add the garnish at the last minute.

Variations: chopped mint can be added with the peas, or a little mint and tarragon cooked with the vegetables.

Add one or two tomatoes and a small piece of diced peeled dessert or cooking apple to the lentils and other vegetables.

Add a little chopped celery or celeriac to the lentils and other vegetables.

A chopped slice of bacon, or bacon stock improves the flavour of this soup or use vegetable stock instead of water.

If the sieved soup is too thick dilute with a little more water before adding the peas.

A modern touch: liquidize the soup instead of sieving it.

The soup can be cooked in a large bowl in the microwave,. Use boiling water or boiling stock to shorten the cooking time then follow directions in your microwave manual for timing.

War Galantine

This is the second recipe I have selected from Mrs. C. S. Peel's *Eat-Less-Meat Book*. As we are unused to covering food with a floured cloth I have also given the method of cooking the galantine in a basin. In the recipe Mrs. Peel advises 'the cloth must be wrung out in boiling water before flouring or the flour will not adhere'. I think cooks of that day must have had very tough hands to 'wring out in the boiling water'. It is more comfortable to leave the cloth until cool enough to handle then wring it out. The glaze mentioned in the recipe would be a little aspic jelly (see page 194), which should be set sufficiently to have reached the stage of a thick syrup.

The galantine is given more flavour by the addition of the onions and herbs, see under Variations.

SERVES 4 TO 6

115 g/4 oz beef, minced	salt and freshly ground black pepper
225 g/8 oz cooked lentils	150 ml/¼ pint beef stock
115 g/4 oz sausagemeat	TO COOK:
175 g/6 oz fine breadcrumbs	stock or water
1 egg	

Mix all the ingredients together, form into a roll, tie loosely in a well-floured cloth so leaving room for the roll to swell in cooking. Place in boiling stock or water to cover and simmer for 2 hours; at the end of this time remove from the pan.

Unroll the cloth then wrap it once again around the warm roll but this time it should be a tight fit. Press firmly to form the galantine into a good shape. When cold unwrap and glaze with the aspic jelly.

Variations: add 50 g/2 oz of chopped nuts to the other ingredients or coat the cold galantine with nuts instead of glaze.

Chop 2 medium onions, cook in 25 g/1 oz hot dripping or lard until nearly tender. Add to the other ingredients with 1 tablespoon chopped mixed herbs or 1 teaspoon dried mixed herbs. 1 or 2 crushed garlic cloves can be cooked with the onions and/or 1 to 2 teaspoons curry powder or paste stirred into the hot onions.

Place the ingredients into a well-greased 1.2 litre/2 pint basin, cover and steam for 2 hours over steadily boiling water.

Apple, Spice and Currant Roll

This recipe comes from a wartime book written by the staff of the National Training College, then in Buckingham Palace Road. The appropriate title was *Thrift for Troubled Times*. Instructions for preparing cloths with flour are on page 69.

SERVES 4 TO 6

225 g/8 oz plain flour
1 teaspoon baking powder
100 g/3½ oz dripping*
water to bind
FOR THE FILLING:
1 large cooking apple, peeled, cored
   and finely chopped
25 g/1 oz currants

½ teaspoon mixed spice, or to taste
25 g/1 oz brown sugar
FOR THE TOPPING:
1 to 2 tablespoons granulated sugar

* shredded suet can be used instead of dripping, in which case increase the cooking time to 2 ½ hours. Hard margarine is excellent in this recipe, steam for the same time as for dripping.

Sift the flour and baking powder into a mixing bowl, rub in the dripping. Add sufficient water to make a soft rolling consistency. Roll out into an oblong shape. Spread the filling ingredients over the dough, damp the edges with water and roll the long sides loosely, like a Swiss roll. Put into a floured cloth (page 69). Steam over boiling water for 2 hours. Unwrap, sprinkle with the sugar and serve hot with custard.

Variation: use a 1.2 litre/2 pint greased pudding basin and cut the dough into 3 rounds, the first to fit the base of the basin, the second slightly larger and the third the size of the top of the basin. Put in the first round, add half the filling then the second round, the last of the filling ingredients then the third round. Cover tightly and steam as above.

A modern touch: cook in the basin for approximately 8 minutes on 66% of full output in a microwave.

Snowdon Pudding

This is a traditional Welsh recipe that was used in many homes in Britain during the war; it was an ideal way to use up stale bread. Its Welsh name is Pwdin Eryri and as far as I know originated at a hotel at the foot of Mount Snowdon. The pudding was exceptionally light in texture as it contained no ordinary flour. The large juicy raisins of the period were ideal, when stoned, as they were slightly sticky.

SERVES 4 TO 6

FOR COATING THE BASIN:
25 g/1 oz butter, softened
115 to 175 g/4 to 6 oz raisins, stoned
FOR THE PUDDING:
85 g/3 oz suet
175 g/6 oz soft white breadcrumbs
25 g/1 oz rice flour or cornflour
50 to 85 g/2 to 3 oz light brown or
    caster sugar
4 tablespoons orange marmalade
1 teaspoon finely grated orange zest

1 teaspoon finely grated lemon zest
2 eggs
1 tablespoon lemon juice
1 tablespoon orange juice
FOR THE SAUCE:
1 lemon
150 ml/1/4 pint water
25 g/1 oz cornflour
300 ml/1/2 pint white wine or water
50 g/2 oz caster sugar

Coat the inside of a 900 ml to 1.2 litre/1 1/2 to 2 pint pudding basin with the butter then press the raisins against the butter. Grate or shred the suet. Mix all the ingredients for the pudding together, put into the basin and cover tightly. Steam steadily over boiling water for 1 3/4 hours. Turn out and serve with the sauce.

For the sauce: pare the top zest from the lemon, put into the saucepan with the water and simmer for 10 minutes. Strain the liquid and return to the pan. Halve the lemon and squeeze out the juice, blend the cornflour with the wine or water. Add to the saucepan with the lemon juice and sugar, stir over a medium heat until thickened. Pour a little more sauce on top of the pudding and serve the rest separately.

A modern touch: as stoneless small raisins are less sticky it is better to grease the basin lightly with a small amount of the butter then blend the raisins with the remaining butter, they then adhere to the base and sides of the basin. The pudding can be cooked in a microwave. Cover with clingfilm and pierce a hole in this. Stand the basin on an upturned saucer. Allow 7 minutes at 66% of full output.

Condensed Milk Fruit Cake

This cake was mentioned by several people, who remembered elderly relatives telling them they used condensed milk to eke out their limited amount of sugar during the Great War. Unfortunately no-one had the exact recipe, so I had to do some testing to try and reproduce the description given me. The baking temperature is important, for if the oven is too hot a very hard crust develops early and prevents the heat reaching the centre of the cake. It is remarkably pleasant in texture.

SERVES 8

115 g/4 oz butter or margarine
50 to 85 g/2 to 3 oz granulated sugar
225 ml/7$\frac{1}{2}$ fl oz sweetened
   condensed milk
175 g/6 oz raisins or mixed dried fruit

2 medium eggs
300 g/10 oz self-raising flour or
   plain flour with 2$\frac{1}{2}$ teaspoons
   baking powder
1 teaspoon mixed spice

Preheat the oven to 160°C/325°F/Gas Mark 3/150°C with a fan oven. Grease and flour or line an 18 cm/7 inch cake tin with greased greaseproof paper.

Put the butter or margarine into a saucepan, melt over a low heat then add the sugar and milk. Stir over the heat until the sugar has dissolved. Remove from the heat but add the dried fruit while the mixture is warm. Leave until cold. Whisk the eggs and add gradually to the milk mixture.

Sift the flour, or flour and baking powder with the spice. Stir into the other ingredients. Spoon into the cake tin and bake for approximately 1 hour 20 minutes or until firm. Cool for 5 minutes in the tin then turn out on to a wire cooling tray.

A modern touch: the condensed milk mixture is very sticky, so use a non-stick saucepan if possible or melt the ingredients in a bowl in the microwave.

1920 to 1929

flappers and flapjacks to dumplings

George V and his wife, Queen Mary had worked tirelessly for the country during the war years. The activities of their eldest son, Edward, Prince of Wales, were of enormous interest to the public – he was a handsome and dashing young man, who enjoyed a very social life. In 1923 Lady Elizabeth Bowes-Lyon (the Queen Mother) married the King's second son, the Duke of York. There was great public rejoicing over this event and again in 1926 when their daughter Elizabeth (Queen Elizabeth II) was born.

In 1920 the League of Nations (the fore-runner of the United Nations) had been launched in London. America did not join this. In the same year the Irish Free State was formed.

The pilots of the Royal Flying Corps (now the Royal Air Force) had won admiration during the war and flying was to become more and more sensational. In 1926 Alan Cobham flew to Cape Town and back; this was followed by flights to Australia.

Life in Britain from 1920 to 1929

At first things looked rosy, for there was plenty of work but even by 1920 the first signs of a trade slump appeared, this continued more or less throughout the decade. Money became short for many people - even the rich suffered from increased death duties.

Women were seeking new opportunities; no longer were they content to work as domestics, they wanted to be employed in shops and offices. When trade became bad they were the first to be sacked.

Fashions changed dramatically. Young women had short haircuts and wore short skirts. Critics found these **'both immodest and immoral'**. Corsets were being discarded. Young men and women were known as **'the bright young things'** or **'flappers'**. They seemed determined to live a carefree life, to compensate for the tragedies of the past years.

In 1923 the B.B.C. got their new London studios. George V opened the Empire Exhibition, his speech was broadcast. Over 6 million people heard his voice as well as those at Wembley Stadium. A radio licence cost 10s. (50p) a year.

By 1925 Noel Coward had three plays running in London.

This was a time when films, and film stars, were of great interest. Charlie Chaplin was mobbed in 1921 when he visited London and there was mass hysteria when the young Rudolf Valentino died. The first talking picture - The Jazz Singer - appeared in 1927.

1926 saw the first General Strike. It lasted nine days.

There was no National Health scheme, many people paid 6d (2½p) per week to the doctor to be 'on the panel' - a kind of health scheme. Others could not afford even this. Many kind doctors treated them free.

In 1928 the voting age for women was lowered to 21, so making them equal with men.

The Kitchens

There were great strides in the improved designs of gas and electric cookers.

In 1920 the Ideal Home Exhibition showed homes of the future, which included more modern kitchens and good bathrooms, plus appliances like dishwashers.

The Foods of Britain

Food rationing continued to February 1921. Canned foods were in demand and so were dried soups.

Favourite Drinks

The drinks of the past were still popular, but mixed cocktails had made their appearance and gin and vermouth was a modern favourite.

Meals of 1920 to 1929

These were much simpler than in times past. The traditional British fare was very much in fashion, even in restaurants. The French chefs of pre-war years had left Britain during the war and our own British chefs had not acquired the skills of the future.

Breakfast

For those with money: although the great selection of foods, known in the past, were less prevalent, most people enjoyed a cooked breakfast. Bacon and egg was the favourite dish. This could be served with fried potatoes, fried black pudding or sausages, mushrooms and fried bread. Cold breakfast cereals were on the market. Porridge was still the breakfast dish for many, especially in Scotland.

For the poor: few cooked meals, bread with margarine and tea.

Luncheon

For those with money: for some families this was the main meal of the day. The menu would be as for dinner, below. Children came home from school, for there were few school dinners served. Where families had an evening dinner the mid-day meals could consist of a light snack.

For the poor: vegetable soup might be made or a reconstituted dried soup, for these were cheap. Potatoes and a little meat. Few other vegetables.

Teatime

The elegant 'At Homes', which vanished in wartime, never returned. The tea dances that had been popular in a few places in the years before the war did not come back either. In many cases, especially where women were alone, teatime consisted of tea and a biscuit.

For those with money: High Teas were served in many comfortable homes, especially in the North of England and Scotland. This meant a cooked main course or cold meat (generally ham) or canned fish, like salmon or sardines with salad, served with bread and butter, cake and tea.

For the poor: in cases where one or both parents were in work, teatime would be a more modest version of the meal of richer people. As the decade continued, and more and more became out of work, their meals would revert to the bread and margarine days.

Dinner

For those with money: simplified three-course meals, consisting of soup or an hors d'oeuvre, followed by a main course, pudding or cheese.

Wines might be served but these were still expensive for most people.

For the poor: a meal of little or no meat, with potatoes and another vegetable if they grew them. Canned peas were a great standby.

Cookery Influences

Mrs. Beeton's book was now considered dated and was used far less, although prized as a family 'heirloom'. Women's magazines were gaining in importance, all carried cookery articles and up-to-the-minute recipes. *Good Housekeeping* magazine was launched in 1922 and this quickly became a great favourite.

1920 to 1929

The Recipes

Giblet Soup

In the 1920's poultry was sold with the giblets, which were used to make stock and occasionally a giblet pâté. Food rationing was still in force until 1921 and there were food shortages. I can remember my mother telling me she used giblets to make a meaty soup. It was so satisfying that it was served as a main dish.

SERVES 4

giblets from a chicken or duck
1.5 litres/2½ pints water
2 medium onions, chop 1 onion
   and finely dice the second
2 medium carrots, chop 1 carrot
   and finely dice the second

1 small turnip, chop half the turnip
   and finely dice the remainder
2 small leeks, thinly sliced
small bunch parsley
few sprigs thyme
salt and freshly ground black pepper

Put the giblets into a saucepan with the water, the chopped vegetables, 1 sliced leek and the herbs tied in a piece of cotton. Cover the pan and simmer steadily for 1 hour. Strain the liquid and return to the saucepan. Dice the meat from the giblets, add to the stock with the diced vegetables, remaining leek and seasoning to taste. Cover the pan again and cook for a further 20 minutes or until the vegetables are tender. Serve with toast.

Variations: when chestnuts are in season a few skinned nuts can be simmered with the giblets as well as the vegetables.

Add 1 to 2 tablespoons long grain rice to the stock with the chopped giblets and diced vegetables; cook for 20 minutes.

Purée of Giblet Soup: simmer the giblets with all the vegetables, which can be roughly chopped. When tender sieve the ingredients to make a smooth purée. Return to the saucepan, add a little milk and extra seasoning. Reheat and top with chopped parsley.

The ingredients can be liquidized but make sure all bones are removed from the neck of the bird.

Stewed Eels

While Jellied Eels are well-known as a favourite dish of true Londoners, stewed eels are less well-known. They were often sold by street traders with Parsley Sauce.

SERVES 4

about 900 g/2 lb eels
900 ml/1½ pints water
4 medium onions, left whole
salt and freshly ground black pepper
2 teaspoons vinegar or lemon juice
2 fresh bay leaves
good pinch allspice

FOR THE PARSLEY SAUCE:
25 g/1 oz butter
25 g/1 oz flour
225 ml/7½ fl oz milk
fish stock, see method
2 tablespoons chopped parsley

Ask the fishmonger to skin and bone the eel. If this has not been done wash the fish and soak for at least 15 minutes in well-salted cold water. After this it is easier to strip away the skin. Slit the eel(s) and carefully cut away the backbone(s). Cut into 2.5 to 5 cm/1 to 2 inch lengths. Put into a saucepan with the water and other ingredients. Cover the pan and simmer gently for 45 to 55 minutes, or until tender.

Meanwhile heat the butter in another pan, stir in the flour then gradually add the milk. Stir over a low heat until thickened; add enough stock from cooking the eel to give the desired consistency. Add the parsley and seasoning.

When served from the fishmongers or barrows the cooked eel, without the onions, was placed into the rather runny sauce and topped with mashed potatoes.

When serving at home arrange the eel on a dish with the onions. Serve the sauce and mashed potatoes separately.

Variations:

Jellied Eels: cook the eels as above (the onions could be omitted); remove from the liquid and boil this briskly until reduced to 300 ml/½ pint. Pour over the fish and leave to set. For a firmer jelly dissolve 7 g/¼ oz of gelatine in the hot liquid before pouring over the fish.

Eels Meunière: skin and slice the uncooked eel, coat in a little seasoned flour, then beaten egg and soft fine breadcrumbs. Fry steadily in a generous amount of hot butter until tender. Sprinkle with lemon juice and parsley and serve as a light main dish or an hors d'oeuvre.

Bloater Pie

Many people of today have never tasted a bloater, which is a pity, for they have an excellent flavour. Bloaters are produced from lightly salted and smoked herrings. Because they are smoked whole, rather than being split like kippers, their texture is more moist. Smoked fish was popular in the 1920's because it kept better than fresh fish, so was safer to buy.

SERVES 4

4 to 6 bloaters

2 eggs

40 g/1½ oz butter or margarine

1 small onion, finely chopped

2 celery sticks, finely chopped

25 g/1 oz plain flour

300 ml/½ pint milk

3 tablespoons single cream

salt and freshly ground black pepper

2 teaspoons chopped tarragon
 or parsley

FOR THE TOPPING:

675 g/1½ lb boiled potatoes

4 tablespoons milk

25 g/1 oz butter

2 tablespoons chopped parsley

Preheat the oven to 190°C/375°F/Gas Mark 5/180°C with a fan oven. Skin the fish and remove all the bones. Break the flesh into large flakes. Hard-boil then slice the eggs. Heat the butter or margarine in a saucepan, add the onion and celery and cook gently for 5 minutes, stir in the flour then add the milk and cream. Bring to the boil and stir briskly until the sauce thickens. Remove from the heat, add the fish, seasoning, tarragon or parsley and sliced eggs.

Spoon into a greased 1.2 litre/2 pint pie dish. Mash the potatoes, heat the milk and butter then gradually beat into the potatoes with the parsley. Season and spoon over the fish. Bake for 30 minutes then serve with a mixture of cooked diced carrots, turnip and swede.

Variations: use smoked haddock instead of bloaters but poach the fish first until just tender.

Cooked flaked white fish can be used instead of bloaters.

Stewed Eels (page 79)

Boiled Beef and Carrots

This is an excellent hot dish for cold weather and the meat is equally good served cold with pickles and salad or in sandwiches. Many public houses of the day made a speciality of sandwiches filled with hot salted beef. In the past capable cooks would have prepared the beef themselves by soaking it for some days in the pickling liquid of water, salt, sugar and saltpetre with various spices, such as cloves, allspice and cinnamon. By the 1920's many more women had become less willing to do these tasks themselves and were happy to buy ready-prepared beef from the butcher.

It is essential that the joint is soaked overnight, or for some hours, in cold water before cooking. The salted meat tends to shrink in cooking so allow for this. The following quantity would provide sufficient meat for both a hot and cold meal.

SERVES 4 TO 6

approximately 2 kg/4 1/2 lb joint of salted brisket or silverside	675 g/1 1/2 lb small carrots
	450 g/1 lb small onions
freshly ground black pepper or	bouquet garni
1/2 teaspoon white or	2 teaspoons brown sugar
black peppercorns	

Soak the beef as instructed above. Put into a saucepan with water to cover. Bring the water to the boil then remove the meat and discard the liquid, (this stage is not essential but it is an added way of ensuring that the beef is not too salty). Return the beef to the pan and cover with fresh water. Bring this to the boil, add the pepper or peppercorns and a few of the carrots, plus all the onions, the herbs and sugar. Cover the pan and lower the heat. In spite of the title of the dish the liquid must NOT BOIL but should just simmer steadily throughout the cooking time. Allow 40 minutes per 450 g/1 lb but, as quality of meat varies, check carefully before serving.

The remainder of the carrots should be added to the beef 20 to 30 minutes (dependent upon size) before the end of the cooking time.

Serve with the freshly cooked carrots, boiled potatoes and some of the strained unthickened liquid or use this to make a Mustard Sauce (page 169).

Variations: make dumplings as the recipe on page 90 and cook in the liquid with the beef. Use other vegetables in season.

The pudding could be cooked in a microwave for about 6 minutes on the setting that gives 66% of full output. Allow to stand for 2 minutes before turning out. Meanwhile heat the ingredients for the sauce in a basin in the microwave.

All-in-One mixture: if using soft butter or margarine put all the ingredients into a mixing bowl or electric mixer or food processor and mix together. Many recipes add an extra 1 teaspoon baking powder to compensate for the lack of aeration given by efficient creaming. I do not do this, for I dislike the taste of baking powder and find I get a very acceptable light sponge without it.

Custard Sauce

French menus often give this sauce under the name of English Cream or English Custard. It should be beautifully smooth and rich in flavour. This is achieved by using more egg yolks than whites and incorporating a little cream.

SERVES 4 TO 6

2 large eggs	600 ml/1 pint milk
3 egg yolks	150 ml/5 fl oz double cream
1 to 2 tablespoons caster sugar	

Break the eggs into a basin, add the yolks and sugar and mix thoroughly. Warm the milk, do not allow it to boil, add to the eggs then stir in the cream. Strain into the top of a double saucepan or clean basin and stand over hot, but not boiling, water. Stir briskly or whisk over a low heat until the custard is sufficiently thick to coat the back of a wooden spoon. Serve hot or cold.

If serving cold cover the basin or sauceboat.

A modern touch: liquidize the custard if it shows any signs of curdling. This makes it beautifully smooth but a little less thick, so you may have to reheat it for a very short time.

Steamed Lemon Pudding (page 98)

Steamed Lemon Pudding

Steamed puddings were one of the favourite cold weather dishes of this era. Many of the pudding recipes contained a high percentage of breadcrumbs to ensure a light texture. Recipes often gave dripping as an alternative to butter or margarine, for the joints of the period had a high percentage of fat which produced good dripping. This would be clarified (cleaned) and used in puddings, baking, frying and roasting. As no egg is in the recipe it would have been ideal for the period before 1921, when many unrationed foods were still scarce.

SERVES 4

FOR THE PUDDING:

50 g/2oz self-raising flour or plain flour with ½ teaspoon baking powder
50 g/2 oz margarine or dripping
25 g/1 oz caster sugar
1 tablespoon golden syrup
115 g/4 oz soft breadcrumbs
1 teaspoon finely grated lemon zest
1 tablespoon lemon juice
6 tablespoons milk

FOR THE SAUCE:

1 teaspoon arrowroot
150 ml/¼ pint water
1 tablespoon golden syrup
1 teaspoon finely grated lemon zest
2 tablespoons lemon juice
25 g/1 oz caster sugar, or to taste

Sift the flour, or flour and baking powder. Melt the margarine or dripping. Mix all the ingredients for the pudding together. Grease a 600 to 900 ml/1 to 1½ pint basin, spoon in the mixture. Cover tightly and steam steadily for 1½ hours. Turn out and serve hot with the sauce.

For the sauce: blend the arrowroot and water, pour into a saucepan, add the rest of the ingredients and stir over a moderate heat until thickened and clear.

A modern touch: cook the pudding in a microwave. Use the setting that gives 66% of full output. The sauce can be cooked in a basin in the microwave.

Bread Pudding

There was always much competition among practical cooks as to who made the best Bread Pudding. It was a favourite way of using up stale bread and it did produce a very satisfying pudding, which could be sliced and taken to work or school. Shredded suet was firmly established by this era but many housewives would prefer suet from the butcher, which they grated.

After the end of food rationing in 1921 people were much more careful about wasting any food. The bread used for the pudding can be with or without crusts; in each case the total weight should be as given below.

SERVES 8

450 g/1 lb bread	1 to 2 teaspoons allspice
450 ml/³/₄ pint milk	½ teaspoon grated or ground nutmeg
115 g/4 oz suet, shredded or grated	2 eggs
175 g/6 oz mixed dried fruit	FOR THE TOPPING:
115 g/4 oz sugar, preferably brown	25 g/1 oz butter, melted
2 tablespoons marmalade	1 to 2 tablespoons brown sugar

Preheat the oven to 180°C/350°F/Gas Mark 4/170°C with a fan oven. Grease a 23 cm/9 inch square tin. Break the bread into small pieces, put into a bowl. Heat two-thirds of the milk, pour over the bread and leave to soak for 30 minutes then stir briskly until a smooth mixture. Add the rest of the ingredients and mix well.

Spoon into the tin, brush with the melted butter and bake for 2¼ hours. At the end of the first hour reduce the heat to 160°C/325°F/Gas Mark 3/150°C with a fan oven. Sprinkle with the brown sugar. Serve hot or cold.

Variation: use melted butter or margarine instead of suet.

Flapjacks

These biscuits, based on rolled oats, were popular early this century and still are a favourite with most people. When cooked store in an airtight tin away from any other biscuits, so they keep firm and crisp.

MAKES: 12 TO 16

85 g/3 oz butter, margarine or lard
2 tablespoons golden syrup

50 g/2 oz soft brown sugar
175 g/6 oz rolled oats

Preheat the oven to 180°C/350°F/Gas Mark 4/160°C with a fan oven - or see Variations. Grease and flour an 18 to 20 cm/7 to 8 inch square tin.

Put the fat, syrup and sugar into a saucepan and melt over a low heat. Remove from the heat and stir in the rolled oats. Spoon into the tin and smooth flat on top. Bake for approximately 25 minutes or until evenly golden brown. Allow to cool for 2 to 3 minutes then cut into 12 to 16 portions. Leave for another 10 to 15 minutes then carefully lift out of the tin on to a wire cooling tray. When quite cold put into an airtight tin.

Variations: for a sticky Flapjack preheat the oven to 160°C/325°F/Gas Mark 3/150°C with a fan oven and bake for about 30 minutes.

Chocolate Flapjack: stir 50 g/2 oz grated plain chocolate into the hot mixture before adding the rolled oats.

Nut Flapjack: add 50 g/2 oz chopped walnuts or other nuts to the mixture.

1930 to 1939

hard times and soup kitchens

This was a decade full of drama. In 1935 the country celebrated the Silver Jubilee of George V. The King and Queen had a wonderful reception as they drove through the streets of London to St. Paul's Cathedral. Sadly he died in 1936. He was succeeded by his son, Edward VIII. Edward was never crowned for in December he renounced the throne to marry Mrs. Wallis Simpson. The former Duke of York became George VI and, with his wife Elizabeth, was crowned in 1937.

1933 brought the first reports of Nazi activities in Germany and in 1938 German forces, under Adolf Hitler, annexed Austria.

The Prime Minister, Neville Chamberlain, flew to Munich to meet Hitler and returned saying 'I believe it is peace in our time'. He was proved wrong, for later that year the Germans marched into Czechoslovakia and then in 1939 into Poland which is when Britain declared war on Germany.

Life in Britain from 1930 to 1939

By 1930 unemployment in Britain had reached over two million. In an effort to help the situation the Prince of Wales launched a 'Buy British' drive.

The cotton industry was declining, they blamed short skirts and the lack of petticoats and had a **National Cotton Week**. Skirts did become longer but critics declared that these were **'an infringement of liberty and comfort'**.

In 1933 Lyons, the caterers, opened the new London Corner House.

In 1934 Britain celebrated a double tennis victory at Wimbledon. Dorothy Round won the women's singles and Fred Perry the men's.

In 1936 the B.B.C. added sound to television pictures. In October of the same year there was the Jarrow march to Parliament as a protest at lack of work.

August 1939, just before the declaration of war, children were being evacuated from large cities to the safety of the country.

The Kitchens

There were improvements in the design of gas and electric cookers. Some were made with glass doors to the oven so cooks could see the food inside. By 1939 about 25% of homes owned a refrigerator. Quick boiling kettles and electric toasters were readily available. Some kitchens were being made more modern.

The Foods of Britain

The slimming craze of the decade meant a serious drop in the sale of potatoes. There was interest in the making of ice cream as people considered the possibility of owning a refrigerator.

People were cooking traditional dishes and showed little interest in new ideas. Baking was popular again.

Prepared Foods

Packet sponge and cake mixes were plentiful.

When war was declared most people tried to accumulate a good stock of canned foods in readiness for the food rationing to come.

Favourite Drinks

Most forms of alcohol were drunk at this time. It had become quite correct for women to visit a public house with their male companions.

Wine with meals was not very usual for the majority of people. They had drinks, such as sherry or gin and tonic or gin with orange juice, before the meal, rather than with the food. Any wines drunk would be French or German. Madeira, which had been popular earlier in the century was rarely seen.

Meals of 1930 to 1939

These were very similar to those served in the previous decade, except for the mass of unemployed people whose diet was so very restricted.

The dishes that follow are indicative of the tastes of this period. Mutton was rarely seen and lamb was sold instead. Roast chicken was the great treat for most families.

Breakfast

Much greater use of uncooked packet cereals.

Cookery Influences

Manufacturers of gas and electric cookers and food products started to produce attractive and practical books; many more people bought women's magazines and followed their cookery articles. Some of these gave step-by-step recipes to help the increasingly large number of women who were learning to cook. Elizabeth Craig was one of the popular writers of cookery books and articles. Domestic science lessons in schools became important.

Andre Simon was a great source of inspiration and instruction to chefs, professional cooks and wine lovers at this time and for several decades in the future.

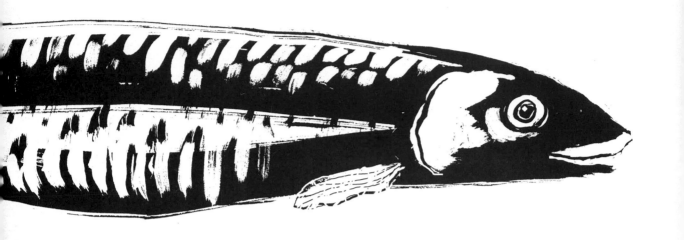
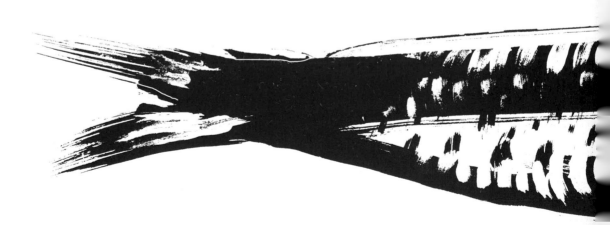

1930 to 1939

The Recipes

Soused Herrings

The word 'souse' means to drench with water, or other liquid, and this is exactly what happens to fresh herrings in this dish. The fish is drenched with diluted vinegar. The slow cooking and extra ingredients give the herrings an excellent flavour. Serve hot or cold with salad.

In the 1930's we were told of the many benefits of eating fresh herrings, plus the other fish produced from them, i.e. kippers, bloaters and buckling. Fresh herrings and kippers are still available, although warnings have been given from time to time about dwindling supplies. Sadly bloaters and buckling have become very scarce.

SERVES 4

4 large or 8 small herrings	250 ml/8 fl oz brown malt vinegar
2 medium onions, thinly sliced	250 ml/8 fl oz water
2 dessert apples, cored and sliced, optional	1 teaspoon mixed pickling spices
	good pinch ground ginger, optional
4 to 8 fresh or 2 to 4 dried bay leaves	salt and freshly ground black pepper

Preheat the oven to 140°C/275°F/Gas Mark 1. The setting is suitable for a fan oven. If the fishmonger has not removed the heads and backbones of the fish do this. Open them out flat and discard the intestines but keep the soft or hard roes. Place several onion rings plus 1 or 2 apple slices, a whole fresh bay leaf or half a dried one on each fish. Roll firmly from the head end to the tail, encourage the tails to stand upright. Secure with wooden cocktail sticks. Place in an ovenproof dish, add the remaining onions, apples and the rest of the ingredients. Cover and cook for 1¼ to 1½ hours, depending upon the size. To serve the fish lift from the liquid. Strain some of this and use in a salad dressing.

The roes can be placed on the fish before rolling or added to the vinegar liquid or fried in a little butter and served as a light snack.

A modern touch: to give a more delicate flavour use red wine vinegar instead of malt and flavour this with chopped lemon grass, strips of red and green pepper and a few juniper berries.

Cod's Roe and Bacon

Breakfast was an important meal up to the beginning of the Second World War. The mixture of fish and bacon is interesting and the dish was popular with lovers of fish.

SERVES 4

8 streaky bacon rashers, derinded

450 g/1 lb cooked cod's roe, skinned and sliced

Cook the bacon rinds in the frying pan to extract the fat. Remove then add the rashers. Cook to personal taste and keep hot. Add the slices of roe, fry in the bacon fat for 2 minutes on either side. Serve with the bacon.

Bacon and Apple Rings: I was told an uncle of mine cooked this mixture when in the trenches during the First World War. Fry cored rings of cooking apple with the bacon. In fact the apple is an excellent accompaniment to the cod's roe and bacon and also with bacon and black pudding (another favourite breakfast dish).

Mock Fish Cakes

This recipe comes from The *OLIO Cookery Book* by L. Sykes. The book was popular before and during the 1930's, for the recipes were practical and economical. The strange name 'OLIO' means 'mixture, medley or collection'.

SERVES 4

225 g/8 oz potatoes, weight when boiled

115 g/4 oz cooked or canned butter beans

1 teaspoon lemon juice, if available

2 teaspoons anchovy sauce or

bloater paste

salt and freshly ground black or cayenne pepper

little plain flour

FOR FRYING:

25 g/1 oz lard

Mash the potatoes and beans until smooth, add the lemon juice and sauce or paste together with seasoning to taste. Form into 8 small flat cakes with floured fingers. Coat in a little flour. Heat the lard and fry the cakes until crisp and brown.

Poached Salmon

In spring and summer hot or cold poached salmon was considered a most luxurious and delicious dish for special occasions. If serving cold it was served with mayonnaise but when hot the perfect accompaniment was Hollandaise Sauce (old recipe books often call it Dutch Sauce). Fresh salmon in the 1930's was the wild fish and therefore in season only from March to August. It was not until the 1970's that salmon farms were established and salmon became an 'all-the-year-round' fish.

Undoubtedly farmed salmon has a good consistent taste but wild salmon, at its best, is the finer fish.

SERVES 6 OR MORE AS AN HORS D'OEUVRE

1 whole fresh salmon about
   1.4 kg/3 lb in weight
1.5 litres/2½ pints water or
   fish stock as page 16 or
   Court Bouillon, see below

TO GARNISH:
lemon slices, parsley and/or fennel
sliced cucumber

Most homes, where a large amount of cooking was done, had a fish kettle in the 1930's and this was ideal for whole fish; for it could be placed on the rack and lowered into the liquid so there was no fear of it breaking.

Clean the fish by washing it well, slit down the stomach and remove the intestines. It has always been traditional to leave both the head and tail on the fish. Scrape away the scales from the body with the back of a knife. Place the fish in the cold liquid in the container. Bring to simmering point and then time the cooking. Allow 7 minutes per 450 g/1 lb for a fish up to 1.4 kg/3 lb. For a larger fish add an extra 5 minutes per 450 g/1 lb. If placing the fish in hot liquid allow 1 or 2 minutes extra cooking time.

Carefully remove the fish from the cooking container. Remove the skin, but keep the fish intact. Garnish and serve.

To make Court Bouillon: for a salmon weighing approximately 1.4 kg/3 lb peel and thinly slice a medium onion and a medium carrot. Remove 2 or 3 slices of top zest from a lemon. Add to 1.2 litres/2 pints of water or fish stock and 300 ml/½ pint white wine with 1 bay leaf, a small sprig of parsley or fennel and a little seasoning.

Steak and Kidney Pie

As a young home economist I seemed to spend a lot of time answering queries about making good pastry. It seemed to me to be every cook's ambition to be a perfect pastry cook. The majority of housewives were happy to top the meat with shortcrust pastry but some were more ambitious and made puff pastry as page 178 instead.

SERVES 4 TO 6

Shortcrust Pastry made with
175 g/6 oz flour, etc. as page 82
FOR THE FILLING:
675 g/1 ½ lb chuck or other stewing
steak, diced
225 g/8 oz ox or lamb's kidneys, diced
25 g/1 oz plain flour

salt and freshly ground black pepper
50 g/2 oz beef dripping or fat
450 ml/³/₄ pint beef stock
150 ml/¹/₄ pint red wine or more stock
TO GLAZE:
1 egg, beaten

Make the pastry, wrap this and put in a cool place to relax. Mix the steak and kidney together. Blend the flour with the seasoning and coat the meat. The easiest way to do this is to put the seasoned flour into a large bag, add the meat and shake firmly.

Heat the dripping or fat in a large saucepan, add the coated meat and cook steadily for about 10 minutes, stir throughout this time. Gradually add the stock, bring to the boil and stir until slightly thickened then pour in the wine or more stock. Cover the saucepan; cook gently for 1 ½ hours, or until the meat is nearly tender. Cool.

Preheat the oven to 200°C/400°F/Gas Mark 6/190°C with a fan oven.

Spoon the meat with a little of the gravy and a pie support into a 1.5 litre/2 ½ pint pie dish. Save the rest of the gravy to serve with the pie. Roll out the pastry and cut out narrow bands to fit around the edge of the pie dish. Roll the rest of the pastry to cover the filling. Moisten and seal the edges and flute neatly. Make a slit on top for the steam to escape. Use any pastry left over to make a rose or tassel and pastry leaves; press on top. Brush all the pastry with the egg. Bake for approximately 40 minutes. If the pastry is becoming too brown lower the heat slightly.

Variation: use Puff Pastry. In this case start the cooking in a preheated oven set to 220°C/425°F/Gas Mark 7/210°C with a fan oven. Lower the heat after 20 minutes.

Omelette en Surprise

During 1938 and 1939, before the start of the Second World War, I was a Home Economist with Frigidaire, giving demonstrations throughout Britain. At that time Frigidaire were the leading manufacturers of refrigerators. This dish was one I often made as the grand finale to impress the audience, who were certain the ice cream would melt in the heat of the oven. In 1939 only about a quarter of households owned a refrigerator and I was trying to show what delicious ices and other delectable dishes could be made at home.

Years later people were inclined to say that this dish (also known as a Norwegian Omelette) was exactly the same as Baked Alaska on page 190; they are similar but not the same.

SERVES 4 TO 6

Victoria Sandwich as page 36

approximately 3 tablespoons liqueur,
    such as crème de menthe

ice cream, made as page 29

FOR THE SOUFFLÉ MIXTURE:

1 or 2 egg yolks

85 g/3 oz caster sugar

few drops vanilla extract

3 egg whites

TO COAT:

1 to 2 tablespoons sifted icing sugar

Preheat the oven to 230°C/450°C/Gas Mark 8/220°C with a fan oven. Cut the sponge to fit into an ovenproof serving dish. Soak in the liqueur. Make sure the ice cream is very hard, keep it in the freezing compartment of the refrigerator until the last minute.

Beat the egg yolk(s), sugar and vanilla until thick and creamy. In a separate bowl whisk the egg whites until stiff, fold the whites into the egg yolk(s). Put the ice cream on the sponge then coat with the egg mixture. Make sure this completely covers the ice cream. Dredge with the icing sugar. Place in the oven for 3 minutes or until golden coloured then serve at once.

A modern touch: in view of the short cooking time the eggs are virtually uncooked, so take care you know the source of supply (see page 265).

It is better to keep the ice cream in the freezer, rather than the freezing compartment of the refrigerator.

Trifle (page 119)

While the sugar is boiling whisk the egg white until very stiff. Gradually pour the sugar syrup on to the egg white in a steady stream, whisking all the time. Cool slightly then spread over the top and sides of the cake to give a thick coating. Decorate with the walnut halves.

Coconut Pyramids

As a young home economist I had to make cakes to serve to the audience at afternoon cookery demonstrations. These and the Battenburg Cake on page 124 were always greeted with enthusiasm.

MAKES ABOUT 16

few sheets of rice paper, if available	175 g/6 oz desiccated coconut
2 whites from small eggs	2 teaspoons cornflour, or
115 g/4 oz caster sugar	amount necessary

Preheat the oven to 160°C/325°F/Gas Mark 3/150°C with a fan oven. Place the rice paper on baking trays or lightly grease the trays.

Whisk the egg whites until frothy, add the sugar and coconut. Mix thoroughly. The mixture should be the right consistency to handle, so add the cornflour steadily to achieve this texture. Mould into Pyramid shapes with damp fingers and place on the rice paper or greased trays.

Bake for 10 to 12 minutes, or until the tips of the cakes are golden brown. Leave until sufficiently cool to handle then carefully cut around the rice paper; lift the cakes from the trays. Place on a wire cooling tray.

These keep well for several days in an airtight tin.

Variation: sweetened condensed milk was extremely popular in the 1930's and another version of Coconut Pyramids was to blend one 405 g/14 oz can of the milk with 225 to 250 g/8 to 9 oz desiccated coconut (the right amount to give the consistency described above). Form into pyramid shapes and bake as above.

1940 to 1949

poor man's goose, monday jug

George VI, Queen Elizabeth and their two daughters remained in Britain through the war years. The King and Queen visited badly bombed areas to sympathise with the people about their terrifying experiences. Buckingham Palace, like so many homes in Britain, was damaged during the bombing.

Winston Churchill became Prime Minister in 1940 and was the voice of encouragement throughout the war.

In 1940 Germany had invaded Denmark and Holland, and the British troops stationed in Norway were captured. In May of the same year the German invasion continued into Belgium and France. The French capitulated and this meant that our expeditionary forces were forced back to the northern sea coast. They were rescued by the Royal Navy, aided by a flotilla of small boats, in the famous Dunkirk evacuation. This meant that Britain now stood alone against Germany.

Later that year the Germans occupied the Channel Islands. In 1941 they invaded Russia.

December 1941 saw the unexpected Japanese attack on America at Pearl Harbour, so Britain joined America in declaring war on Japan. America, Britain and Russia became allies against Germany. The whole world was now at war, to remain so until 1945.

After all the unhappiness and worries of the war years, and the restrictions that followed the end of the hostilities, the marriage of Princess Elizabeth to Prince Philip of Greece in November, 1947 and the birth of their son Charles in 1948 were two happy occasions for the Royal family and the people of Britain.

Life in Britain from 1940 to 1949

1940 saw the beginning of bombing against many parts of Britain. This continued throughout the war years.

The Home Guard was formed from older men, those too young to be drafted into the forces, and anyone who could help defend Britain in the case of an invasion.

Many people's lives consisted of hard work, voluntary service and sheltering from bombing in vulnerable areas. Tube stations were the night-time home of many Londoners throughout the war. This meant catering services had to be provided. When areas had been destroyed by bombing out-door emergency catering was rushed there. Catering was arranged at centres for members of the A.R.P. and other Civil Defence workers. I helped at Bradford all night once a week. Most of this work was by volunteers.

Clothes and soap rationing were other problems of the era.

There were dances for the forces and young people, especially when the American forces came to Britain.

In 1944, in spite of the demands of wartime, the National Health Service was introduced and Parliament passed a law raising the school leaving age to 15. In years to come it was raised again to 16.

May 1945 saw the end of the war in Europe and was celebrated as V.E. Day. In August the Japanese surrendered and V.J. Day followed.

In October 1946 B.B.C. radio began **Woman's Hour** and B.B.C. television began after a lapse of six years. Programmes were shown for a limited number of hours.

The winter of 1946 and spring of 1947 brought exceptionally cold weather. The R.A.F. had to drop food supplies to stranded villages.

Women rejoiced when the rather dreary utility clothes ceased to exist and delighted in the new feminine Dior designs.

There was plenty of work for men and women during, and after, the war.

The Kitchens

Obviously no new cookers and other domestic appliances were made during the war but the manufacture of refrigerators and other goods began almost immediately it ended. The equipment at this time was not for the British but for export. The rather frightening slogans **'export or die'** and **'work or want'** replaced those of wartime.

Pressure cookers came on the market in 1949 and were hailed with delight. We were urged to save fuel and the short cooking times when using these cookers were ideal.

The Foods of Britain

Rationing came into force at the beginning of January 1940. It was a gradual process - bacon or ham, butter and sugar came first; in March meat was rationed. This was the most worrying of all foods, for supplies were never plentiful and often the fresh meat ration of 1s.2d (6 p) per person each week had to be supplemented with some corned beef.

Rationing of tea, margarine, cooking fat and cheese began in July 1940.

In 1941 jam, marmalade, treacle and syrup came on ration and in 1941 rationing of fresh eggs, milk and sweetmeats began.

These strict controls lasted throughout this decade and into the 1950s.

Comments are often made in modern times that the British were healthier during the war years than they are today. What are the reasons?

As a member of the Food Advice Division of the Ministry of Food from 1942 onward I was in contact with the public. I think therefore the answers are simple.

a) for many poor children the school dinners and milk, free cod liver oil and orange juice when young, provided them with a more nutritious diet than they had ever experienced. There were British restaurants in many towns so older people would be sure of a satisfying meal. Canteens provided meals for factory workers.

b) expectant mothers of all classes had cod liver oil and orange juice so they were kept fit.

c) mothers and fathers of all classes took nutrition seriously and made sure the family ate their rations plus the fresh vegetables and fruits available. People who had been out of work now had jobs, so more money to spend on food.

d) there were few sweetened snacks available; children nibbled carrots between meals. Sweetmeats were rationed to 350 g/12 oz per person per month.

e) although restricted in selection our vegetables and fruits were **fresh** since all were British grown.

I consider the war years to be the time when British cooks began to be imaginative and create new dishes. Had they not done so they would have been very hungry.

They also learned to cook vegetables correctly, and eat more salads, to ensure they had essential vitamins. Citrus fruits were not imported during the war, except for very infrequent supplies of oranges that were for children.

After the war ended supplies of whale-meat, snoek (a South African canned fish, not unlike tuna) and even horse-meat were foods the Ministry of Food tried to encourage us to eat, to help out the small amount of meat. None were popular.

In 1946 bread became rationed, due to a world shortage of grain, and in 1947 rationing of potatoes was introduced. This was because of poor supplies, due to the terrible winter weather of 1946 to 1947.

Prepared Foods

Dried egg and dried milk could be said to be prepared foods and both were welcome additions to the rations.

Canned corned beef and Spam, obtainable on the points system, were helpful.

Favourite Drinks

This should really be headed 'obtainable drinks', for alcohol, like most other commodities, was scarce. Supplies were more available for the forces and their recreational establishments.

Meals of 1940 to 1949

The selection of recipes from pages 134 to 154 give an idea of what could be made during these years. You would be a very brave person to try and make out menus. You did the best with the foods available.

Radio talks and television demonstrations had up-to-the-minute suggestions for dishes that could be made. I gave many radio talks and started on B.B.C television in November 1947 on the first women's magazine programme, Designed for Women. I continued to be the cook on this programme for 15 years.

Emergency Cooking

The Ministry of Food provided plans to make emergency cookers in the event of severe devastation in an area due to bombing. These were generally built and used by members of the Women's Royal Voluntary Service (W.R.V.S.). This meant that hot food and drinks could be provided to people whose homes were not habitable at the time.

Cookery Influences

The Ministry of Food's leaflets, newspaper articles and broadcasts of recipes were the main sources of information, together with the demonstrations given throughout Britain by the Ministry of Food Advisers. Magazines printed economical cookery recipes and so did some food manufacturers for, even if their products were not available, they wanted to keep their names before the public.

There was some cookery education in schools, although this was limited by rationing restrictions. The B.B.C. broadcast recipes, as did Woman's Hour after it was launched in 1946. Philip Harben and I began cookery demonstrations on B.B.C. television from Alexandra Palace, Wood Green in 1947.

1940 to 1949

The Recipes

Russian Borsch

When Russia was attacked by Germany, and we became their ally, Russian dishes were of great interest. We made a number of economical versions of this soup during the years of shortages but when food became slightly more plentiful, and people had a little more time for cooking, at the very end of the 1940's, we were able to make a more authentic dish. The beetroot soup should be topped with soured cream. Sadly cream was not available until 1953, so we had to make do with 'souring' the top of the milk.

SERVES 4 TO 6

8 oz/225 g stewing steak, finely diced
1.5 litres/2½ pints water
3 medium onions, finely diced
3 medium carrots, finely diced
salt and freshly ground black pepper
small bunch parsley
2 potatoes, finely diced
350 g/12 oz cooked beetroot,

finely diced
2 medium tomatoes, skinned and deseeded then chopped
2 teaspoons sugar
50 g/2 oz cabbage heart, finely shredded
TO GARNISH:
little top of the milk
squeeze lemon juice or little vinegar

Put the steak in a saucepan with the water, 1 of the onions and 1 of the carrots. Season lightly. Add half the parsley. Cover the pan and simmer gently for 1 hour. Strain the stock and keep the meat.

Put the remaining onions, carrots and parsley into a saucepan with the beef stock. Cover and simmer for 25 minutes, add the potatoes, beetroot, tomatoes and sugar and simmer for a further 10 minutes.

Lastly add the cabbage and cook fairly quickly for 5 to 6 minutes, so the cabbage retains its firm texture. Taste and add extra seasoning and the diced stewing steak. Heat thoroughly, spoon into bowls or soup plates and add the soured milk just before serving.

To sour milk or cream: add a very little lemon juice or vinegar to the top of the milk or lightly whipped fresh cream.

A modern touch: commercially soured cream or crème fraîche is readily available and makes an excellent topping to the soup.

Potato and Bacon Omelette

Potatoes were one of the most important foods during the war years. We used them grated raw in puddings and cooked in a wide variety of dishes. It was an unexpected blow when potato rationing was introduced during 1947 - due to terrible winter weather which prevented spring crops being planted.

When dried eggs were first introduced most of us disliked them, they seemed to have a musty taste. This was due to the way we mixed them. It took a little time to appreciate the fact that the proportion of dried egg powder to water was very important. This is stressed in the recipe below.

The wording about the amount of fat repeats the words used during all years of rationing.

SERVES 1 OR 2

1 bacon rasher, derinded and chopped
15 to 25 g/½ to 1 oz fat
1 large cooked potato, sliced or diced

salt and freshly ground black pepper
2 fresh or reconstituted dried eggs*

* **To reconstitute dried eggs:** to give the equivalent of a fresh egg, measure out 1 absolutely level tablespoon dried egg powder. Add 2 full tablespoons of cold water. Stir briskly until smooth.

Heat the bacon rind and as much fat as you can spare in a frying pan or omelette pan. Add the bacon and potato. Cook for a few minutes. Remove the bacon rind (this can be saved and used as a garnish for soup). Beat and season the eggs, pour into the pan and heat for about 30 seconds, then tilt the pan so the liquid egg runs to the sides. When set fold or roll away from the handle, halve and tip on to one or two plates.

Monday Jug

Each week from Monday to Friday there was a five minute broadcast after the 8 a.m. news. This was called The Kitchen Front. Many people participated in this programme, including Dr. Charles Hill, known as the Radio Doctor, who later became Lord Hill and Chairman of the B.B.C. I was one of the people who gave several broadcasts. The B.B.C. put some of the favourite recipes into a small book, which I found at the Imperial War Museum. I have used the measurements given in the broadcast and book. Fat was not used in these dumplings.

This was a suggested way of using up the Sunday joint. If you were a fairly large family, where people ate out during the week at canteens, British restaurants and/or school the meat rations would allow you to buy a Sunday joint. Any meat left would be used in various ways on Monday and this was one suggestion.

SERVES 4

600 ml/1 pint water or stock
4 carrots
small bunch sweet herbs*
salt and 5 peppercorns or shake
   freshly ground black pepper
115 to 175 g/4 to 6 oz cold joint,
   cut into small pieces
2 tablespoons brown sauce**
1 ½ level tablespoons plain flour

FOR THE DUMPLINGS:
6 heaped tablespoons plain flour
   (approximately 175 g/6 oz)
1 teaspoon baking powder
pinch salt
1 tablespoon chopped parsley
water to bind

* parsley, thyme, rosemary
** Worcestershire sauce or similar

Put half the water or stock into a saucepan, bring to the boil then add the carrots, herbs and seasoning; cook until nearly tender. Add the meat with the brown sauce. When thoroughly hot blend the flour with the remaining water or stock, stir into the ingredients in the saucepan and continue to stir over a moderate heat until the gravy is thickened.

For the dumplings: sift the flour, baking powder and salt into a mixing bowl, add the parsley and enough water to make a soft dough. Drop spoonfuls into the hot liquid in the stew and cook briskly for 10 minutes or until the dumplings are well risen. Dish up and serve with potatoes, greens and a little home-made chutney.

Faggots

Before the Second World War one could go to most butchers or delicatessens and buy ready-cooked Faggots (small savoury meat cakes) with Pease Pudding. These were some of the early 'take-away' foods that were popular in England, just as Haggis was in Scotland. In most cases you had to take your own basin to carry away the moist Pease Pudding. Faggots disappeared during meat rationing but, if you were lucky enough to purchase pig's liver and heart from the butcher, you could make your own.

SERVES 4 TO 6

2 medium onions
300 to 350 g/10 to 12 oz pig's liver
115 g/4 oz pig's heart
115 g/4 oz streaky bacon, cut in
   one piece
600 ml/1 pint water
salt and freshly ground black pepper

$1/4$ teaspoon ground ginger
1 teaspoon chopped sage, or to taste
$1/2$ teaspoon chopped thyme,
   or to taste
50 g/2 oz soft breadcrumbs
1 reconstituted dried or fresh egg

Leave the onions whole; put into a saucepan with the liver, heart, bacon, water and a little seasoning. Cover the pan and simmer gently for approximately 45 minutes or until the ingredients are just tender. Strain the stock and retain this.

Put the onion and meat through a fine mincer, add the remainder of the ingredients and season again. If a little dry add some of the stock. The mixture should be an ideal consistency to form into 12 small balls, use the remainder of the stock for the gravy.

Preheat the oven to 190°C/375°F/Gas Mark 5/180°C with a fan oven. Grease an 18 to 20 cm/7 to 8 inch square tin and pack the balls in this. Cover the tin and bake for 1 hour. Serve hot with Pease Pudding (page 140) and mixed vegetables.

Variation: when possible use fat belly of pork instead of bacon.

A modern touch: chop the ingredients in a food processor.

Pease Pudding

Pease Pudding was not difficult to prepare during the years of rationing, for dried peas were one of the ingredients you could purchase on points. Each month everyone had 16 points in addition to the normal rations. These points would allow you to buy a can of fish, such as salmon, or a meat product or dried fruit or dried vegetables, such as peas.

Only on rare occasions could we buy meat for Faggots with which Pease Pudding was the perfect accompaniment. Often people would prepare the pudding and serve it with rashers of bacon or a small amount of meat for we were advised to make use of pulses (peas, beans and lentils) as additional sources of protein. Covering basins was quite a problem in wartime, for paper was scarce and every wrapper from butter or lard was carefully hoarded.

SERVES 6

225 g/8 oz dried peas	1.2 litres/2 pints water
2 small onions, chopped	salt and freshly ground black pepper
small bunch parsley	25 g/1 oz butter or margarine
several sprigs thyme	or dripping
few mint leaves	1 egg

Put the dried peas into a container and cover with plenty of water. Leave soaking overnight then strain and discard the water. Place the peas, onions, herbs, water and seasoning into a saucepan. Bring to the boil, cover the pan and simmer gently for 2 to 2½ hours or until the peas are tender. Lift the lid towards the end of the cooking time to allow any surplus liquid to evaporate.

Sieve the mixture then add the fat and egg. Place into a well-greased basin covered with greaseproof paper or margarine paper and steam for 1 hour. Turn out and serve hot.

A modern touch: use a food processor instead of a sieve.

A delicious Pease Pudding can be made with fresh or frozen peas. Use 550 g/ 1¼ lb, the finely chopped onions, herbs and a little water. Cook until tender; make sure all the liquid evaporates. Sieve or process then blend with the fat and egg. Steam as above for 40 minutes.

Beef Ragoût

This was the type of beef stew that had been popular for decades but this particular recipe is similar to one from a pressure cookery book I wrote for Harrods in 1949. Small compact pressure cookers had come on the market and they were a blessing for, as well as food shortages, we had fuel cuts. A pressure cooker enabled a stew to be cooked in less than 30 minutes, so saved an enormous amount of fuel. The flavour and texture of the food correctly cooked under pressure is excellent. Today a more generous amount of meat could be used.

SERVES 4 TO 6

25 g/1 oz dripping or lard
450 g/1 lb stewing steak, diced
2 bacon rashers, derinded and diced
2 medium onions, cut into rings
4 medium carrots, sliced
1 small turnip, diced
115 g/4 oz small mushrooms
2 medium tomatoes, skinned
    and chopped

300 ml/½ pint stock or water
salt and freshly ground black pepper
1 tablespoon chopped parsley
½ teaspoon chopped thyme
    or pinch dried thyme
25 g/1 oz plain flour
150 ml/¼ pint red wine or extra stock

Heat the dripping or lard in the base of the cooker, add the meat and bacon and turn in the fat for 5 minutes. Put in all the vegetables, stir to mix with the meat then add the stock or water, seasoning and herbs. Fix the lid of the cooker, bring to full pressure over a high heat.

When pressure has been reached lower the heat and cook for 15 minutes, the exact timing depends upon the tenderness of the meat and the size of the pieces. Reduce pressure by placing the cooker under running cold water, then remove lid.

Blend the flour with the wine or extra stock, stir into the other ingredients and continue stirring over a moderate heat until the sauce has thickened.

A modern touch: people do not possess or use pressure cookers much today, so after browning the meat and vegetables place in a casserole, cover and cook for 2 to 2½ hours in a preheated oven set to 160°C/325°F/Gas Mark 3/150°C with a fan oven.

Jugged Hare

If you lived in a city or town it was difficult not to feel envious when you heard of country people being able to obtain rabbits, hares and other game. Those people would reply that in most towns of any size there were British restaurants where people could have an economical meal without surrendering food coupons; this facility was not available in the country. The dish was named because in the past it was cooked over the fire in a deep jug-shaped container.

SERVES 6

1 hare, jointed and with the blood
  and liver
2 tablespoons vinegar
1 litre/1¾ pints water
salt and freshly ground black pepper
50 g/2 oz butter or lard
3 medium onions, sliced
3 medium carrots, sliced
1 or 2 garlic cloves, crushed
50 g/2 oz plain flour
150 ml/¼ pint port wine or red wine

3 tablespoons redcurrant jelly
FOR THE FORCEMEAT BALLS:
50 g/2 oz butter
115 g/4 oz soft fine breadcrumbs
2 tablespoons finely chopped parsley
2 teaspoons finely chopped thyme or
  1 teaspoon dried thyme
1 teaspoon finely grated lemon zest
2 teaspoons lemon juice
1 egg yolk

Keep the blood and liver of the hare on one side. Place the hare joints into a container, add the vinegar and enough cold water to cover. Soak for 1 hour. Meanwhile put the liver into a saucepan with the 1 litre/1¾ pints cold water, add a little seasoning. Cover the pan and simmer for 40 minutes, strain, retain the liver and 900 ml/1½ pints of the liquid.

Remove the hare from the vinegar and water, dry very well. Heat half the butter or lard in a large saucepan add the hare and fry steadily for 10 minutes. Turn over from time to time. Arrange in a deep casserole. Heat the remainder of the fat and gently fry the vegetables and garlic for 5 minutes. Stir in the flour, allow to cook for a few minutes then gradually add the 900 ml/1½ pints stock from cooking the liver, the blood and wine. Stir as the sauce comes to the boil and thickens. Dice the cooked liver and add to the sauce with the redcurrant jelly. Simmer gently for 15 minutes then sieve or liquidize.

Preheat the oven to 150°C/300°F/Gas Mark 2/140°C with a fan oven. Pour the sauce over the hare. Cover the casserole and cook for 3 hours or until the hare is tender. Serve with the Forcemeat Balls, redcurrant jelly and garnish with fried croûtons.

For the Forcemeat Balls: melt the butter and blend with the rest of the ingredients. Form into 12 small balls. Place on a baking sheet or ovenproof dish and bake for 35 minutes.

Variation: redcurrant jelly, like many other preserves was scarce during rationing so a sweet plum jam or even grated cooked beetroot could be added to give the desired sweetness.

A modern touch: this is one classic way of cooking hare, the liver gives interest to the sauce. There are many modern ingredients that would give a more subtle taste to the sauce. Add 2 teaspoons finely grated root ginger and/or 2 tablespoons diced sun-dried tomatoes and/or a dash of soy sauce.

Flavour the Forcemeat Balls with 1 tablespoon finely chopped lemon grass.

For a small family buy a young hare (leveret), use the saddle (back) as a roasting joint and cook as chicken (page 111). Jug the legs only, which means using half the quantity of sauce given above but include the liver and blood. The Forcemeat Balls blend equally well with the roasted and casseroled hare.

Poor Man's Goose

There were a whole selection of recipes for Mock Duck and Mock Goose during the years when we never saw either of these birds. This particular recipe, based upon a vegetable marrow, was both satisfying and pleasant. Liver was unrationed but quite difficult to obtain from the butcher. When not available other meats could be used, see under Variations. Onions were very difficult to buy in wintertime so, unless you had grown them, leeks often had to be substituted.

SERVES 4 TO 6

1 medium marrow	1 teaspoon dried sage
FOR THE FILLING:	225 g/8 oz lambs' liver, finely diced
50 g/2 oz dripping or lard	50 g/2 oz soft breadcrumbs
4 to 6 medium onions, chopped	salt and freshly ground black pepper
2 bacon rashers, derinded and chopped	1 fresh or reconstituted dried egg
1 tablespoon chopped sage or	

Preheat the oven to 180°C/350°F/Gas Mark 4/170°C with a fan oven. Peel the marrow and cut in half lengthways. Remove all the seeds and centre fibres.

Heat half the dripping or lard in a saucepan, add the onions and cook gently for 5 minutes. Add the bacon and cook for a further 5 minutes, stir during this time. Remove the pan from the heat, stir in the remaining ingredients. Mix together then spoon into both halves of the marrow.

Press these together and tie the filled marrow with string or secure with several skewers. Place into a roasting tin. Melt the remaining fat and spoon over the marrow. Bake, without covering, for 1 hour.

Serve with Apple Sauce (page 150), a thickened gravy and seasonal vegetables.
Variations: when liver was not available I suggested that people substitute sausage meat or diced Spam or corned beef or make a vegetarian version by adding a small can of baked beans.

Another version of the dish was made by buying about 1 kg/2¼ lb lambs' liver, (quite a feat), placing the slices on a board to give a flat layer then covering the slices with the stuffing above (minus the diced liver). The slices were rolled around the filling and secured with a great deal of string. The rather untidy 'goose' was roasted as the recipe above.

Vegetable Goulash

This paprika flavoured dish was a recipe I demonstrated on a number of occasions during the years of rationing. Sometimes I made a version with meat, or, dare I say it, with whalemeat (which the Ministry of Food promoted). I was asked for a vegetarian version too. An advantage of Goulash was that we could use bottled tomatoes as there were no imported ones. If we did not bottle the fruit we had to be tomato-less from October to June the next year when the British crop began again.

SERVES 4 TO 6

50 g/2 oz lard or dripping
3 large onions or use leeks if onions are
    not available, chopped or thinly sliced
1 to 2 tablespoons paprika, depending
    upon personal taste
750 ml/1 ¼ pints vegetable stock
    or water
salt and freshly ground black pepper
2 tablespoons chopped parsley
1 teaspoon chopped thyme
1 teaspoon chopped rosemary

450 g/1 lb jar bottled tomatoes with
    the liquid as page 154
350 g/12 oz carrots, sliced
1 small turnip, cut into small dice
1 to 2 parsnips, cut into small dice
1 small swede, cut into small dice
550 g/1 ¼ lb potatoes, a quarter thinly
    sliced, the remainder thickly sliced
TO GARNISH:
chopped parsley

Heat the lard or dripping in a saucepan, add the onions or leeks and cook gently for 5 minutes. Stir in the paprika, it improves the flavour if it is stirred over a very low heat for 1 minute. Pour the stock or water into the pan, bring to the boil, add a little seasoning, the herbs and tomatoes. Heat for 2 or 3 minutes.

Add the carrots, turnip, parsnip(s), swede and thinly sliced potatoes to the boiling liquid. Cover the pan and cook steadily for 15 minutes, stir briskly to encourage the potatoes to break and thicken the stew. Check there is sufficient liquid then add the thicker potato slices and cook for a further 15 to 20 minutes, or until all the vegetables are tender. Taste and adjust the seasoning. Garnish with more parsley.

This dish is sufficiently satisfying to be served by itself with a cooked green vegetable. **Variation:** use chopped fresh tomatoes instead of the bottled variety. In this case a little extra stock or water may be needed before adding the thickly sliced potatoes.

Date, Nut and Apple Slices

I well remember demonstrating this dish at Harrods at the beginning of 1948. It was to celebrate the return of imported nuts for Christmas in 1947. In addition to the nuts I rejoiced at being able to use real lemon juice instead of the quite awful lemon substitute available during the wartime years. Fats were still rationed but I found most people would prefer to make a special dessert now and again with the right ingredients.

SERVES 6

FOR THE FILLING:

150 ml/¼ pint water

2 tablespoons clear honey

225 g/8 oz cooking dates,
    finely chopped

1 tablespoon lemon juice

115 g/4 oz dessert apples, weight
    when peeled and finely chopped*

50 g/2 oz Brazils or other nuts,
    coarsely chopped

FOR THE CRUST:

115 g/4 oz fine semolina

115 g/4 oz self-raising flour or plain flour
    with 1 teaspoon baking powder

1 teaspoon finely grated lemon zest

115 g/4 oz butter or margarine

25 g/1 oz caster or soft brown sugar

50 g/2 oz Brazils or other nuts,
    finely chopped

* type that cook well, e.g. Cox's

Preheat the oven to 190°C/375°F/Gas Mark 5/180°C with a fan oven. Lightly grease a 20 to 23 cm/8 to 9 inch flan dish. Place a metal baking tray in the oven when preheating this. This helps to crisp the base of the crust.

For the filling: heat the water with the honey in a saucepan, add the dates and simmer until these are softened and form a purée. Stir in the remainder of the filling ingredients then allow to cool.

For the crust: sift the semolina with the flour, or flour and baking powder, add the lemon zest. Rub in the butter or margarine, stir in the sugar and nuts. Press half the mixture into the base of the dish. Spread the filling over this then cover with the remainder of the crust mixture. Place on the baking tray and bake for 40 to 45 minutes. If the top is becoming too brown lower the heat slightly after 30 minutes. Serve hot or cold.

Scottish Apple Crumble

This recipe comes from an excellent Ministry of Food wartime leaflet for caterers, which I have adapted for domestic use. It gave two recipes for an Apple Crumble, the one for England and Wales used all flour but the more interesting Scottish recipe used some rolled oats.

SERVES 4 TO 6

FOR THE APPLE BASE:
550 g/1 ¼ lb cooking apples, weight
    when peeled, cored and sliced
3 tablespoons water
50 g/2 oz caster or soft brown sugar
½ to 1 teaspoon mixed spice

FOR THE CRUMBLE TOPPING:
150 g/5 oz rolled oats
85 g/3 oz plain flour
85 g/3 oz margarine
115 g/4 oz soft brown sugar

Preheat the oven to 180°C/350°F/Gas Mark 4/170°C with a fan oven. Put the apples with the water, sugar and spice into a 900 to 1200 ml/1 ½ to 2 pint pie dish. Cover and bake for 15 minutes.

Mix the rolled oats with the flour, melt the margarine, add to the oat mixture with the sugar. Mix well then spread evenly over the apples. Bake for a further 30 minutes, or until the topping is crisp and brown.

A modern touch: increase the amount of margarine to 150 g/5 oz for a richer topping.

Ginger Crumble: mix 50 g/2 oz sultanas and 3 tablespoons finely diced preserved ginger with the apples. Sift ½ to 1 teaspoon ground ginger with the flour.

Coconut and Oat Crumble: omit 25 g/1 oz rolled oats and 25 g/1 oz flour; add 50 g/ 2 oz desiccated coconut instead.

Christmas Pudding

This is the pudding recipe I demonstrated at Harrods Food Advice Bureau for Christmas 1946. The war had ended in 1945 but still we were very short of food and certainly had no luxuries such as lemons, imported almonds and candied peel and some of the extras I like to add to my puddings today. However this was a great improvement on the puddings made during the war years and it proved to be very popular. I have listed the quantity of spices and essences as in the original recipe, they may seem very generous but we tended to use plenty of flavourings to compensate for the lack of other ingredients. Obviously these can be cut down. The instructions for covering the puddings are those I gave to my audience.

SERVES 6 TO 8

115 g/4 oz breadcrumbs
50 g/2 oz flour, plain or self-raising
1 teaspoon mixed spice
1 teaspoon ground cinnamon
50 to 115 g/2 to 4 oz shredded suet
    or margarine, melted*
50 to 115 g/2 to 4 oz sugar, preferably
    dark brown*
1 small carrot, grated
1 small apple, peeled and grated
2 level tablespoons marmalade

1 tablespoon golden syrup or
    black treacle
450 g/1 lb mixed dried fruit**
1 to 2 fresh or reconstituted dried eggs
1 teaspoon vanilla essence
1 teaspoon lemon essence
1 teaspoon almond essence
8 tablespoons beer or brandy or whisky

* use the larger amount for a richer pudding
** or as much as you can spare

Grease one 1.2 to 1.5 litre/2 to 2½ pint basin or two smaller ones. Mix all the ingredients together, wish hard for good times ahead as you stir.

Spoon the mixture into the basin(s) and cover with a good layer of greased greaseproof paper. Put a pleat in the paper, for although Christmas puddings do not rise like light puddings, the ingredients swell in cooking. If you have insufficient covering then make a flour and water paste, as given below, place this on the small amount of greaseproof paper available. It keeps the pudding dry. You could of course use floured pudding cloth(s).

Steam a large pudding for at least 5 hours and the smaller ones for at least 3 hours. Remove any damp paper and cover with fresh dried paper or remove the soft flour and water paste. If you have insufficient paper then cover the puddings with cloths. On Christmas Day steam for another 1½ to 2 hours. You will need to make more flour and water paste if you have no paper.

Flour and water paste: blend about 115 g/4 oz flour with enough water to make a rolling consistency. Roll out to a round the size of the top of the pudding basin(s). Place over a scanty amount of greaseproof paper. You will need about 50% more than this for two smaller basins.

Gooseberry Fool

How we welcomed summer fruits in wartime after the scarcity of fruit in the winter! Our Fruit Fool of the '40's was far less rich than it would have been in the past as it was illegal for cream to be produced at that period.

Because we were so busy there was little time to sieve the cooked fruit so it remained a thick purée with small pieces of gooseberry - quite correct for originally the title was a Fruit Foulé (meaning chopped fruit).

SERVES 4

450 ml/15 fl oz thick sweetened
   gooseberry purée
450 ml/15 fl oz sweetened custard

Blend the cool fruit and custard together. Spoon into glasses and serve as cold as possible.

Variations: use half thick custard and half whipped cream or even all whipped cream.

Use other fruits such as blackcurrants, raspberries or plums with apples.

A modern touch: some Greek yoghurt or fromage frais instead of cream gives a dessert that is lower in calories.

Gingerbread with Apple Sauce

During the war producers of butter and margarine did not use their trade names on packets but some kept their well-known names alive by publishing recipe leaflets. Generally they stated the recipes were 'with the approval of the Ministry of Food'. This recipe comes from a special leaflet dated 1942, which encouraged British families to entertain American service personnel. The flour in wartime was known as National flour, and was much darker than the white flour of today. In many recipes the dried egg powder was sifted with the flour but a recipe can be adapted to use a fresh egg. This economical gingerbread is nicest served warm with hot apple sauce.

SERVES 8

FOR THE GINGERBREAD:
300 g/10 oz self-raising flour or
    plain flour with 2½ teaspoons
    baking powder
1 level teaspoon bicarbonate of soda
1 teaspoon mixed spice
1 teaspoon ground ginger
good pinch salt
1 tablespoon dried egg powder*
175 g/6 oz golden syrup

85 g/3 oz margarine or cooking fat
300 ml/½ pint milk*
FOR THE APPLE SAUCE:
300 ml/½ pint water
2 tablespoons golden syrup
3 tablespoons sultanas, or
    other dried fruit
550 g/1¼ lb dessert apples,
    weight when peeled and sliced

* if using a fresh egg use 2 tablespoons less milk

Preheat the oven to 180°C/350°F/Gas Mark 4/170°C with a fan oven. Grease or line an oblong tin measuring approximately 20 to 23 x 15 cm/8 to 9 x 6 inches.

Sift all the dry ingredients together. Melt the syrup and margarine or lard in a large saucepan, cool slightly then beat in the dry ingredients.

Spoon into the tin and bake for 45 minutes or until firm to the touch. Cool in the tin for about 5 minutes then turn out, slice and serve with the sauce.

For the Apple Sauce: put the water and syrup into a saucepan, bring to the boil then add the dried fruit and apple slices. Lower the heat and simmer steadily in an uncovered pan until the slices are tender but unbroken.

Variation: a sweetened purée of cooking apples could be served instead of the sauce above.

Scottish Apple Crumble (page 147)

Wartime Carrot Cake

Many people have remarked to me that they find it strange that the Ministry of Food and anyone who gave recipes during wartime included so many cakes. The reason was that we had to try and provide variety at all times - not easy on the rations. This cake illustrates two points. The first that many cakes were made with a little vinegar when one had no fresh or dried eggs to spare and secondly that we often relied on carrots to give flavour, sweetness and texture in cakes and puddings.

SERVES 6

225 g/8 oz self-raising flour or
    plain flour with 2 teaspoons
    baking powder
115 g/4 oz margarine or cooking fat
115 g/4 oz caster or soft brown sugar,
    or type available
50 g/2 oz sultanas or other dried fruit
85 g/3 oz carrots, grated
1½ tablespoons malt vinegar
approximately 6½ tablespoons milk

Preheat the oven to 180°C/350°F/Gas Mark 4/170°C with a fan oven. Grease and flour an 18 cm/7 inch cake tin.

Sift the flour, or flour and baking powder, into a mixing bowl. Rub in the margarine or fat, add the sugar, fruit and carrots. Mix the vinegar with the milk then add to the other ingredients to give a sticky consistency. Spoon into the cake tin and bake for 1 hour 10 minutes or until firm.

Jam Cake

The Ministry of Food recipe suggested using jam as the sweetening in a cake instead of sugar. Obviously it was not very sweet so would not meet today's tastes but it does illustrate how inventive we had to be. People often query the fact that potatoes were used in baking but forget how many Continental cakes include potato flour. We never lined cake tins if we could avoid it, for greaseproof paper was so scarce. An ultra-economical cake like this could be turned out of a greased and floured tin with the greatest of ease.

SERVES 4 TO 6

115 g/4 oz boiled old potatoes
225 g/8 oz self-raising flour or
    plain flour with 2 teaspoons
    baking powder
1 level teaspoon bicarbonate of soda

1 teaspoon mixed spice
50 g/2 oz lard or margarine
2 tablespoons jam
2 reconstituted dried or fresh eggs
50 g/2 oz currants or sultanas

Preheat the oven to 180°C/350°F/Gas Mark 4/170°C with a fan oven. Grease and flour a 20 cm/8 inch round or 18 cm/7 inch square cake tin. Sieve the potatoes; sift all the dry ingredients together. Rub the lard or margarine into the flour mixture. Add the potatoes, jam, well-beaten eggs and currants or sultanas. Spoon into the cake tin and bake for 50 minutes or until firm. Turn out on to a wire cooling tray. Serve freshly baked.

Variation: add 50 g/2 oz sugar and another 2 tablespoons jam to the mixture.
Apricot jam is particularly suitable.

Wartime Preserves

One very important task for the Food Advisers of the Ministry was to encourage the public to preserve as much summer produce as possible, ready for winter when there was a great scarcity. We had to depend upon British grown varieties.

Most people made some jam if they could spare the sugar. Often a small allocation of extra sugar was made available for this purpose. The Food Advisers always demonstrated standard recipes, for it was important that the completed jars of jam had a 60% sugar content, so the preserve kept well. When I was working in the East Anglia area, at the beginning of my time with the Ministry of Food, I was sent to supervise the making of large amounts of jam by groups of women. The jam was not meant for their consumption but to be stored to meet the jam ration. Not all the ladies were happy with the Ministry's advice, they wanted to use their own 'pet' recipes - but this was not possible.

Bottling fruit, like plums, or apples, generally had to be done in water, not syrup, for there was no extra sugar for this purpose.

Bottled tomatoes: there was more interest in bottling tomatoes than anything else, for these added so much flavour to cooked dishes. The best way to bottle them was in their own juice, without extra liquid. Pack the whole or halved tomatoes into the sterilized bottling jars with a pinch of salt and sugar. Fix the lids but give screw bands half a turn back to allow for the expansion of the glass. Stand on the rack in a sterilizer filled with cold water. Take 1½ hours to bring the water up to 87.5°C/190°F (steady simmering) and maintain this temperature for 30 minutes. Remove from the sterilizer and tighten the screw bands.

A modern touch: nowadays one can freeze tomato purée but bottling is better for whole or halved tomatoes.

Pickled red cabbage: shred the cabbage finely with a stainless steel knife. Discard hard stalks. Put a layer of cabbage into a dish then a layer of kitchen salt, continue like this, ending with salt. Leave for 24 hours; drain away the moisture. For a less salt flavour rinse in cold water then drain again.

Heat 1 tablespoon mixed pickling spices (or as required) in each 600 ml/1 pint malt vinegar; strain then cool. Put the cabbage into a container, cover with the vinegar. Leave for several hours, turn over once or twice. Pack into cold sterilized jars; top with the vinegar and cover.

1950 to 1959

vol-au-vents and hostess trolleys

In 1951 King George VI had a serious lung operation. Because of this Princess Elizabeth and Prince Philip were deputising for him on a State visit to Australia and New Zealand but they only reached Kenya before they were forced to return by the King's death. In January 1952 viewers saw the King say goodbye to his daughter at the airport, so it was a shock when, a week later, it was announced he had died in his sleep.

On June 2nd 1953 Elizabeth was crowned Queen. It was a unique experience to see the ceremony on television and share the enthusiasm of the crowds as they cheered Queen Elizabeth II and Prince Philip with their two young children on the balcony of Buckingham Palace. The newspapers hailed the period as the New Elizabethan Age and prophesied great things ahead.

Edmund Hilary, a New Zealander, and Sherpa Tensing reached the summit of Mount Everest on June 1st 1953.

1959 saw the signing of the Treaty of Rome by Belgium, France, West Germany, Holland, Italy and Luxembourg to form the European Common Market.

Trouble on the seas came in 1958 with disagreement between Britain and Iceland about fishing rights.

Cheese and Wine Parties

With the end of cheese rationing in 1954 this easy way of entertaining became the vogue. At first there were only British cheeses but gradually Dutch, Danish and French varieties appeared. Many people bought wines for the first time and wine and cookery writers had many letters asking about a wise selection. Fanny and Johnny Cradock's T.V. programmes included advice on wine.

Cookery Influences

Elizabeth David's first cookery book produced great excitement, for she brought a new approach to the appreciation of food and cooking with her vivid descriptions of Mediterranean ingredients. It was like the sun coming out after the grey days of rationing. I know the book fired me with great desire to sample the ingredients and see the scenery she described so expertly. There followed other equally outstanding books by the same author.

The Cradocks made their first television appearances and the elegance of the B.B.C's set, Fanny's evening dresses and the information on wine, as well as food, was something new to viewers.

The television cookery demonstrations of Philip Harben and myself became increasingly well-known as more and more bought T.V. sets. I first demonstrated an Alaska and my good friend, that delightful and accomplished T.V. chef Philip Harben, showed his FRIED ICE CREAM and it is so unusual that I've given the recipe here.

PHILIP HARBEN'S FRIED ICE CREAM

Cut the ice cream into individual portions. Make sure these are very hard. Make the batter (page 52). Heat deep fat (today we would doubtless use oil) to 190°C/ 375°F (a cube of 24-hour bread should turn golden in 30 seconds). Quickly dip the ice cream in the batter, it should have a thin but complete coating, drop into the fat or oil. Fry for 1 to 2 minutes until golden. Drain on kitchen paper and serve at once. Do not fry more than two portions at one time so the fat retains it temperature.

A modern touch: instead of coating the ice cream with batter wrap neat portions in filo pastry and return to the freezer for a short time then fry as above. Do not brush the pastry with melted butter or oil. This version is delicious with Raspberry Sauce (page 30).

1950 to 1959

The Recipes

Tomato Soup

At the beginning of the 1950's it was such a pleasure to have tomatoes throughout the year that home-made Tomato Soup became a general favourite. There were many recipes but this is the one I prefer. As more herbs became popular and we realized the value of plum tomatoes these were used, see under Variations.

SERVES 6

675 g/1½ lb ripe tomatoes, skinned
25 g/1 oz butter or margarine
1 medium onion, chopped
1 or 2 streaky bacon rashers, derinded and chopped
1 garlic clove, crushed
300 ml/½ pint water
2 teaspoons chopped parsley

½ teaspoon chopped thyme
½ teaspoon finely grated lemon zest
1 teaspoon brown sugar
salt and freshly ground black pepper
TO GARNISH:
little cream
chopped parsley or chives

Chop the tomatoes into small pieces. Heat the butter or margarine in a saucepan, add the onion and cook gently for 5 minutes. Add the bacon and garlic and cook for a further 2 minutes, take care the bacon does not become crisp. Put in the tomatoes, mix with the other ingredients and cook very gently for 4 minutes. Pour in the water, add all the other ingredients, including the bacon rinds if available. Cover the pan and simmer for 20 to 25 minutes.

Lift out the bacon rinds then sieve or liquidize the soup (this may not remove all the seeds from the tomatoes). Taste and adjust the seasoning and add more sugar if necessary. Garnish and serve.

Variations: use plum tomatoes when available; a 427 g/15 oz can of plum tomatoes can be substituted for the fresh fruit.

When tomato paste became available in the late 1950's to 1960's a tablespoon of this enhanced the flavour and colour of the soup.

Use finely chopped basil with, or instead of, parsley.

Top with yoghurt instead of cream. We began to use yoghurt a great deal in the 1960's. Crème fraîche or soured cream, both plentiful in the 1990's, are ideal toppings on the soup.

Cock-a-leekie

This is a very old Scottish traditional soup-cum-main dish. The chicken gives flavour and body to the soup, and part of the flesh can be added, leaving the main part of the chicken for the main course of that meal or for a subsequent day. I remember making the dish several times during this decade as butchers were offering both boiling fowls, ideally suitable for the soup, as well as younger chickens too. This recipe is as it would have been in the 1950's for it uses the dried prunes which needed to be soaked overnight before cooking. Poultry was always sold with giblets in those days so the chicken stock would have been made with these.

SERVES 4 TO 6

12 large prunes
1 small boiling fowl
1.5 litres/2½ pints chicken stock
few parsley sprigs
1 or 2 thyme sprigs

salt and freshly ground black pepper
450 g/1 lb leeks, very thinly sliced
TO GARNISH:
chopped parsley

Cover the prunes with cold water and soak overnight. Next day simmer in the soaking water until nearly tender, then strain.

Put the boiling fowl into a saucepan with the stock, herbs and seasoning. Cover the pan and simmer for about 2 hours, or until the bird is tender. Lift the bird out of the stock, strain this. Pour 900 ml/1½ pints back into the saucepan, add the leeks and the prunes and cook for 20 minutes or until the leeks are tender. Cut one or two slices from the breast of the chicken, dice this finely, add to the soup and heat. Garnish and serve.

A modern touch: this is an excellent dish made with a small young chicken. In this case use about 1 litre/1¾ pints stock and simmer for 1 hour only. Modern tenderized prunes do not need soaking. The dried prunes can be added to the stock and leeks, they will be adequately softened within 20 minutes.

Rollmop Herrings

Some people would purchase Rollmops from a delicatessen counter or fishmonger, others preferred to prepare them at home. They were at their most popular in the 1950's and early 1960's as an easy-to-serve hors d'oeuvre, particularly with those people who did not eat shellfish and so avoided the inescapable Prawn Cocktail. If you make them yourself it is important that the herring fillets are completely free from bones.

SERVES 4

4 salted herrings
2 medium onions, very thinly sliced
1/2 to 1 lemon, thinly sliced
few peppercorns or shake freshly
    ground black pepper

2 dried bay leaves
approximately 225 ml/7 1/2 fl oz white
    vinegar
water, see method
2 teaspoons sugar

Soak the herrings overnight to remove the excess salt. Drain and rinse in plenty of fresh cold water. Remove the heads, tails and all bones.

Split each fish into 2 fillets. Spread the onions over the flesh side of the fillets then roll from head to tail. Secure the rolls with wooden cocktail sticks. Place in a large jar with the lemon, peppercorns or pepper, bay leaves and enough vinegar to come half way up the jar. Fill up with water, add the sugar. Cover and shake the jar gently so the vinegar and water mix well. Leave for 3 to 4 days for the flavour to mature.

To serve lift the fish out of the liquid, remove the cocktail sticks, garnish with a little salad and serve. Some of the liquid could be used in a salad dressing.

Fish Pie

Although fish pies had been made for generations they achieved greater popularity in the late 1950's when a far more varied range of fish became available. During the 1940's the selection and quality was poor and this continued into the early 1950's.

The greater the selection of fish and flavouring the more interesting the pie becomes.

SERVES 4

675 g/1½ lb white fish or a mixture
   of white fish and smoked haddock
salt and freshly ground white pepper
sprig parsley
1 bay leaf
1 shallot or small onion, sliced
40 g/1½ oz butter
40 g/1½ oz plain flour

300 ml/½ pint milk
little cream, optional
1 tablespoon chopped parsley
few drops anchovy essence
FOR THE TOPPING:
450 g/1 lb cooked and
   creamed potatoes
little extra butter

Put the fish into a saucepan with sufficient cold water to just cover, the seasoning, herbs and shallot or onion. Bring to the boil and simmer gently until the fish is barely cooked. Leave until cool, then lift the fish out of the liquid and flake. Retain the liquid.

Preheat the oven to 180°C/350°C/Gas Mark 4 or 170°C with a fan oven. Heat the butter in a saucepan, stir in the flour then add the milk. Stir briskly over the heat until a thick sauce, then stir in enough cream and strained fish liquid to make a coating consistency. Add the parsley, essence and fish.

Spoon into a 1.2 litre/2 pint dish. Top with the potato and dot this with a little butter. Bake for 35 minutes.

Variations: add sliced hard-boiled eggs and peeled prawns to the fish and sauce.

Top the potatoes with grated cheese.

A modern touch: flavour the liquid in which the fish is cooked with lemon grass or a little diced ginger.

Fried Scampi

It is said that it was members of the forces, stationed in Italy, who first extolled the virtues of scampi - large prawns caught in the Adriatic. Our own Dublin Bay prawns are just as good. When they first appeared we had to shell, coat and fry them ourselves but in the years that followed commercially prepared frozen foods began to make their appearance and it was not long before frozen scampi, already coated ready for cooking, were on sale throughout Britain. Italian recipes tend to coat the fish with seasoned flour and not egg and crumbs.

SERVES 4

24 scampi, shelled
40 g/1 ½ oz plain flour
salt and freshly ground black pepper
8 tablespoons olive oil

TO GARNISH:
lemon wedges
parsley

Dry the scampi well, mix the flour with seasoning and toss the fish in this. Heat the oil in a large frying pan and fry the fish for 5 minutes, until golden on the outside. Never over cook them, for this makes the flesh tough. Lift out of the pan and drain on kitchen paper. Garnish and serve with Tartare Sauce (page 171). Scampi are very good served on a bed of fried sliced zucchini (courgettes).

Variation: coat with a little seasoned flour, then beaten egg and fine soft or crisp breadcrumbs. Fry as above or deep fry at 170°C/340°F for 3 to 4 minutes.

Mayonnaise

Many members of the general public became more interested in preparing mayonnaise when they discovered it was quicker to make in a liquidizer (blender) than by hand. In the 1950's we were just learning about the merits of virgin olive oil for salad dressings and the oil was being sold more widely. Since 1950 other kinds of oil have been used with, or instead of, olive oil, such as corn oil - popular at the time - also sunflower oil or nut oils such as walnut and almond.

We had never heard of the possibility of there being salmonella in eggs so we used them uncooked quite happily.

SERVES 4 TO 6

2 egg yolks
salt and freshly ground black or
    white pepper
½ teaspoon made English or
    French mustard
pinch sugar, optional

up to 300 ml/10 fl oz extra virgin
    olive oil, or other oil
1 to 2 tablespoons white wine
    vinegar or lemon juice
1 tablespoon boiling water

By hand: put the egg yolks into a dry basin, add the seasonings and sugar, if using this. Whisk or beat until well mixed. Gradually beat in the oil, drop by drop. When the sauce shows signs of thickening the oil can be added a little more quickly. When the required amount of oil has been added gradually whisk in the vinegar or lemon juice.

The boiling water can then be added, it lightens the texture of the mayonnaise. Check the seasonings before serving.

In a liquidizer: put the egg yolks and seasonings into the dry goblet. Switch on to medium speed for a few seconds. Remove the centre cap in the lid or, if this is not possible, tilt the lid, so the oil can be added gradually. Switch on again to medium speed and add the oil steadily, **not rapidly**. Pour in the vinegar or lemon juice in the same way and then the boiling water, if using this.

Variations: a food processor can be used instead of a liquidizer.

A lighter mayonnaise can be made in either the liquidizer or food processor using 2 whole eggs instead of the 2 egg yolks. This is not possible when making it by hand.

Marinated Fish

Although professional chefs had been in the habit of marinating some meats, poultry and fish before cooking, this was a process that did not become particularly popular until towards the end of the 1950's. I think we had endured tasteless food during the 1940's and early 1950's so that most of us longed for dishes with a stronger flavour.

SERVES 4

FOR THE MARINADE:

1 teaspoon made mustard
1 small onion, finely chopped
1 garlic clove, crushed
2 tablespoons olive oil

1 tablespoon white wine vinegar
1 tablespoon chopped parsley

4 portions of white fish or herrings
   or trout

Mix all the ingredients for the marinade in a long dish. Add the white fish. If using herrings or trout remove the heads, slit the fish and take out the intestines. Save the herring roes. Put the herrings with their roes or trout into the marinade. Leave for 2 hours. Turn over once or twice.

Preheat the grill. Lift the fish from the marinade, drain and place in the grill pan. Cook quickly on either side, then lower the heat and cook for a further 5 to 7 minutes or until the fish is tender.

Serve with mixed vegetables and the Mustard Sauce (page 169).

A modern touch: add 2 teaspoons soy sauce and 2 teaspoons grated root ginger to the other ingredients in the marinade.

Mustard Sauce

Mustard seeds have been known for thousands of years. It is chronicled that the Romans fermented the seeds for making wine. The primary object of mustard though is to enhance the flavour of other foods and it blends surprisingly well with a great variety of ingredients from fish and meat to cheese and salad dressings. Mustard loses some potency if added to a sauce too soon so stir this in just before serving.

SERVES: DEPENDENT ON THE RECIPE

300 ml/½ pint stock, see method
25 g/1 oz butter
25 g/1 oz plain flour
1 level teaspoon English mustard
   powder or to taste

3 tablespoons white malt or
   white wine vinegar, or half water
   and half vinegar
salt and freshly ground white pepper

Choose the kind of stock according to the dish with which the sauce is to be served and strain it before use. A fish stock is correct when making the sauce as an accompaniment for this, such as herrings (page 106), failing this use chicken stock. The stock from cooking Boiled Beef (page 88) is ideal for the sauce but in this case be sparing with the salt.

Heat the butter in a saucepan, stir in the flour and then the stock. Bring to the boil and stir or whisk until a smooth thickened mixture. Blend the mustard powder with the vinegar, add to the sauce and cook for 2 to 3 minutes. Season to taste.

Variations: use 1 level tablespoon cornflour instead of the flour, blend this with the stock and add to the butter. Cook as before.

Cream of Mustard Sauce: use milk instead of stock or half milk and half stock. Blend the mustard powder with more milk or double cream. Remove the pan from the heat and stir in 1 or 2 teaspoons white wine vinegar or lemon juice. Heat gently but do not allow the sauce to boil.

A modern touch: with the variety of mustards available today the sauce can be changed in flavour as required. Grained English mustard gives an interesting appearance and an excellent taste.

Fish and Chips

Fried fish and chips have always been, and still are, one of the most popular meals in Britain. Towards the end of the 1950's a far better selection of fish appeared again. Also there was plenty of fat for frying, so housewives began to cook fish and chips at home, rather than go to the fried fish shop. The fish was generally shallow fried and the potatoes cooked in a 'chip pan' (an ordinary saucepan with a frying basket).

SERVES 4

FOR FRYING:
lard or cooking fat
4 portions of white fish, such as hake,
    cod, fresh haddock, huss or
    rock salmon*

FOR COATING:
1 tablespoon flour
salt and freshly ground black pepper
1 egg, whisked

2 tablespoons crisp breadcrumbs

FOR THE CHIPS:
450 to 675 g/1 to 1½ lb potatoes,
    cut into chips

TO GARNISH:
lemon slices
parsley

*also known as catfish. Inexpensive and very
    popular at this time*

Put approximately 50 g/2 oz of the lard or fat into a frying pan and enough into the chip pan to half-fill it when melted. Never over-fill any utensil for frying.

Frying the fish: dry this well. Mix the flour and seasoning and shake over the fish. Dip the portions in the egg; roll in the breadcrumbs until well coated. Heat the fat in the frying pan. Fry thin fillets for 2 to 3 minutes on either side, and thicker portions for 4 to 5 minutes on either side. Lift out of the pan and drain on absorbent paper. Garnish and serve with Tartare Sauce (page 171) or tomato ketchup, chips and a cooked green vegetable.

Cooking the chips: place the chips in cold water until ready to cook, drain and dry well. Double frying is essential for good chips.

Heat the fat in the pan to 170°C/340°F (a cube of day-old bread turns golden in 1 minute). Lower the frying basket into the hot fat - this makes sure the potatoes do not stick. Half-fill the basket with potatoes and fry steadily until tender. They will not be brown. Lift out and continue until all the potatoes are cooked.

Just before the meal reheat the fat to 190°C/375°F (a cube of day-old bread turns golden in 30 seconds). Fry for 2 minutes or until crisp and golden brown. Remove from the pan, drain on absorbent paper and serve at once.

A modern touch: use one of the oils recommended for frying.

As frying is less popular in modern times the wartime tips about oven 'frying' may be useful. Preheat the oven to 200°C/400°F/Gas Mark 6/190°C with a fan oven. Grease and heat a large metal tray. Thinly slice the potatoes, rather than cut them into chips. Place in a single layer on the tray, brush with a few drops of oil. Cook for 10 minutes. Add the coated portions of fish. Cook fillets for 12 to 15 minutes and thicker portions for 18 to 20 minutes.

Tartare Sauce

Generally this is based on Mayonnaise, as the recipe on page 167, but sometimes I use Hollandaise Sauce (page 110) instead. This gives a more delicate sauce which blends well with fish salads. The quantity of ingredients given below can be adapted to suit personal taste.

Mayonnaise (page 167) or	2 tablespoons finely chopped gherkins
Hollandaise Sauce (page 110)	2 tablespoons finely chopped capers
2 tablespoons finely chopped parsley	

Mix all the ingredients together. Serve cold with cold or hot dishes.

Variations: 1 or 2 chopped hard-boiled eggs or egg yolks can be stirred into the sauce as well as the ingredients above.

1 to 2 tablespoons very finely chopped mild onion or shallot can be added in addition to the ingredients above.

A modern touch: Aioli (Garlic Mayonnaise): peel and finely crush 2 to 4 garlic cloves by hand or in a liquidizer or food processor. Blend well with the egg yolks or eggs before making the Mayonnaise (page 167).

Hamburgers

During the Second World War many of us entertained American servicemen and women. They were excellent company and extremely generous, for they rarely visited a British home without a gift of chocolate or other delicacy. We listened to their memories of life 'back home', including descriptions of the dishes made by their mothers and wives. I never understood their enthusiasm for Hamburgers. But during my time with the Ministry of Food I had made them, eking out the precious beef with breadcrumbs or grated raw potato or rolled oats and fried onion, when one was available. They were edible, but in no way would I enthuse about them. After meat rationing ended in 1954 I decided to make true burgers with freshly minced good quality steak - according to advice in my favourite American book of the time - *The Joy of Cooking* - by Irma S. Rombauer and Marion Rombauer Becker. Later I tasted innumerable Hamburgers in America - I am still not an enthusiast but who am I to argue with the millions who love them. This is the classic recipe.

SERVES 4

450 g/1 lb lean beef*
salt and freshly ground black pepper
little butter or pork fat, see method

Hamburger buns
salad, tomato ketchup, etc., see method
I have used rump and sirloin steaks and best quality topside and rib of beef

Mince the beef just before cooking or have this freshly minced by the butcher. You can incorporate a little seasoning but many experts do not recommend this. If the meat is very lean grease a heavy frying pan with a little butter or pork fat. If the meat contains a fair percentage of fat do not grease the pan.

Slowly heat the pan, the Hamburgers should sizzle when added. Cook for 2 to 3 minutes on either side. Some experts advise seasoning the Hamburgers when turned over on the second side. Meanwhile split and toast the buns. Fill with the burgers, salad and add tomato ketchup, fried sliced onions or slices of cheese. Serve at once.

Tournedos Rossini (page 174)

Tournedos Rossini

The pâté on top of the steaks turns this into a truly delicious dish. After meat rationing ended in 1954 most people celebrated by purchasing good sized joints or steaks, for these were the foods they had missed most. Butchers of the day were willing to turn fillet steaks into tournedos (rounds) but it is quite easy to do this at home. Prepare the pâté well beforehand, for it should have time to stiffen and become cold. You could use a commercial pâté but during the 1950's these were not as plentiful as they became in the '60's and '70's when pâté was a favourite hors d'oeuvre.

SERVES 4

Calves' Liver pâté as page 176,
    use about a third of the quantity
    given in the recipe
4 fillet steaks
salt and freshly ground black pepper,
    optional

25 to 50 g/1 to 2 oz butter, melted
FOR THE CROÛTES:
25 g/1 oz butter
4 rounds of bread, size of the tournedos
TO GARNISH:
watercress

Make the pâté and leave until firm. Take some of the pâté from the container and cut it into 4 neat squares or rounds. If the butcher has not prepared the tournedos purchase steaks about 3.75 cm/1½ inches in thickness. Form into rounds with your fingers or cut into shape with a pastry cutter. Secure the rounds with fine string or small wooden cocktail sticks. Season the meat lightly.

Preheat the grill, place the steaks on the grid of the grill pan. Brush the top of the meat with some of the butter and grill rapidly for about 2 minutes. Turn over and brush the other side with more butter then continue cooking to taste. Suggested cooking times are: **rare:** 5 to 6 minutes, **medium:** 8 minutes, **well-done:** 10 minutes.

Tournedos should be so tender that, although the steaks may be a little thicker than those given on page 174, the times above are adequate. With medium or well-done meat brush the steaks again with butter, so the meat does not become dry.

While the steaks are cooking heat the rest of the butter in a frying pan and cook the bread until crisp and brown on both sides. Remove the string or cocktail sticks. Place the tournedos on the croûtes and top with the cold pâté. Garnish with sprigs of watercress and serve with seasonal vegetables.

Variation: for extra luxury place small pieces of cooked truffle around the pâté.

Steak Diane

This seemed a very appropriate steak dish after the end of meat rationing. We had been used to small quantities of meat for many years and this did not strike us as being 'mean' with the quantity. The term 'minute' steaks means they do take only 1 minute cooking on either side. You can choose between sirloin, entrecôte or rump steaks but they must be cut very thinly. Later in the 1970's, when electric frying pans became the fashionable piece of equipment, this was a good dish to cook at the table.

SERVES 4

85 g/3 oz butter
1 or 2 shallots or small onions, finely chopped
2 tablespoons chopped parsley

4 minute steaks
salt and freshly ground black pepper
1 to 2 teaspoons Worcestershire sauce
2 tablespoons brandy

Heat the butter in a large frying pan, add the shallots or onions and half the parsley and cook for 2 to 3 minutes, or until the shallots or onions are nearly tender. Put in the steaks, these can be seasoned before cooking, but that is a matter of personal taste. Fry for a minute on either side, then add the sauce and seasoning if that has not been added earlier. Heat for a few seconds. Pour in the brandy, stir to mix with the other ingredients then ignite. Top with the remaining parsley and serve. In restaurants French-fried (chipped potatoes) and peas were the usual accompaniments.

A modern touch: use half butter and half oil. If using a non-stick pan you can reduce the amount of fat in the recipe by half.

Calves' Liver Pâté

Calves' liver gives a delicate flavour to a pâté. For a more robust taste use lambs' or pig's liver. The cooking time may vary, see under Variations. Aluminium foil would become available in 1966 and this made an ideal covering for pâtés as they cook. A 'bain-marie' means that the dish is placed in a container of water that comes half way up the cooking container. I use cold water, for in this case it not only keeps the food moist, it helps to prevent it cooking too quickly.

SERVES 4 TO 6

450 g/1 lb calves' liver, sliced
115 g/4 oz pork or streaky bacon
2 eggs
150 ml/5 fl oz double cream
2 tablespoons brandy or dry sherry
2 tablespoons veal or beef stock as
   page 16

1 teaspoon chopped thyme or
   pinch dried thyme
pinch grated or ground nutmeg
salt and freshly ground black pepper

Preheat the oven to 160°C/325°F/Gas Mark 3/150°C with a fan oven. Grease a 900 ml/1½ pint ovenproof terrine or small casserole.

Mince the liver and pork or bacon. For a very smooth texture put through the mincer twice. Add the rest of the ingredients and mix thoroughly. Spoon into the container, cover with well-greased greaseproof paper or greased foil. Stand in the bain-marie and cook for 1½ hours. Serve the pâté with hot toast and butter.

Note: if storing the pâté for any length of time cover with a layer of melted butter to keep out the air.

Variations: substitute lambs' liver and cook for the same time as above. If using pig's liver cook for 1½ hours. Pâtés have a good flavour if 1 teaspoon finely grated lemon zest is added.

Chicken Liver pâté uses chicken livers and add a flavouring of 2 teaspoons finely grated orange zest to the other ingredients. For some people chicken livers have a slightly bitter taste so add 1 to 2 teaspoons brown sugar.

Cook any of the mixtures in 4 to 6 individual soufflé or ramekin dishes. Allow 45 minutes at the temperature given above and 55 minutes for pig's liver.

Quiche Lorraine

When I demonstrated this pastry dish on B.B.C. television at the very end of the 1950's a number of the crew were fascinated by the name and spelling. Quiches were unknown to the majority of people in Britain at that time. I think the fact that they became accepted with such pleasure was because a sweet Custard Tart was very much part of our traditional fare, so quiches were simply a savoury version of a well-known pudding.

SERVES 6 TO 8

Shortcrust Pastry made with
    225 g/8 oz flour, etc. as page 82
FOR THE FILLING:
4 to 5 back or streaky bacon
    rashers, derinded
175 g/6 oz Gruyère or Cheddar
    cheese, grated

25 g/1 oz Parmesan cheese, grated
2 eggs
3 egg yolks
225 ml/7 ½ fl oz milk
150 ml/5 fl oz single cream or extra milk
salt and freshly ground black pepper

Preheat the oven to 200°C/100°F/Gas Mark 6/190°C with a fan oven. Make the pastry, roll out and line a 23 to 25 cm/9 to 10 inch flan tin or dish, measuring at least 2.5 cm/1 inch in depth. Bake 'blind', as described on page 188 for 15 to 20 minutes or until firm and pale golden in colour. If using a ceramic dish place on a preheated metal baking tray in the oven, this makes sure the bottom pastry is firm and crisp. Reset the oven to 160°C/325°F/Gas Mark 3/150°C with a fan oven.

While the pastry is cooking fry or grill the bacon until crisp then cut into narrow fingers. Place the bacon and cheese into the partially cooked pastry case.

Beat the eggs and egg yolks, add the milk, cream and seasoning. Strain over the bacon and cheese. If by chance there seems too much custard mixture do not discard this. Bake the flan for about 5 minutes and the custard level in the flan drops, so any extra liquid can be added. Cook for 35 to 40 minutes or until the filling is set. Serve hot or cold.

A modern touch: as more ingredients became available the fillings for quiches varied from asparagus, mixed mushrooms, vegetables, and cooked fish.

Quiches freeze very well, especially if some cream is used in the filling.

Puff Pastry

When all fats came off ration in May 1954 there was a great surge in the baking of pastry, cakes and puddings. I had been asked to give a demonstration of making puff pastry at the Food Advice Bureau at Harrods several years before this, as a number of people wanted to make Vol-au-Vents for special occasions and had saved butter for the pastry. I too had to save fat from my demonstration rations in order to meet the requests. The pastry was not as good as it would be today, as the flour of the early 1950's was still far from light but, even so, I think it made one realise just how delicious good puff pastry is.

SERVES: DEPENDENT ON THE RECIPE

225 g/8 oz unsalted butter, see method
225 g/8 oz strong or plain flour
pinch salt

I or 2 teaspoons lemon juice
ice cold water

In order to make sure you have 100% fat in the butter wrap it in gauze and squeeze out any liquid then weigh out the right amount. This step is not essential but it is part of the right technique.

Sift the flour and salt, add the lemon juice and sufficient water to make an elastic and pliable dough.

1. Roll out the dough on a lightly floured surface to make a neat oblong shape.
2. Place the block of butter in the centre of the dough.
3. Bring up the two bottom corners to cover the butter (the pastry then looks like an opened envelope).
4. Bring down the top two corners to cove the butter and dough (it now looks like a closed envelope).
5. Turn the pastry at right angles, rib the dough with a rolling pin (this means depressing it at regular intervals, which equalizes the pressure of air).
6. Roll out again to an oblong and repeat stages 3, 4 and 5. Continue like this until the pastry has 7 foldings and 7 rollings but do wrap in clingfilm and chill well between several of these stages.

Vol-au-Vents

The great chef of the 18th and early 19th century 'Carême' when describing Vol-au-Vents stated ' this entrée is pretty good without a doubt; it is almost always eaten with pleasure for its extreme delicacy and lightness but to cook it perfectly demands the utmost care'.

In the 1950's I found that enthusiastic cooks were so delighted to be able to use good ingredients once more, after the long years of rationing, that they were very willing to learn about puff pastry and then to use this to make light cases that really did 'melt in the mouth'.

MAKES: ABOUT 12

Puff Pastry made with
225 g/8 oz flour, etc. as page 178

TO GLAZE:
1 egg or egg yolk, but see under Sweet Fillings

Preheat the oven to 230°C/450°F/Gas Mark 8/220°C with a fan oven. Damp a baking sheet with cold water.

For medium sized cases roll out the pastry until about 1.25 to 2 cm/½ to ¾ inch in thickness. Cut into rounds of approximately 6.5 to 7.5 cm/2 ½ to 3 inches in diameter with a pastry cutter. Take a second pastry cutter, measuring approximately 3.75 cm/1 ½ inches in diameter, press this firmly into the centre of each pastry round. Make sure the cutter only goes half way down the pastry.

Put the cases on the baking tray. Beat the egg or yolk and brush over the top of the pastry. Bake for approximately 10 minutes then lower the heat to 190°C/375°F/Gas Mark 5/180°C with a fan oven and cook for a further 5 minutes or until the cases are golden in colour and firm.

Carefully lift out the centre part of each round with the tip of a knife. Put the small rounds on one side; they are the 'lids' of the cases. If by chance you find a little uncooked pastry return the cases to the oven, at the lower setting, for a further 3 or 4 minutes to dry out.

To serve: add the filling and garnish, perch the 'lids' at a jaunty angle.

Hot Vol-au-Vents: put hot fillings into hot cases just before serving.

Cold Vol-au-Vents: make sure pastry and fillings are cold before putting together.

Variations: the cooking time will vary according to the size of the cases. Small cocktail sized Vol-au-Vents take about 8 minutes total cooking time, whereas a single large case, which is ideal for a main dish, takes about 10 minutes at the higher setting and nearly 15 minutes at the lower setting.

Savoury Fillings

Mix cooked diced chicken or other poultry or game birds or shellfish with a fairly thick sauce of your choice. Cooked mushrooms and other cooked vegetables are delicious in a cheese sauce or tomato purée.

Scrambled eggs make a good filling. Give these colour and interest with the addition of diced cooked red and green peppers, asparagus tips and diced mushrooms.

Crisp raw diced bamboo shoots and crisp salad ingredients can be mixed with thick mayonnaise or seasoned yoghurt or crème fraîche.

Sweet Fillings

Jam or conserve with whipped cream to decorate; fresh berry fruits with ice cream.

The uncooked pastry can be brushed with lightly beaten egg white, instead of the yolk or whole egg and dusted with caster sugar before baking or dust the rim of the cooked cases with sifted icing sugar.

A modern touch: home-made puff pastry freezes well. If using ready-prepared frozen pastry allow 450 g/1 lb to take the place of home-made based on 225 g/8 oz flour, etc.

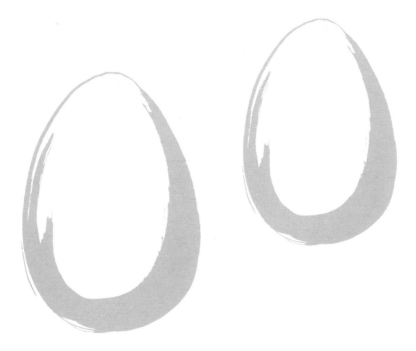

Vol-au-Vents and Quiche Lorraine (pages 179 and 177)

it does not dry. Continue like this until you have 5 or 6 sheets prepared. Place on to the lightly greased baking tin. Cover with the apple filling, then the remainder of the butter coated sheets of pastry. Seal the edges well and brush the top of the strudel with more melted butter.

Bake for 40 minutes but reduce the heat slightly after about 25 minutes, if the pastry is becoming too brown. You need adequate cooking time to cook the apples. Top with sifted icing sugar before serving. This is equally good hot or cold.

Variations: substitute olive or sunflower oil for butter in the filling and pastry.

With a little practise you can form the filo pastry strudel into the traditional horseshoe shape of a true strudel.

Strudel dough: sift 150 g/5 oz strong or plain flour and a pinch of salt into a bowl. Add 1 tablespoon melted butter or olive oil, 1 egg yolk and enough warm water to give a pliable dough. Knead until smooth. Return to the bowl, spread with ½ tablespoon melted butter or oil, cover and leave for 30 minutes. Spread a large cloth over the table, sprinkle with flour then roll the dough until reasonably thin, after which pull and stretch until shaped into a large paper thin oblong. Spread the apple filling over this then roll the dough around it. Form into a horseshoe shape and bake as above but brush the strudel with melted butter or oil before baking once or twice during cooking.

Lemon Meringue Pie (page 188)

Lemon Meringue Pie

As a Lemon Meringue Pie depends upon adequate fat to make good pastry, fresh eggs and fresh lemons for the filling, we had to wait until well into the 1950's, until all these essential ingredients came back again.

SERVES 6

FOR THE PASTRY:
175 g/6 oz plain flour
pinch salt
100 g/3½ oz butter or margarine
1 tablespoon caster sugar
1 egg yolk
few drops water
FOR THE FILLING:
1 large or 2 small lemons

water, see method
25 g/1 oz cornflour
25 g/1 oz butter
85 g/3 oz caster sugar, or to taste
2 egg yolks
FOR THE MERINGUE:
2 egg whites
50 to 115 g/2 to 4 oz caster sugar,
   see method

For the pastry: sift the flour and salt, rub in the butter or margarine, add the sugar, egg yolk and enough water to make a firm rolling consistency. Cover and chill for a short time.

Preheat the oven to 190°C/375°F/Gas Mark 5/180°C with a fan oven. Roll out the pastry and line a flan tin or dish measuring 20 to 23 cm/8 to 9 inches in diameter and at least 3.75cm/1½ inches in depth.

To bake blind: fill the pastry shape with greaseproof paper and baking beans or with foil. Cook for 15 minutes or the pastry is firm and just pale golden in colour. Remove the paper and beans or foil.

If serving the pie hot reduce the heat of the oven to 160°C/325°F/Gas Mark 3/ 150°C with a fan oven.

If serving the pie cold reduce the heat to 120°C/250°F/Gas Mark ½ - this setting is also quite satisfactory for a fan oven.

For the filling: while the pastry is being prepared and baked make the filling. Grate the zest from the lemon(s), squeeze out the juice. Measure and add sufficient water to give a total of 300 ml/½ pint.

Blend the cornflour with this liquid, pour into a saucepan, add the lemon zest, butter and sugar. Stir over a low heat until thickened. Remove from the heat and whisk in the egg yolks. Return to the heat again and cook very slowly for 2 minutes.

Spoon the hot filling into the hot pastry.

Whisk the egg whites until stiff, they should stand up in peaks. If serving hot you can use just 50 g/2 oz sugar but if serving cold you have a better meringue if the larger amount of sugar is added. Gradually beat most of the sugar into the egg white, fold in the remainder then spoon or pipe over the lemon filling. Make sure the meringue completely covers the filling – if the filling is exposed it causes 'sweating' and softens the meringue.

Bake for 20 to 25 minutes for a hot pie or 1 hour if serving the pie cold.

Syllabub

Although this light dessert has never been quite as popular in homes as it should be, it remains a great favourite of mine. I showed how to make this on television when cream was available once more. The dessert should be slightly liquid in consistency.

SERVES 6

450 ml/15 fl oz double cream
150 ml/5 fl oz single cream
4 teaspoons lemon juice

1 to 2 teaspoons brandy, optional
1 to 2 tablespoons caster sugar

Whip the double cream until it stands in soft peaks. Gradually stir in the remaining ingredients.

Spoon into glasses and chill well.

Variations: the dessert can be topped with crystallized rose or violet petals.

Use a little thick smooth raspberry purée instead of lemon juice.

Baked Alaska

I first demonstrated this on B.B.C. television in the late 1950's as a dish for a festive occasion and on the same occasion Philp Harben produced his Fried Ice Cream, which I mention on page 160.

Everyone in the studio held their breath at his daring, for the programmes were live in those days - no chance of a re-take if things went wrong. His secret was to ensure the fat was at the right temperature before coating the ice cream, and work quickly so it remained very hard. Even so this is not a dish for the beginner. Home freezers were not yet on the market, therefore the ice cream had to be stored in the freezing compartment of a refrigerator.

SERVES 4 TO 6

Victoria Sandwich as page 36 or
   the Light Sponge page 38
175 g/6 oz fruit or canned fruit such
   as sliced peaches
ice cream, made as page 29

FOR THE MERINGUE:
4 egg whites
few drops vanilla extract
115 to 175 g/4 to 6 oz caster sugar,
   depending upon personal taste

Preheat the oven to 230°C/450°C/Gas Mark 8/220°C with a fan oven. Cut the sponge to fit into an ovenproof dish. Top with the fruit, canned fruit should be well-drained. Chill the ice cream well.

Whisk the egg whites and vanilla until very stiff, you should be able to turn the mixing bowl upside down without fear of the whites sliding out. Gradually beat in the sugar. Place the ice cream on top of the fruit then cover this with the meringue. For a more professional appearance you could pipe, rather than spread, this over the ice cream. Place in the oven for 3 minutes or until golden coloured then serve at once.

A modern touch: in view of the short cooking time the eggs are virtually uncooked, so take care you know the source of supply (see page 265).

It is better to keep the ice cream in the freezer rather than the freezing compartment of the refrigerator.

1960 to 1969

the prawn cocktail, black forest gâteau and fondue set

Queen Elizabeth gave birth to two sons during this decade. Prince Andrew was born in 1960 and Prince Edward in 1964.

In spite of the unrest in parts of Africa the Queen and Prince Philip carried out a very successful visit to Ghana in 1961.

In June 1963 a Russian woman, Valentina Tereshkova, became the first female to go into space.

In November of the same year the American President John Kennedy was shot and killed while on a visit to Dallas, Texas.

In 1965 Winston Churchill died. He was given a state funeral.

Professor Barnard carried out the world's first successful heart transplant in South Africa in December 1967.

In 1969 Neil Armstrong, the American astronaut, took the first step on the moon.

Life in Britain from 1960 to 1969

Young people were making the news again, some were called 'flower people' or 'hippies'. The less desirable element divided themselves between Mods and Rockers and had many altercations. London was said to be the fashion capital of the world for men and women.

In 1961 the Beatles made their debut at the Cavern Club in Liverpool, within a short time after this event they became world famous.

During this decade advertising of cigarettes on television was banned.

In May 1968 the liner QE2 was launched.

The Kitchens

Interesting kitchen furniture was being made and suddenly there was a wealth of kitchen appliances. Automatic electric cookers appeared, these enabled the cook to put food in the oven then set the timer. The oven would automatically switch on and off at pre-set times.

Electric hotplates, and other appliances for keeping food hot, allowed the cook to prepare dishes ahead; dish-washers took the drudgery out of washing-up. Food processors mixed, chopped and puréed various foods.

Home freezers were on sale. Their influence was felt more in the 1970's. At this stage cookery articles concentrated on the correct technique of freezing and suggested 'batch-cooking', i.e. preparing double amounts of food, eating some when freshly cooked and freezing the rest.

The Foods of Britain

This was the decade that heralded changing eating habits. British people were becoming accustomed to eating out. By 1960 there were 2,000 coffee bars. Many Chinese and Indian restaurants opened. They appealed to young people for they were 'trendy', the food was interesting and comparatively cheap. Quick-food restaurants flourished as did Italian Trattorias.

Supermarkets were bringing new foods into the country. As supermarkets flourished private grocers, greengrocers and butchers were finding their trade decreasing.

Garlic was at last being accepted by the British.

Pasta dishes found great favour with the young, who gradually converted their parents. Rice dishes, such as Paella, were new favourites.

Olive oil was more readily available. In the past it was only found in a chemist's shop.

Yoghurt was becoming increasingly popular.

Convenience Foods

Canned foods were still enjoying large sales, although frozen foods were fast overtaking them. The fact one could buy frozen, as well as fresh, prawns helped to create the popularity of the Prawn Cocktail.

Tubes and cans of tomato purée were a great asset. The concentrated purée added flavour to many dishes.

Favourite Drinks

The younger generation were discovering Coca-Cola. It had been imported into Britain from America from the beginning of the century.

Vermouth was the drink for many adults. There was an appreciable increase in the amount of wine being drunk in restaurants and at home.

Meals of 1960 to 1969

This was the first decade in which the family meal, where everyone gathered together around the dining-room table, seemed to be on the wane.

Individual members of the family were following their own activities, rather than going out as a family unit.

Often people had informal meals in the kitchen and T.V. Dinners was the theme of many cookery articles.

Breakfast

This was the first decade in which I heard parents grumble that their youngsters were in a hurry in the morning and left little time for a good breakfast. Breakfast cereals were taking over from cooked meals.

Luncheon

For some people the meal was similar to the lunches of the past but pasta dishes

had become such a favourite for informal meals, as well as for special occasions, that they became an ideal choice for lunch (page 214).

Teatime

As more women worked this meal was slowly disappearing, except at weekends. Instead of 'old-fashioned' cakes, cookery writers tended to give gâteau recipes that were equally suitable for a dessert or for tea.

Dinner

Formal dinner parties were more popular than in the 1950's, for the range of labour-saving appliances had taken away much of the work. Some of the recipes that follow were exceptionally popular at the time.

Cocktail Parties

These were a feature of both the late 1950's and the 1960's. They were considered a good way of entertaining a larger number of people than one could accommodate at a dinner party. A choice of drinks would be offered, except at Christmas time or the summer when people might serve **Mulled Wine** or a **Wine Cup** (page 230).

Small **Vol-au-Vent** cases (page 179) were a favourite, so were hot cocktail sausages, **Kebabs** - cocktail sticks with diced cheese and pineapple or prawns and cucumber or tiny rolls of ham filled with cream cheese – were some ideas of the 1960's. The sticks would be pressed into cabbage hearts or grapefruit. Small lengths of crisp celery would be filled with Stilton cheese and stoned dates with cream cheese and almonds. Gherkins, tiny onions, salted nuts, crisps and olives would be available.

The more sophisticated would prepare **Aspic Canapés**. Small pieces of smoked salmon, anchovies, piped cream cheese, sliced hard-boiled eggs and other foods would be arranged on squares of toast and coated with aspic.

Aspic Jelly

This is a lengthy process, that only chefs would undertake. The majority of people bought packet aspic, dissolved it in hot water, or a good stock (page 16), then allowed it to cool to a syrupy consistency. It then was brushed or carefully spread over the food. When set a second coating of aspic could be applied.

Open Sandwiches

Another favourite of the 1960's. A diversity of foods would be arranged carefully on buttered rye or other bread. When well made these looked as appetising as they tasted.

Cookery Influences

There were cookery books from gifted authors, such as Jane Grigson and Robert Carrier on sale. My own *Cookery in Colour* was published and the 1960's was a very busy decade for me, with more books, and a long tour of Australia where I gave demonstrations to many people and appeared on television in that exciting country. A new and modern edition of Mrs. Beeton's book appeared. The television programmes of Fanny and Johnnie Cradock were increasingly popular, for they showed new dishes for dinner parties and other occasions. The Cradocks and I gave cookery demonstrations throughout Britain in theatres and city halls.

Graham Kerr was a new name to British television; he gave informal demonstrations, for he used to join the audiences and chat to them when he had finished his excellent cookery demonstrations.

Cookery lessons in schools were now renamed Home Economics. Evening and daytime vocational adult cookery classes at technical colleges and school became very popular.

1960 to 1969

The Recipes

Cheese Straws

When there was ample butter and Parmesan cheese again we could make these delicate rich biscuits for cocktail parties or to serve with pre-dinner drinks or heated canned Turtle Soup. The oven heat is high so check baking carefully. I have suggested reducing the heat in a fan oven slightly more than usual.

MAKES ABOUT 48

115 g/4 oz plain flour
1 teaspoon dry English mustard
    powder, or to taste
salt and cayenne pepper
115 g/4 oz butter

85 g/3 oz Parmesan cheese,
    finely grated
1 egg yolk
TO GLAZE:
1 egg white

Preheat the oven to 220°C/425°F/Gas Mark 7 or 200°C with a fan oven. Grease several baking sheets.

Sift the flour with the mustard, a good pinch of salt and shake of cayenne. Rub in the butter, add the cheese. Mix well. Beat the egg yolk and add sufficient to make a slightly sticky dough, chill well.

Roll out on a lightly floured board to a thickness of 6 mm/¼ inch. Cut into strips about 6 mm/¼ inch in width and 7.5 cm/3 inches in length.

Put onto the baking sheets. Whisk the egg white until frothy, brush over the straws. Bake for 7 to 10 minutes. Cool until firm enough to handle. When cold store in an airtight tin.

Variations: if the cheese is dry you may need a very little water as well as egg yolk.

Some dough can be made into rings. When baked and cold place several straws into each ring.

There was a vogue for coating the ends of the straws in a very little mayonnaise then coating one end with finely chopped parsley and the other end in paprika.

A modern touch: top sheets with baking parchment, rather than greasing them.

Cheese Fondue (page 204)

Escargots

During the 1960's many restaurants included escargots on their menus. I had quite a number of letters from people asking for the secret of preparing garden snails for this delicacy. Escargots are an hors d'oeuvre of which I am very fond, I can never decide whether it is the plump snails or the moist garlic butter that is the attraction. The snails and their shells were sold in cans and all one had to do was to make the garlic butter, as below, put this into the shells with the snails and heat in the oven at the temperature given below.

In a small café in France I tasted this version of the dish where the snails were embedded into slices of French bread. I christened the dish 'snails in a nest'. This makes an excellent snack or hors d'oeuvre to a meal.

SERVES 4

1 long baguette	115 g/4 oz butter
3 garlic cloves or a roasted head of garlic, see below	salt and freshly ground black pepper
	24 snails

Preheat the oven to 200°C/400°F/Gas Mark 6/190°C with a fan oven. Cut the loaf into 12 fairly thin slices, scoop out a little of the crumb in the centre of each slice. Peel and crush the garlic and blend with 85 g/3 oz of the butter and seasoning. Spread some garlic butter into each hollow, top with 2 snails then cover with the rest of the garlic butter. The slices around the snails can be spread with the remaining plain butter. Place on a baking tray and bake for 6 or 7 minutes. Serve piping hot.

Variations: add chopped chervil or parsley and a squeeze of lemon juice to the garlic butter.

Roasted garlic: cut the top off a whole head of garlic, exposing just the tips of the cloves. Brush with plenty of olive oil and bake for 20 minutes in a preheated oven set to 190°C/375°F/Gas Mark 5/180°C with a fan oven. The garlic becomes as soft as butter and could be used in the recipe above. The flavour is milder than ordinary crushed garlic.

Prawn Cocktail

When this hors d'oeuvre made its appearance it was hailed with delight by busy people planning dinner parties. It was easy to prepare and could be made ahead. It was offered in restaurants too. The 1960's was an era when British catering had yet to establish the deservedly high reputation of the 1990's. All too often one would find that indifferent prawns were encased in a mixture of salad dressing and an excess of tomato ketchup, which passed for Mary Rose dressing.

A Prawn Cocktail can be adapted in many ways and the basic recipe of those far off days is followed by ways in which I have varied it as new and interesting ingredients appear on the market. Choose the best quality prawns available. If you HAVE to use frozen prawns allow them to defrost thoroughly then drain and dry them well. Remember to shred beautifully crisp lettuce finely, it has to be eaten with a small spoon.

SERVES 4

FOR THE MARY ROSE DRESSING:
3 to 4 tablespoons mayonnaise
1 to 1 ½ tablespoons tomato purée*
1 tablespoon double cream
1 teaspoon lemon juice
½ tablespoon dry sherry, optional
few drops Tabasco sauce, optional
salt and freshly ground white pepper

225 to 300 g/8 to 10 oz prawns,
    weight when shelled
¼ small lettuce heart
TO GARNISH:
lemon slices

* if you use tomato purée from a tube or can, add ½ to 1 teaspoon sugar to give a delicate sweetness or mix half tomato purée and half best quality tomato ketchup. I like a fresh tomato purée, so I skin, halve and deseed 1 or 2 ripe tomatoes and sieve or liquidize the pulp. This can be mixed with a teaspoon concentrated tomato purée or ketchup.

Mix the ingredients for the sauce, add the prawns. Cover the container and keep well chilled. Just before the meal shred the lettuce very finely, put into 4 glasses and top with the prawn mixture. Place the lemon slices on the rim of the glasses.

Variations: a pleasant touch of crispness is given by adding a small portion of finely diced celery heart, red or green pepper, fennel bulb or dessert apple to the prawn mixture.

Add more flavour to the dressing with 2 teaspoons finely chopped dill or fennel leaves or sun-dried tomatoes or crushed and chopped lemon grass. Use soy sauce instead of Tabasco.

Use crème fraîche or thick Greek yoghurt instead of double cream.

Blend a diced avocado with a little oil and lemon or vinegar dressing put on the lettuce then top with the prawn mixture.

Flaked crabmeat or diced lobster or lightly cooked diced scallops can be used instead of prawns or blend a mixture of shellfish.

Potted Shrimps

People who have never tasted the sweet flavour of tiny shrimps are missing a treat. It has always been one of the delights of living on the coast, particularly in and around Morecambe Bay in the Lake District, to catch shrimps, rush home to boil them and eat them warm. Potted shrimps are a more sophisticated method of serving the fish. Clarified butter is preferable but not essential.

SERVES 4

115 g/4 oz clarified butter	cayenne and/or freshly ground
1.2 litres/2 pints cooked shrimps	white pepper
	pinch grated or ground nutmeg

To clarify butter: put the 115 g/4 oz butter into a saucepan with water to cover. Heat until the butter has melted then leave until cold. Remove the solid butter from the top of the water.

Peel the shrimps, if cold place in to boiling water for a few seconds so the outsides become warm.

Heat the butter carefully. Mix half the melted butter, pepper(s) and nutmeg with the shrimps. Spoon into small dishes. Top with the remaining butter. Chill well. Serve with hot toast and lemon wedges.

Sole Veronique

During this decade a number of people became interested in some of the wonderful classic French recipes for cooking fish. Sole is so often the fish recommended but this recipe can be made with cheaper fish, such as plaice or whiting fillets. The whole success of the dish, like so many other classic dishes of the period, was the care given to produce a good flavoured stock and cooking liquid for the fish.

SERVES 4

FOR THE FISH STOCK:

3 peppercorns

few parsley sprigs

1 small onion, sliced, optional

150 ml/¼ pint water

150 ml/¼ pint dry white wine or
   more water

2 medium sole, filleted, retain heads,
   bones and skin

FOR COOKING THE FISH AND THE SAUCE:

1 small shallot, finely chopped

3 tablespoons dry white wine

salt and freshly ground black pepper

25 g/1 oz butter

25 g/1 oz plain flour

150 ml/5 fl oz double or single cream

115 g/4 oz white grapes, skinned
   and deseeded

TO GARNISH:

few grapes, not skinned, and watercress

Put the ingredients for the stock into a pan, add the fish heads, bones and skins. Cover the pan and simmer for 20 to 30 minutes, Strain the liquid and measure off 150 ml/¼ pint. Keep any excess, it might be needed for the sauce.

Preheat the oven to 190°C/375°F/Gas Mark 5/180°C with a fan oven. Fold the 8 fillets of sole, put into a dish, add the 150 ml/¼ pint stock plus the shallot, wine and a little seasoning. Cover and cook for 20 minutes or until the fish is just tender. Lift the fillets on to a heated serving dish, cover and keep warm. Strain the cooking liquid into a measuring jug.

Heat the butter in a saucepan, stir in the flour then add the strained stock from cooking the fish with enough fish stock to give 250 ml/8 fl oz liquid. Stir as the mixture comes to the boil and thickens. Remove from the heat, stir in the cream and grapes. Heat gently, without boiling. Taste and add more seasoning if required. Serve the fish with the sauce and garnish the dish with grapes and watercress. Serve with new or creamed potatoes or cooked rice and mixed vegetables.

Variation: the fish can be poached in a covered pan on top of the cooker.

Cheese Fondue

Cheese Fondue was a logical extension of the cheese and wine parties of the previous decade. There were three main reasons why these had been chosen as a form of entertaining. Firstly they entailed very little preparation. This was important, for domestic help was proving difficult to find and expensive too. Secondly, after years of limited choice, a wide selection of cheeses had come on the market. Lastly the British were discovering the pleasures of drinking wine.

The cheeses given in the recipe are the classic ones for a Swiss fondue but any good cooking cheese can be used. Attractive fondue sets were displayed in stores and shops - they were favourite wedding and Christmas presents. A wide ceramic pot is best. It is more difficult to keep at the right heat in a metal one.

SERVES 4 TO 6

15 g/½ oz butter, preferably unsalted	freshly ground black pepper
1 garlic clove, halved	1 to 2 tablespoons brandy or kirsch,
300 ml/½ pint dry white wine	optional
225 g/8 oz Emmenthal cheese, grated	little grated nutmeg, optional
225 g/8 oz Gruyère cheese, grated	TO DIP INTO THE FONDUE:
1 level teaspoon cornflour, optional	toast, bread, vegetables

Rub the inside of the fondue pot with the butter and then the garlic. Add most of the wine and place over the fondue heater. When the wine begins to bubble gently start to stir in a little cheese. If using cornflour, which helps (with the correct heat) to stop the mixture curdling, blend this with the last of the wine and pour into the pot with the first lot of cheese. Continue adding cheese, stirring all the time. When it has melted then add the extra ingredients. Keep warm over a very low heat but even then stir briskly from time to time.

Cut toast or bread or cooked raw vegetables into small portions. Using fondue forks spear the 'dippers' and swirl around in the hot cheese mixture.

Variation: to make fondue without a special heater use a ceramic bowl and stand over a pan of gently simmering water.

Flavour the cheese mixture with tiny pieces of sun-dried tomato, chopped lemon grass or a little lemon juice or pieces of roasted red pepper.

Roast Joints

After the end of meat rationing in 1954, joints began to appear in butcher's shops. Most families returned to the pre-war habit of Sunday roast dinner. This trend continued right through the 1960's, although there was growing interest in dishes from other countries.

The following is just a nostalgic reminder of the classic accompaniments to the various meats. The post-war joints still contained a fairly high percentage of fat. Their flavour therefore was good and they produced splendid dripping.

Roast Beef

To celebrate the return of the nation's favourite meat, most people bought expensive sirloin or rib but some preferred the more economical topside.

The beef would be served with Yorkshire Pudding, commercially made horseradish cream or horseradish sauce or mustard, roast potatoes and other seasonal vegetables. Thin gravy is considered correct with roast beef.

Yorkshire Pudding

Serves 4 to 6

For a light Yorkshire Pudding the oven should be preheated to 220°C/425°F/Gas Mark 7/210°C with a fan oven. Sift 115 g/4 oz plain flour with a pinch salt, gradually add 2 eggs and 270 ml/9 fl oz milk or milk and water. Beat until smooth. If using just 1 egg increase the liquid by 2 tablespoons. Heat 25 g/1 oz dripping or lard in an oblong Yorkshire Pudding tin, pour in the batter and cook for 15 minutes then lower the heat to 190°C/375°F/Gas Mark 5/180°C with a fan oven and cook for a further 10 to 15 minutes.

If using small tins (more popular in later eras) grease the tins, heat for 2 minutes, add the batter and cook for 5 to 8 minutes at the high heat then lower the heat and cook for a total of 12 to 15 minutes, depending upon the depth of the mixture.

Roast Mutton and Lamb

The favourite joints were leg or shoulder of lamb. For small families a rack of lamb would be chosen. The end of mutton was approaching and lamb took its place.

Mutton would be served with Onion Sauce, redcurrant jelly, roast potatoes and seasonal vegetables. A thick gravy was usual.

Lamb would be served with Mint Sauce and similar gravy and vegetables as mutton. Unusual stuffings and Crown Roasts were favourites of the future.

Onion Sauce

Serves 4 to 6

Peel and finely chop 2 large onions. Heat 50 g/2 oz butter in a saucepan and cook the onions gently until nearly soft, do not allow to brown. Stir in 40 g/1 ½ oz plain flour and 600 ml/1 pint milk (or use a little cream instead of all the milk). Bring to the boil and cook until thickened, season to taste.

Mint Sauce

Serves 4 to 6

Finely chop a handful of young mint leaves. Add 1 to 2 tablespoons caster sugar (amount depends upon personal taste) then gradually stir in several tablespoons of brown or white malt vinegar. Allow to stand for a time so the flavours mature.

A modern touch: put all the ingredients into the liquidizer.

Roast Pork

Fillet (from the leg) or part of the leg, loin or spare rib were the popular joints of the period. Blade, hand and spring were cheaper joints. For good crackling score the skin, brush with a little melted lard or oil and sprinkle sparingly with salt. Instead of this the whole skin can be lifted off the meat and cooked separately.

Sage and Onion Stuffing and Apple Sauce were the usual accompaniments and the joint would be served with roast or boiled potatoes, seasonal vegetables and a thick gravy.

Sage and Onion Stuffing

Serves 4 to 6

Peel and chop 2 large or 3 medium onions, simmer for 10 minutes in 150 ml/¼ pint water, or until the onions are softened and most of the liquid has evaporated. Strain and blend the onions with 50 g/2 oz soft breadcrumbs, 2 teaspoons chopped sage (or 1 teaspoon dried sage), 50 g/2 oz shredded suet or melted margarine and 1 egg. Season well. Cook in a separate dish from the meat for approximately 40 minutes at 190°C/ 375°F/Gas Mark 5/180°C with a fan oven.

Apple Sauce

Serves 4 to 6

Peel, core and slice 450 g/1 lb cooking apples, put into a saucepan with 3 tablespoons water and simmer until soft. Add 1 to 2 tablespoons soft brown or caster sugar, 25 g/1 oz butter can be added for a richer sauce.

A modern touch: place the sauce in a liquidizer to give a smooth purée.

Roast Veal

This was not as popular as the other meats. The favourite joints were fillet, leg, loin or shoulder. Breast and neck are less expensive joints. The meat is very lean so should be **barded** before cooking. This means it should have strips of fat bacon inserted through the joint.

Veal is served with sausages and bacon (like chicken), a Parsley and Thyme Stuffing which is often made into Forcemeat Balls (as under Jugged Hare page 142) and thick gravy.

Good Gravy

Serves 4 to 6

In the 1950's special sauces were not a usual choice, families preferred gravy.

Pour away all the dripping from the roasting tin except for 1½ tablespoons, save any residue that drops from the meat.

For a thin gravy: blend 1½ level tablespoons plain flour with the dripping in the tin. Stir over a low heat on top of the cooker until the mixture turns brown. Gradually blend in 600 ml/1 pint meat stock or strained vegetable water. Bring to the boil and cook for several minutes, stirring well. Season to taste then strain.

For a thicker gravy: follow the directions above but use 2 to 3 level tablespoons plain flour.

Variations: in the 1950's there were several aids for gravy. You could buy stock cubes that were mixed with water, or gravy flavourings.

Cooks recommended using a little Madeira, port or red wine or sherry instead of all stock.

Glazed Bacon or Ham

Joints of bacon or ham were popular throughout this decade. While the meat could be boiled, as instructions on page 90, most people preferred to adorn it with an attractive glaze. The best method of preparation was to par-boil the meat, then complete the cooking in the oven. If preferred the joint could be roasted for the whole period, see below.

SERVES: DEPENDENT ON THE SIZE OF JOINT

bacon or ham joint (page 90)
glaze, see below

Calculate the cooking time but deduct 30 minutes from the total. Soak and simmer as instructed on page 90.

At the end of the cooking time remove the bacon or ham from the liquid, cut away the rind. Leave the fat on the joint and score this in a neat design. Preheat the oven to 190°C/ 375°F/Gas Mark 5/180°C with a fan oven.

Blend the ingredients for the glaze; press against the fat and roast the joint for 30 minutes. Serve hot or cold.

Glazes

The amounts are sufficient for 2 kg/4 to 4½ lb joint.

Ginger and Treacle: blend 2 level tablespoons black treacle with 3 tablespoons soft brown sugar, 1 to 2 teaspoons ground ginger, 2 tablespoons very finely diced preserved ginger and 1 tablespoon syrup from the jar of preserved ginger. Garnish with slices of preserved ginger.

Honey and Orange: blend the finely grated zest of 2 oranges with 3 tablespoons clear honey, 2 tablespoons Demerara sugar, 1 tablespoon plain flour and 1 tablespoon orange juice. Garnish with orange segments put on cocktail sticks and pressed into the joint before serving.

Pineapple and Lemon: blend 1 teaspoon finely grated lemon zest with 175 g/6 oz light brown sugar, 3 tablespoons pineapple juice, 1 tablespoon lemon juice and 2 level tablespoons plain flour sifted with ½ teaspoon cayenne pepper. Garnish the joint with pineapple rings.

Variation: Roasted Bacon or Ham: soak the meat overnight in cold water to cover; drain and dry thoroughly. The bacon or ham can be cooked without covering but it dries less if lightly covered with foil or cooked in a roasting tin with a lid. When wrapping in foil add an extra 10 minutes to the total cooking time. With a covered roasting tin add an extra 5 minutes.

Spread a little softened butter or oil over the lean part of the joint before roasting.

Fast roasting: this is only suitable for prime gammon joints. Preheat the oven to 200°C/400°F/Gas Mark 6/190°C with a fan oven. Allow 20 to 25 minutes per 450 g/1 lb and 20 minutes over. Shallow joints generally need the shorter cooking time whereas thick joints of smaller diameter require the longer cooking time. Lower the heat to 190°C/375°F/Gas Mark 5/180°C with a fan oven after the first 1 hour's cooking time. If glazing the joint deduct 30 minutes from the total cooking time.

Slower roasting: suitable for all joints. Preheat the oven to 180°C/350°F/Gas Mark 4/170°C with a fan oven. Allow 25 to 30 minutes per 450 g/1 lb for gammon and 25 to 30 minutes over but 45 minutes per 450 g/1 lb for collar and forehock and 45 minutes over. If glazing the joint deduct 30 minutes from the total cooking time.

Shish Kebabs

Kebabs became fashionable in the 1960's. The optimistic British were prepared to defy the uncertain summer weather and invest in barbecue equipment. Shish Kebabs, shortened to Kebabs, also known as Shashlyk or Brochettes, were one of the dishes chosen. A cooker manufacturer included a turning spit in the oven and long metal skewers began to appear in kitchen shops.

SERVES 4 TO 5

approximately 675 g/ 1 ½ lb lean
    tender meat - beef or lamb
2 to 3 tablespoons sunflower or
    other oil
good pinch ground allspice
good pinch ground cumin

pinch saffron powder, optional
1 red or/and 1 green pepper
8 to 12 small button mushrooms
8 small tomatoes
4 to 5 long metal skewers

It is essential that a barbecue is glowing red before trying to cook any food. A grill should be preheated.

Cut the meat into 3.75 cm/ 1 ½ inch cubes. Brush with the oil and sprinkle with the spices. Cut the pepper(s) into neat dice, discard the core and seeds. Trim the mushrooms. Brush the skewers with a little oil. Thread the meat and all the other ingredients on the skewers, arrange them to give a colourful effect. Brush with a little oil immediately before cooking.

Place the filled skewers over the barbecue, under the preheated grill or oven (if there is a kebab attachment) and cook for 10 to 15 minutes. Turn over once or twice during cooking and baste with more oil. Use long tongs with a barbecue.

Note: it is essential to remove the foods from the hot metal skewers with a fork to eat them. To try and eat them from the skewers would burn one's mouth. The bamboo sticks recommended for Pork Satay on page 315 never become as hot as metal, even so care should be taken.

Serve with saffron-flavoured rice or jacket potatoes and mixed salads.

Variations: use diced chicken or lean pork or a mixture of meats plus small sausages. Marinating the meat for a few hours will give extra flavour.

Chicken Maryland

When this dish first became popular in the 1960's it meant buying a small young chicken and asking the butcher to cut it into joints, or doing it at home. Within a relatively short time chicken joints were on sale, so it was possible to choose four breast or four leg portions.

During the latter end of this decade and into the 1970's electric deep fat fryers made their appearance and the people who bought them were introduced to oil, rather than lard, as a frying medium. Chicken Maryland became a dish that was deep, rather than shallow, fried.

SERVES 4

1 small young chicken, jointed or
    4 chicken joints
25 g/1 oz plain flour
salt and freshly ground black pepper
1 egg
50 g/2 oz fine crisp breadcrumbs
FOR THE CORN FRITTERS:
50 g/2 oz self-raising flour or plain flour
    with ½ teaspoon baking powder

salt and cayenne pepper
1 egg
3 tablespoons milk or water
175 g/6 oz cooked or canned sweetcorn
FOR SHALLOW FRYING:
4 tablespoons sunflower
    or ground nut oil

4 small bananas

Dry the chicken joints well, it is not essential to skin them but this is an option. Mix the flour with a generous amount of seasoning and coat the chicken. Beat the egg, brush over the joints and then roll in the crumbs. Press these firmly to the chicken flesh. It is always a good idea to chill coated foods for a time; this makes the coating adhere better. Mix all the ingredients for the fritters together.

Heat half the oil in a large frying pan, fry the joints for 3 to 4 minutes, lower the heat and cook for 10 minutes or until the chicken is tender, crisp and brown. Heat the remaining oil in a second pan and drop in spoonfuls of the batter mixture. Fry quickly for about 2 to 3 minutes. Turn and fry for the same time on the second side. Lift the cooked chicken and fritters on to kitchen paper to drain; keep hot. Meanwhile heat the bananas in the remaining oil in one of the frying pans.

Serve this dish with a crisp salad or green vegetables and creamed potatoes.
Variation: if using a deep fryer heat the oil to 170°C/340°F. Allow 10 to 12 minutes cooking time for the chicken, 4 for the fritters and 1 to 2 for the bananas.

Coq au Vin

In the 1960's good restaurants invariably had Coq au Vin on the menu and very soon the public were asking for the recipe. When I was shown how to make this classic dish in France the chef stressed that a cock, and not a hen bird must be used. I felt that, in the days of anonymous poultry, it would be difficult to be certain you had a cock unless you followed the French habit of obtaining a live bird, or one you had seen killed on a farm, so I never stressed this point in my recipe.

In the 1960's individual chicken joints were not easily obtainable so one had to buy a whole bird and have it jointed or do this yourself. Nowadays you could buy all leg or all breast joints, whichever you prefer.

SERVES 4 TO 6

50 g/2 oz butter	115 to 175 g/4 to 6 oz streaky bacon,
1 tablespoon olive oil	preferably in one piece
12 very small onions or shallots	1 young chicken, weight about
2 garlic cloves, crushed	1.5 kg/3½ lb, cut into joints
225 g/8 oz small button mushrooms	1 tablespoon plain flour

Heat half the butter and half the oil in a large deep frying pan or saucepan. Add the whole peeled onions or shallots and gently cook for 10 minutes or until golden in colour. Turn frequently so they do not burn. Lift on to a dish. Add the garlic and mushrooms and cook for 5 minutes, remove from the pan.

Cut the bacon into small dice; coat the chicken joints in the flour and a generous amount of seasoning; heat the bacon with the remaining butter and oil, put in the chicken and fry steadily until golden brown. Pour in the wine and replace the onions or shallots, simmer for 15 minutes then add the partially cooked mushrooms and garlic. Continue cooking gently for another 5 to 10 minutes or until all the ingredients are tender. Turn the chicken joints around so they become tinged with the colour of the wine. Taste and add extra seasoning if required. Serve with creamed or new potatoes or rice and mixed vegetables or a green salad.

Chicken Maryland (page 211)

Spaghetti alla Bolognese

This dish and Spaghetti all' Amatriciana, below, were the first well-known pasta dishes and they are favourites still. Unless people had been to Italy, or dined in authentic Italian restaurants, they had known little about correctly cooked pasta. It was quite difficult to persuade cooks that perfect pasta meant it should be 'al dente' (firm to the bite). Over the years many different forms of pasta have arrived, together with a never-ending range of sauces and accompaniments, and pasta lovers may make their own (page 182) or buy the freshly made type.

Today pasta, a carbohydrate, is extolled by nutritionists as an ideal food and source of energy. In the early 1960's we were advised not to eat it too often, for it was fattening. How times change!

SERVES 4

FOR THE BOLOGNESE SAUCE:
25 g/1 oz butter
1 tablespoon olive oil
1 medium onion, chopped
1 garlic clove, chopped
2 medium tomatoes, preferably plum
   type, skinned and chopped
175 to 225 g/6 to 8 oz minced beef
1 tablespoon tomato purée
300 ml/½ pint beef stock

150 ml/¼ pint red wine or extra stock
salt and freshly ground black pepper
TO COOK THE PASTA:
2.5 litres/4 pints water
225 g/8 oz spaghetti
25 g/1 oz butter or 1 tablespoon
   olive oil
TO GARNISH:
Parmesan cheese, grated
chopped parsley, optional

Heat the butter and oil in a saucepan, add the vegetables and cook gently for 5 minutes. Stir in the meat and continue stirring as this mixes with the vegetables and becomes golden brown. At the end of 5 to 6 minutes add the rest of the ingredients. Stir briskly until well blended then cover the saucepan, lower the heat and simmer for 40 to 45 minutes. Stir from time to time.

The sauce thickens by evaporation so, if it is still fairly liquid after 35 minutes cooking, remove the saucepan lid. Taste and adjust the seasoning.

Meanwhile boil the water, add ½ to 1 level teaspoon salt. Put in the spaghetti. The way to do this is to hold the long strands in one hand, insert the ends and, when you feel these soften, turn it so more falls into the water. Continue like this until all the spaghetti is completely immersed in the water. Cook steadily in an uncovered pan for the time recommended on the packet. After a short cooking time lift the strands with two spoons or forks to separate them. When cooked strain the pasta. Heat the butter or oil, add the pasta and turn gently so the strands are coated.

Serve topped with the sauce or blend the pasta and sauce. Top with the cheese and parsley.

Variations: add sliced mushrooms, diced red or green pepper, chopped oregano or other herbs to the sauce. A pinch of chilli powder or a small chopped red chilli adds a hot taste. Hungry people may like to increase the amount of pasta in which case increase the water too, i.e. 1.2 litres/2 pints to each 115 g/4 oz.

Spaghetti all' Amatriciana: (often given other names, **e.g. Spaghetti alla Pomodoro.**) Peel and finely chop a medium onion, cut 50 g/2 oz pancetta or streaky bacon into thin strips. Heat 25 g/1 oz butter and 1 tablespoon olive oil in a saucepan, add the onion and cook gently for a few minutes. Put in the pancetta or bacon and continue cooking for 2 minutes. Add 450 g/1 lb skinned and chopped plum tomatoes or a 425 g can chopped tomatoes together with 1 tablespoon tomato purée, a little seasoning and 1 to 2 teaspoons soft brown sugar. Simmer gently in a covered saucepan until the ingredients are softened. If the sauce is becoming too thick add a little water or stock or white wine. The sauce can be liquidized.

Often I add a small piece of diced cooking apple to the other ingredients, and/or a pinch of chilli powder or 1 to 2 teaspoons finely chopped basil.

A modern touch: spaghetti and other pasta can be cooked in a large bowl in the microwave. As water takes a long time to heat in a microwave it is better to boil the water in a kettle, pour it into the bowl, then add the pasta. Follow cooking instructions from your own microwave manual. The cooking time for pasta is not greatly reduced. The sauces can be cooked in a bowl in the microwave successfully. They take an appreciably shorter cooking time than when made in a saucepan.

Paella

Spain was becoming a popular holiday destination and so Paella became a great favourite and I remember having a great number of requests for an authentic recipe. This is my version.

SERVES 4 TO 6

12 to 18 uncooked mussels
TO COOK THE MUSSELS:
1 small onion, chopped
sprig parsley
6 tablespoons water or white wine
FOR THE PAELLA:
3 tablespoons olive oil
1 medium onion, chopped
1 or 2 garlic cloves, chopped
1 small chicken, cut into joints
175 to 225 g/6 to 8 oz long grain rice*

1.2 litres/2 pints chicken stock
¼ teaspoon saffron powder or
   saffron strands
2 to 4 medium tomatoes, skinned
   and chopped
1 red pepper, deseeded and diced
salt and freshly ground black pepper
meat from 1 small cooked lobster, diced
about 12 large prawns, cooked
   and peeled
225 g/8 oz cooked peas

* or use arborio rice

To cook the mussels: wash these well in cold water, strip away any growth on the shells (known as the beard). Discard any mussels that are open and do not close when tapped sharply. Put them into a saucepan with the onion, parsley and water or wine. Place over a fairly high heat and leave until the shells open. Remove from the liquid. This can be strained and used in the Paella. Discard any mussels that remain closed. For this dish the mussels can be removed from both shells or left on a single shell.

Heat the oil in the largest pan possible, add the onion, garlic and chicken and cook steadily until the chicken is golden brown. Stir in the rice and continue stirring until the grains are coated with oil. Mix half the stock with the saffron, pour into the pan and simmer for 10 minutes. Add the tomatoes, red pepper, more of the stock and a little seasoning. Stir very well and continue cooking until the rice is tender. You will need to add more stock during the cooking period for a Paella should be pleasantly moist. Add the mussels, lobster, prawns and peas. Heat thoroughly but do not over-cook, for this toughens shellfish. Taste and adjust the seasoning then serve.

Pommes de Terre Dauphine

When people had mastered the art of making Choux Pastry as page 220, they were interested in the way it could be used other than for sweet pastries. This combination of absolutely smooth potatoes and pastry was very popular during the era when electric deep fryers were a fashionable appliance.

SERVES 4 TO 6

450 g/1 lb old potatoes, boiled
salt and freshly ground white pepper
Choux Pastry (page 220)

little grated or ground nutmeg, optional
FOR FRYING:
oil

Sieve the potatoes or put them through a ricer to make sure they are perfectly smooth, season well. Meanwhile make the pastry as page 220. Use a large saucepan, so there is room to add the potatoes.

Gradually beat the potatoes into the pastry mixture, taste and add more seasoning and the nutmeg. Put the mixture into a large piping bag fitted with a 1.25 cm/½ inch plain pipe.

Heat the oil to 185°C/365°F (when a cube of day-old bread turns golden within 45 seconds). Pipe small balls, about the size of a cob nut, into the very hot oil and fry for about 5 minutes, or until well-risen, firm and golden brown. Drain on absorbent paper and serve.

Variation: add about 25 g/1 oz grated Parmesan cheese to the potato and pastry mixture. Sprinkle the cooked potato balls with more Parmesan just before serving.

Orange Cheesecake: flavour the mixture with orange zest and juice instead of lemon and decorate with whipped cream and mandarin orange segments.
A modern touch: to make the cheesecake lower in fat use sifted cottage cheese instead of the cream or curd cheese and low fat yoghurt or fromage frais instead of cream.

Like most cheesecakes this freezes well.

Choux Pastry

It was the ambition of many cooks of the era to produce perfect choux pastry, so this was one of the recipes I included frequently in my demonstrations. Although the popularity of teatime was slowly declining, except perhaps at weekends when the family were all at home, Cream Buns (page 222) were still a great favourite for they made equally good teatime delicacies or delicious desserts.

SERVES: DEPENDENT ON THE RECIPE

150 ml/¼ pint water	65 g/2½ oz plain flour
50 g/2 oz butter or margarine	2 medium eggs

Pour the water into a medium saucepan, add the butter or margarine and heat until the fat has melted. Remove the pan from the heat, add the flour all at once then stir briskly over a low heat until the mixture forms a firm ball. Allow the mixture to cool.

Whisk the eggs then gradually beat these into the flour mixture; add just enough of the eggs to make a sticky mixture. Use as the recipes, page 222.
Variations: if using the pastry for a sweet dish, as in Cream Buns (page 222), a teaspoon of sugar can be added to the flour.

If used for a savoury dish, such as Gougère, add a pinch of salt to the flour.

Pavlova (page 223)

Black Forest Gâteau

This light chocolate-flavoured sponge filled with cherries, flavoured with kirsch, and whipped cream enjoyed great popularity in homes and restaurants. The new electric mixers were encouraging people to make a number of light sponges and they were excellent for whisking eggs and sugar but home economists had to remind users that in a recipe, such as the one below, the flour and cocoa should be folded in with great care by hand. Over-handling with the mixer would spoil the texture.

SERVES 8

FOR THE SPONGE:
4 large eggs
150 g/5 oz caster sugar
100 g/3 ½ oz plain flour*
15 g/½ oz cocoa powder*
FOR THE FILLING AND DECORATION:
425 g can black cherries in syrup, stoned
2 tablespoons kirsch
300 to 450 ml/10 to 15 fl oz double cream**

50 to 115 g/2 to 4 oz plain chocolate, finely grated**

the eggs and sugar are beaten so well that they aerate the mixture, so a raising agent is unnecessary. You can use self-raising flour or sift 1 level teaspoon baking powder with plain flour if worried about the cake rising well.

** *you will need the larger amounts of cream and chocolate if coating the sides of the gâteau.*

Preheat the oven to 180°C/350°F/Gas Mark 4/170°C with a fan oven. Grease and flour or line a 20 cm/8 inch cake tin with greased greaseproof paper.

Put the eggs and sugar into a large bowl, whisk until thick and creamy. Sift the flour and cocoa twice then gently fold into the egg mixture. Spoon into the tin, bake for 30 to 35 minutes or until firm to a gentle touch. Cool for 3 or 4 minutes in the tin then turn out on to a wire cooling tray. When cold slice horizontally to give 3 layers.

Drain the cherries thoroughly and moisten with half the kirsch. Whip the cream and mix with the remaining kirsch. Sandwich the layers together with whipped cream and most of the cherries. Spread the sides of the cake with whipped cream; save some for the top and piping around the edge of the cake.

Press grated chocolate against the sides of the cake. Decorate the top of the cake with the remaining cream, cherries and chocolate.

A modern touch: this gâteau freezes well.

1970 to 1979

curries and nut roast

In 1970, under Prime Minister, Edward Heath, Britain became a member of the E.E.C.

The first jumbo jet landed at Heathrow in 1970.

In 1977 Queen Elizabeth II celebrated 25 years on the throne. The Silver Jubilee was an occasion for public celebrations and the people showed their affection for the Queen.

In November 1973 Princess Anne married Captain Mark Phillips.

In October 1978 a Polish Cardinal became the first non-Italian Pope since 1552, he would be known as John-Paul II. In September 1979 he visited Ireland to make an appeal for peace.

Life in Britain from 1970 to 1979

In 1970 the voting age was lowered from 21 to 18.

Decimalisation of British currency took place in 1971. This was not greeted with enthusiasm by the people who regretted the passing of £.s.d. and declared it was an excuse for prices to rise.

This was a decade of unrest and strikes; on December 17th 1973 it was announced that industry and commerce would be limited in the amount of electricity consumed and that from the New Year working days were to be limited to a 3-day week. Except for Christmas and the New Year all television services were to close down at 10.30 p.m.

In 1979 Mrs. Margaret Thatcher became Britain's first woman Prime Minister.

Many people were now taking their holidays abroad, Spain being the favourite country.

The Kitchens

The sale of freezers had risen enormously; often people bought capacious cabinets, so searched for foods to fill them. Microwaves, used in some catering establishments, were beginning to be sold for the domestic market.

The need to save fuel led to increased sales of pressure cookers. Many kitchens were re-designed with new streamline fitted units.

The Foods of Britain

Some freezer owners bought large packs of meat. This habit did not last long, for people realised that many of the cuts they acquired were not popular with the family. Most recipes of the era were marked with freezing advice. I gave 'freezer teach-ins' throughout Britain.

Many people became vegetarian. Requests for recipes at first were for vegetarian versions of popular meat dishes. Soon there were new recipes based on lentils, beans, peas (including chick peas), nuts and seeds.

We were urged to eat more fish; seafood was the favourite kind.

Nouvelle Cuisine came to Britain from France. It was widely misunderstood and not surprisingly, for restaurants used it as an excuse to serve minute portions at high prices. The real objective was to omit some cream and flour thickening, etc. in

dishes. This meant one had the true flavour of basic ingredients and, at the same time, enjoyed beautiful food, while keeping slim and healthy.

An ever increasing range of cheeses was available; this dish was popular.

Fried Cheese: coat portions of Camembert or Brie with egg and crumbs, fry quickly and serve with Cranberry Sauce (page 283).

People enjoyed the flavour of chilli, most used the powder but red chilli peppers appeared. There was a greater selection of spices available.

Fruits and Vegetables: aubergines, courgettes, fennel and peppers gaining in popularity as well as sweet potatoes and yams. More fresh herbs used; basil was the herb of the decade. Kiwi fruit, lychees and mangoes becoming well-known. Bananas more and more popular.

The Start of the Macrobiotic Era

It was during the 1970's that the emphasis on choosing ingredients to give greater benefit to health and hopefully to prolong life began. Brown rice, wholemeal flour and bread were recommended together with the greater use of vegetables in daily menus outlined above.

Convenience Foods

There was a rapid increase in the growth of more complex frozen foods, one had a choice of complete dishes as well as frozen ingredients.

More ingredients for Chinese cookery, such as canned water chestnuts, bamboo shoots and bean sprouts.

Greater selection in ice creams and yoghurts. Ice cream was rapidly becoming Britain's favourite dessert. Sales increased enormously in the hot summer of 1976.

Favourite Drinks

As people began buying more wine they looked kindly upon cheaper vintages. The less expensive wines from Australia were gaining in popularity and one heard people happily stating they drank 'plonk'.

Mateus Rosé was a favourite wine during the 1970's. The liking for wine drinks for special occasions in the 1960's became increasingly popular.

Mulled Wine: preheat the oven to 180°C/350°F/Gas Mark 4/170°C with a fan oven.

1970 to 1979

The Recipes

Gazpacho

As regular visitors to Spain know there are several regional variations of this cold soup, but this is my favourite. I had quite a deluge of requests for this, and the Paella on page 216, when Spain became the most popular country for British travellers. The soup can be sieved but it is easier to prepare with the help of a liquidizer or food processor. Do not use canned tomatoes, really ripe Mediterranean type fresh ones give the best result.

SERVES 4 TO 6

2 garlic cloves, crushed
675 g/1 ½ lb tomatoes, skinned*
2 medium Spanish onions, chopped
1 small cucumber, peeled and diced
1 green pepper, deseeded and diced
1 red pepper, deseeded and diced
2 tablespoons Spanish extra virgin
   olive oil, see method

salt and freshly ground black pepper
1 tablespoon lemon juice or white
   wine vinegar
iced water or iced clear chicken stock
several slices of bread

the tomatoes can be deseeded if liquidizing the soup

Either sieve or liquidize all the garlic and tomatoes with half the onions, half the cucumber and half the peppers to make a smooth purée. Put the remaining diced onion, cucumber and peppers into individual dishes so they can be served with the soup.

Add the olive oil, seasoning and lemon juice or vinegar to the purée then enough iced water or stock to make a flowing consistency. Many Spanish recipes use rather more oil than given above, but this is a matter of personal taste. Chill the soup until ready to serve.

Remove the crusts from the bread, dice the crumb and put into a dish. Everyone takes the amount of cucumber, peppers and bread they like as a topping for the soup.
Variation: if you dislike the taste of uncooked onions substitute spring onions or shallots.
A modern touch: add a few tablespoons of uncooked chopped sun-dried tomatoes to the soup. You can freeze the soup and serve it lightly frosted but cannot freeze the firm accompaniments.

Vichyssoise

This became **the** soup to serve during the summer months of the 1970's. Really well chilled it makes a most refreshing start to a meal. The basic recipe below can be varied in a number of different ways.

SERVES 4

450 g/1 lb small young leeks
175 g/6 oz potatoes, weight
    when peeled
40 g/1½ oz butter
750 ml/1¼ pints chicken or
    vegetable stock

salt and freshly ground white pepper
300 ml/10 fl oz double or
    whipping cream
TO GARNISH:
2 to 3 tablespoons finely snipped chives

Take any dark outer leaves and tops from the leeks, slice the remainder, dice the potatoes. Heat the butter in a saucepan and gently cook the leeks and potatoes for 4 to 5 minutes, take care they do not brown.

Add the stock and a little seasoning; bring to the boil. Cover the pan and simmer steadily for 15 to 20 minutes. Allow to become cold then sieve or liquidize with the cream. Adjust the seasoning.

Serve in chilled soup cups and top with the chives.

Variations: instead of all cream use half cream and half white wine.

Crab Vichyssoise: use crab or other fish stock in the soup and top each portion with a good spoonful of white crabmeat and slices of lemon.

Green Vichyssoise: use half young peas and half potatoes, or all peas instead of potatoes. Add 1 or 2 sprigs of mint as the ingredients cook. Top with chives and mint.

Tortilla

I am surprised that this Spanish omelette has never become better known. It makes an excellent hot or cold dish, which can be served as an hors d'oeuvre, main meal or for a picnic. The recipe below is the basic one, which can be varied in many ways.

SERVES 2 TO 4

2 tablespoons olive oil

2 medium onions, finely chopped

25 g/1 oz butter or

   1 extra tablespoon oil

3 medium potatoes, boiled and diced

5 to 6 large eggs

salt and freshly ground black pepper

TO GARNISH:

parsley

Heat the oil in a frying pan or omelette pan, add the onions and cook steadily until almost tender. Add the butter or extra oil and heat, then put in the potatoes. Cook steadily, stirring most of the time, until these are slightly golden.

Beat the eggs with seasoning. Pour over the onions and potatoes and cook steadily until set. Cut into slices to serve. Garnish with the parsley.

Variations: the onions and potatoes can be cooked in a separate pan. In this case use just the 2 tablespoons oil. Heat the 25 g/1 oz butter or tablespoon oil in an omelette pan, add the eggs and cook until they begin to set on the bottom then cover with the piping hot onions and potatoes and continue cooking until the eggs are firm.

Cooked diced peppers, shellfish, diced chorizo or other cooked meat can be added to the onions instead of, or with, the potatoes. Always make sure there is plenty of oil or butter in the pan before adding the eggs.

Caesar Salad

By the 1970's the emphasis was on new ideas and these came from many parts of the world, for people were travelling far more extensively than in the past. This American salad is extremely simple to prepare but there are certain differences of opinion as to the 'right' ingredients. Some experts state that the anchovy fillets are wrong. Personally I feel they give more interest to the salad, so include them. Choose a very crisp lettuce, a cos type is ideal. You can break the leaves slightly but do not shred them.

SERVES 4

1 garlic clove, peeled and halved	2 tablespoons mayonnaise
4 tablespoons extra virgin olive oil	shake freshly ground black pepper
2 large slices of bread, crusts removed, the crumb cut into small dice	1 lettuce heart
	3 tablespoons Parmesan cheese, grated
2 tablespoons white wine vinegar	about 6 canned anchovy fillets, chopped

Infuse the garlic clove in the olive oil for some hours. Lift out the garlic and use this to rub around the sides of the salad bowl. Heat 2 tablespoons of the garlic-flavoured oil in a frying pan, add the diced bread and fry steadily until golden brown and crisp croûtons. Drain on absorbent paper and put on one side.

Blend the remaining oil with the vinegar, mayonnaise and pepper. Place the lettuce into the salad bowl, toss in the dressing, add the grated cheese and anchovy fillets. Just before serving top with the crisp croûtons.

Variations: use crisp pieces of bacon instead of the anchovy fillets.

Although not strictly correct this salad is still delicious if diced tomatoes and sliced cucumber are added.

Some recipes omit the mayonnaise and use a beaten egg yolk to coat the lettuce before adding the dressing; other recipes recommend using just the garlic, olive oil and wine vinegar, as in the recipe, to make a vinaigrette dressing, which is then flavoured with a little Worcester sauce.

Avocado and Seafood Salad

Avocados had become one of the most popular ways to start a meal. Often they were combined with the ingredients in the Prawn Cocktail on page 201. I find the use of a little sherry gives an interesting taste to the dressing.

SERVES 4

FOR THE DRESSING:
2 teaspoons lemon juice
3 tablespoons mayonnaise
2 teaspoons tomato purée
1 tablespoon dry sherry
1 teaspoon Dijon mustard
salt and freshly ground black pepper

FOR THE SALAD:
2 large ripe avocados
green salad ingredients
115 to 175 g/4 to 6 oz peeled prawns
1 tablespoon chopped fennel leaves
TO GARNISH:
lemon slices, tomato slices

Mix the ingredients for the dressing together. Halve the avocados, remove the stones and skin then neatly slice the pulp and place in the dressing. Arrange the salad ingredients on a large flat dish or individual plates. Spoon the avocado mixture in the centre, top with the prawns and fennel. Garnish with lemon and tomato.

Variations: use a mixture of prawns and diced lobster or crabmeat.

Slice the avocados, fan out on the plate and pile the prawn mixture in the centre.

Avocado Ramekins: to make a hot dish substitute double cream for the mayonnaise in the dressing above. Dice the avocado flesh and mix with the dressing and the prawns or other shellfish. Put into individual ovenproof dishes, top with a sprinkling of breadcrumbs and grated cheese. Bake for 10 minutes in a preheated oven set to 190°C/375°F/Gas Mark 5/180°C with a fan oven.

Never over-cook avocados - it gives the flesh a bitter taste.

A modern touch: sherry vinegar could be used instead of sherry.

Seafood Gougère

According to *Larousse Gastronomique* a Gougère is a Burgundian pastry, which is said to have originated in Sens in France; a slightly simplified version of this became a favourite dish in Britain in the 1970's. The Gougère is made from Choux Pastry and formed into a large ring or other shape, baked and then filled with savoury or sweet ingredients.

In the early 1970's cooks were anxious to create original looking dishes and a Gougère 'fitted the bill'. In the same decade fromage frais was becoming better known as people discovered its adaptability and low calorific value.

SERVES 4

Choux Pastry as page 220
salt and freshly ground black pepper
FOR THE FILLING
50 g/2 oz butter
8 to 12 small spring onions, green
  stalks removed
225 ml/7 ½ fl oz yoghurt or
  fromage frais

1 teaspoon Dijon mustard
about 12 cooked mussels as page 275
175 g/6 oz peeled prawns
2 tablespoons dry sherry
115 g/4 oz Gruyère cheese, grated
TO GARNISH:
lemon slices
watercress

Preheat the oven to 220°C/425°F/Gas Mark 7/200°C with a fan oven. Grease an 18 to 20 cm/7 to 8 inch round ovenproof serving dish.

Make the Choux Pastry, season the mixture well. Place the pastry into a large piping bag with a 2.5 cm/1 inch pipe and pipe a neat round on the dish. If more convenient the mixture can be spooned into a ring. Bake for 15 minutes at the setting given then reduce the heat to 190°C/375°F/Gas Mark 5/180°C with a fan oven and cook for a further 20 to 25 minutes, or until firm and golden in colour.

While the Gougère is cooking prepare the filling. Heat the butter, add the onions and cook until tender then put in all the ingredients for the filling. Heat thoroughly but do not over-cook, for this toughens the fish, and do not allow the mixture to boil.

Spoon the hot filling into the centre of the hot pastry ring. Garnish and serve.

Variations: the Gougère can be filled with vegetables in a cheese or tomato sauce.
Substitute diced cooked chicken and ham for the fish.

A modern touch: freeze the cooked pastry ring but not the filling.

Beef Stroganoff

For a short time in the 1970's, when the quality of steak was excellent and soured cream was readily available, this was a favourite dinner party dish and was also an ideal dish to cook on an electric table cooker. As fillet steak became more and more expensive its popularity waned.

In order to achieve the best result you must prepare the ingredients well ahead, as the method below. Only cook the steak for a very limited period then allow it to stand a short time before reheating and serving. Do not freeze this dish.

SERVES 4 TO 6

675 to 900 g/1 ½ to 2 lb fillet steak
salt and freshly ground black pepper
115 g/4 oz butter
1 level tablespoon plain flour
150 ml/¼ pint beef stock
1 tablespoon tomato purée

1 teaspoon French mustard
115 g/4 oz small mushrooms,
   thinly sliced
1 medium onion, finely chopped
300 ml/10 fl oz soured cream

Cut the steak into neat strips, do not make these too thin, for that could result in over-cooking. Season the meat, cover and leave in the refrigerator for 2 or 3 hours.

Heat 25 g/1 oz of the butter in a small pan, add the flour and stir over a low heat until golden brown. Gradually blend in the stock, tomato purée and mustard. Bring to the boil and cook until thickened. It is a good idea to liquidize this sauce just before adding it to the steak, it gives a wonderful smoothness.

Heat another 25 g/1 oz of the butter and cook the mushrooms for a few minutes.

Heat the remaining butter in a large pan and cook the steak with the onion for 4 to 5 minutes only. Stir continually and turn the beef over after 2 minutes. The onion should still retain a certain crispness. Add the thick sauce, cooked mushrooms, soured cream and any extra seasoning required. Cover the pan, remove from the heat and allow it to stand at room temperature for about 30 minutes.

Reheat immediately before serving. Cooked rice and a crisp green salad are perfect accompaniments.

Variation: a small glass of brandy can be added to the ingredients immediately before serving. This should be ignited.

Sweet and Sour Pork

The combination of sweet and sour flavourings for meat was beginning to be appreciated. Some recipes of this period were inclined to have an ultra-thick sauce, for the public had not yet come to appreciate lighter and thinner sauces. In this recipe I have kept the sauce a fairly thin consistency. A wok was still regarded as a 'foreign' cooking utensil.

SERVES 4

226 g can pineapple rings in syrup
450 g/1 lb lean pork
1½ tablespoons white wine vinegar
1 tablespoon sunflower oil*
1 bunch spring onions
1 red pepper, deseeded
1 teaspoon ground ginger

1 teaspoon cornflour
150 ml/¼ pint chicken stock
1 to 2 tablespoons soy sauce,
    according to personal taste
1 tablespoon brown sugar
salt and freshly ground black pepper

* if the pork is very lean use slightly more

Drain the syrup from the pineapple and cut the rings into neat slices. Pour the pineapple syrup into a dish. Cut the pork into thin strips, add to the pineapple syrup with 1 tablespoon of the vinegar and marinate for at least 1 hour. Turn the meat over once or twice.

Drain the meat well, but keep the liquid in which it had been marinated.

Heat the oil in a large frying pan or wok, add the pork and cook steadily for about 10 minutes, stirring well throughout this time. Discard most of the green tops from the spring onions; cut the red pepper into narrow strips. Add the onions and pepper to the pan and continue stirring over the heat for a further 5 minutes, or until the pork is tender. The onions and pepper should retain a fairly firm texture.

Blend the ground ginger and cornflour with the stock and the pineapple and vinegar liquid. Add to the pan with the diced pineapple soy sauce, sugar, the rest of the vinegar and a little seasoning. Allow the liquid to come to the boil and thicken slightly then simmer for about 5 minutes. Taste and adjust the seasoning. This is the time when you could add a little extra vinegar to give sharpness or sugar for sweetness. Serve with cooked rice.

Variations: use this recipe for other meats or poultry such as chicken or turkey.
A modern touch: use 2 teaspoons finely diced or grated root ginger instead of the ground ginger. Add this to the pan with the onions and pepper.

Steak au Poivre

No good restaurant would omit this dish from its menu in the 1970's for it was a great favourite. The pepper coating varied from crushed black or white pepper-corns to the more interesting green ones. Some home cooks simply dusted both sides of the meat with freshly ground black pepper which tasted excellent but did not look as interesting as the crumbly texture of the peppercorns.

The steak can be served without a sauce but I think this complements the pepper taste.

SERVES 4

1 to 2 tablespoons peppercorns, or
   to taste
4 fillet or sirloin steaks
little salt, optional
85 g/3 oz butter

FOR THE SAUCE, OPTIONAL:
150 ml/¼ pint beef consommé
150 ml/5 fl oz double cream
1 to 2 teaspoons chopped chervil
   or parsley
salt and freshly ground black pepper
2 to 3 tablespoons brandy

Crush the peppercorns with a rolling pin, this is better than using a food processor or liquidizer for these are inclined to make them too fine. Press the peppercorns very firmly on to both sides of the meat. A little salt can be sprinkled on one side of the steaks, but this is not essential.

Heat the butter in a frying pan and cook the steaks quickly for about 1 minute on either side; lower the heat and cook steadily to personal taste. The total cooking time for a steak of about 2.5 cm/1 inch in thickness is:

rare: 5 to 6 minutes, **medium:** 8 minutes, **well-done:** 10 minutes.

While the steaks are cooking prepare the sauce. Pour the consommé into a saucepan, heat briskly until reduced to half then add the cream and herbs. Season to taste. Heat well then tip into the pan around the steaks. Lastly add the brandy, warm this and ignite if desired. Serve with cooked mushrooms, potatoes and other vegetables.

Variation: 1 to 2 teaspoons French mustard adds piquancy to the sauce.

Veal Escalopes

In the 1970's there was great enthusiasm for these tender crisply fried veal slices, which you might find on a menu as Weiner Schnitzel. During the passing years of the 1970's and early 1980's veal became less popular when it was realised under what appalling conditions calves were reared to produce milky white meat.

Fortunately the situation has now changed; for many years veal has been reared under humane conditions; this produces meat that is pink in colour but which has just as good a flavour as the earlier white meat.

SERVES 4

4 slices veal fillet, cut from the leg
salt and freshly ground black pepper
approximately 1 tablespoon plain flour
1 egg
little water
50 g/2 oz fine breadcrumbs

FOR FRYING:
50 g/2 oz butter
2 tablespoons sunflower oil
TO GARNISH:
4 thick lemon rings
1 egg, hard-boiled and finely chopped
2 teaspoons chopped parsley
4 canned anchovy fillets

Put each slice of veal between sheets of greaseproof paper and flatten with a rolling pin. Season the flour and lightly coat the meat. Beat the egg with a few drops of water and brush over the meat then carefully coat the meat with the crumbs. Press these firmly against the flesh with a palette knife.

Heat the butter and oil in a large frying pan, put in the veal and fry quickly on either side then reduce the heat and cook for a further 8 to 10 minutes. Veal needs to be well-cooked. Drain on absorbent paper. The traditional garnish for the veal was to put the lemon slices on the meat and top these with the egg, parsley and a curled anchovy fillet.

A modern touch: use fillets of lean pork or turkey or chicken breasts instead of veal.

Crown Roast of Lamb

In the early 1970's this presentation of meat became very popular. It gave cooks a chance to experiment with interesting stuffings and to produce an impressive joint of meat without spending too much money. This particular stuffing blends well with lamb and is a good accompaniment to pork or chicken.

SERVES 6 TO 7

2 racks (best ends) of lamb giving a
    total of 12 to 14 cutlets*
FOR THE APRICOT AND PEPPER STUFFING:
225 g/8 oz dried apricots, thinly sliced
2 tablespoons orange juice
25 g/1 oz butter or margarine
1 medium onion, chopped
1 red pepper, deseeded and diced
50 g/2 oz raisins
115 g/4 oz soft breadcrumbs

1 teaspoon chopped mint
1 tablespoon chopped parsley
1 egg
salt and freshly ground black pepper
TO GARNISH:
cutlet frills
sprigs of mint and parsley

in the 1970's there were plenty of butchers who would prepare the crown, given reasonable notice.

Protect the ends of the meat bones with foil. Put the apricots with the orange juice and leave soaking for at least 30 minutes. Heat the butter or margarine in a pan, add the onion and cook gently for 5 minutes. Put in the pepper and cook for another 5 minutes. Remove from the heat and add all the other stuffing ingredients. Weigh the stuffing and the meat to calculate the cooking time. This is based on meat plus stuffing.

Put the meat on a sheet of foil in the roasting tin, this makes certain no stuffing will be wasted. Spoon all the stuffing into the centre of the crown. Cover lightly with foil, so it will not scorch. Roast the joint as one of the timings given below. Remove the foil from the top of the stuffing 30 to 40 minutes before the end of the cooking time, so it becomes pleasantly brown on top.

To serve the meat remove the foil from the ends of the bones. Put the meat on to a large dish and press cutlet frills on to the ends of the bones. Carve the cutlets and take spoonfuls of the stuffing. Serve with mixed vegetables.

Variation: sometimes the end of the cutlets were garnished with cherries, olives or other brightly coloured ingredients.

There are two ways of roasting this joint.

Fast roasting: preheat the oven to 200°C/400°F/Gas Mark 6/190°C with a fan oven. Allow 15 minutes per 450 g/1 lb and 15 minutes over if you like 'pink' (under-done) lamb. Allow 18 to 20 minutes per 450 g/1 lb for medium to well-done lamb and 20 minutes over. The oven setting can be reduced to 190°C/375°F/Gas Mark 5/180°C with a fan oven after the first 1 hour.

Slower roasting: this is better for defrosted or chilled meat. Preheat the oven to 180°C/ 350°F/Gas Mark 4/170°C with a fan oven. It is difficult to achieve good 'pink' lamb at this setting. For medium lamb allow 30 minutes per 450 g/1 lb and 30 minutes over. For well-done lamb allow 35 minutes per 450 g/1 lb and 35 minutes over. The oven setting can be reduced to 160°C/325°F/Gas Mark 3/150°C with a fan oven after 1 ½ hours.

Crown Roast of Lamb (page 245)

Moussaka

Visitors who had holidayed in Greece always requested recipes for this dish, called Melitzanes Mousakas. It is different from the Turkish version, given under Variations. During the 1970's aubergines tended to have a bitter taste and it was necessary to score the skins, sprinkle with salt and leave for a while. The salt draws out the juices and the bitter taste. This has the added advantage that one needs less oil when frying the slices as they are less watery. Aubergines available today seem to have lost much of the bitterness, so salting is a matter of personal preference.

SERVES 4 TO 6

FOR THE MEAT MIXTURE:
2 medium aubergines
salt and freshly ground black pepper
3 tablespoons olive oil
2 medium onions, chopped
4 medium tomatoes, sliced
450 to 550 g/1 to 1¼ lb minced
    lamb or mutton
FOR THE CHEESE SAUCE:
600 ml/1 pint milk, plus any extra
    required, see method

1 or 2 celery sticks, chopped
1 small onion, sliced
50 g/2 oz butter
50 g/2 oz plain flour
115 g/4 oz Gruyère or Cheddar
    cheese, grated
2 eggs
1 to 2 teaspoons made mustard
FOR THE TOPPING
2 tablespoons oil or melted butter
50 g/2 oz soft breadcrumbs

Slice the aubergines, the skin can be scored and sprinkled with salt as described above. If you do this leave for 30 minutes then drain well and rinse in cold water, dry, slice and season lightly. Heat half the oil in a pan add the aubergine and cook steadily until golden on both sides. Remove from the pan. Heat the remainder of the oil, add the onions and cook for 5 minutes. Put in the tomatoes and meat; season and cook for a further 5 minutes, stir well during this time.

For the sauce pour the milk into a saucepan, add the celery and onion. Bring the milk just to boiling point, remove from the heat and allow to cool, then strain and measure the milk again, make up to 600 ml/1 pint if necessary. Heat the butter, stir in the flour then gradually add the milk. Bring to the boil and stir briskly or whisk until thickened. Remove from the heat, stir in the cheese and then beat in the eggs. Add salt, pepper and mustard to taste.

Preheat the oven to 160°C/325°F/Gas Mark 3/150°C with a fan oven.

Arrange layers of aubergine, meat mixture and sauce in a large casserole, ending with a layer of sauce. Mix the oil or butter with the crumbs and spoon over the sauce. Cover the casserole and bake for 1 hour then remove the lid and cook for a further 15 to 20 minutes, or until the top is brown. Serve with a salad or green vegetables and cooked rice or pasta.

Variations: the proportion of sauce is high, the amount can be reduced if you like a firm consistency. The baking time will be the same.

Patlican Musakasi: the Turkish Moussaka is a very good way to make use of cooked lamb, mutton or beef. Mince 350 to 450 g/12 oz to 1 lb cooked meat. Peel and thinly slice 4 medium aubergines, about 6 medium potatoes and 4 medium onions. Slice 450 to 675 g/1 to 1½ lb unskinned tomatoes.

Preheat the oven as given in the recipe above.

Each kind of vegetable is cooked separately then removed from the frying pan. Fry the aubergine slices in 1½ tablespoons of oil. The tomatoes are not pre-cooked.

Arrange a layer of tomatoes in a casserole then add layers of well-seasoned vegetables and meat, end with a good layer of tomatoes. Bake for 1 hour. This Moussaka is so firm in texture that it can be cut into wedges rather like a cake. Serve with salad.

A modern touch: both versions of Moussaka freeze well.

Chilli con Carne

This dish did not become widely served until the early 1970's and I think I am right in saying it was an introduction to the hot taste of chilli to most people in Britain. Small chilli peppers were not sold in many supermarkets and greengrocers at the time so the flavouring was given by chilli powder.

SERVES 4

2 tablespoons sunflower oil
1 teaspoon ground cumin
1 tablespoon chilli powder, or to taste
2 medium onions, chopped
1 to 2 garlic cloves, crushed
450 g/1 lb chuck steak, minced
450 ml/³/₄ pint beef stock

1 green pepper, deseeded and
   diced, optional
3 medium tomatoes, skinned
   and chopped
1 teaspoon chopped oregano
salt and freshly ground black pepper
1 x 400 g can red kidney beans

Heat the oil in a saucepan, add the ground cumin and chilli powder and heat very gently for a minute. This brings out the flavour of the spices. Stir in the onions and cook steadily for 5 minutes then add the garlic and meat. Continue stirring for a further 5 minutes or until the meat is golden. Add the stock with the rest of the ingredients, except the canned beans. Cover the pan and simmer steadily for 45 minutes. Stir once or twice during this period and check there is sufficient liquid.

Drain the beans, add to the mixture and continue cooking for a further 10 minutes. Serve with rice or noodles.

The dish is very good as a topping for a Pizza (page 290) or an accompaniment to a Tortilla (page 236). Soured cream is an excellent topping for the dish.

Variation: use 175 to 225 g/6 to 8 oz dried red kidney beans, soak overnight then drain and place in a saucepan with fresh water to cover. It is essential the water boils for 10 minutes to destroy any harmful enzymes in the beans. After this add a little seasoning, cover the pan and simmer gently for about 1 hour. If worried about using the chilli powder it is simple to omit this and use a chilli sauce instead. This can be added gradually with the stock so you gauge the flavour without any trouble.

A modern touch: use one or more chilli peppers instead of the chilli powder.

Chicken Korma

Towards the very end of the 1970's this spiced chicken dish became popular and it has become more and more popular as the years pass. This is not surprising, for it has a very pleasing spiced flavour but is not over-hot.

SERVES 4

FOR THE KORMA PASTE:

2 teaspoons poppy seeds
150 ml/¼ pint water
2 onions, finely chopped
1 garlic clove, crushed
2 teaspoons finely grated root ginger
1 teaspoon turmeric
1 red or green chilli, finely chopped*
2 tablespoons grated fresh coconut or
   1 tablespoon desiccated coconut
½ teaspoon ground cinnamon
pinch grated or ground nutmeg
3 cloves or pinch ground cloves
1 tablespoon chopped coriander

FOR THE CHICKEN DISH:

50 g/2 oz ghee**
1 onion, finely chopped
1.8 kg/4 lb chicken, jointed
150 ml/5 fl oz yoghurt
300 ml/½ pint water
1 tablespoon lemon juice
2 tablespoons coriander leaves
salt and freshly ground black pepper

* the seeds can be removed before chopping the pod.

** put the butter with water to cover into a saucepan. Heat slowly until the butter melts. Leave until cold then remove the butter from the liquid and weigh out amount required.

Put the poppy seeds into a basin. Boil the water, pour over the seeds and leave for about 20 minutes, strain and discard the water. Gradually put the ingredients for the paste into a mortar and grind with a pestle, or liquidize into a food processor.

Heat the butter or ghee in a large pan, add the korma paste and gently cook for 3 minutes, this gives a more definite flavour to the spices. Add the onion and stir over the heat for 5 minutes. Put in the chicken with the yoghurt and water. Stir well, so the paste and onion blend with the liquid. Cover the pan and simmer for 1 to 1¼ hours, or until the chicken is tender and the sauce thick. Check once or twice to make sure there is enough liquid. Just before serving stir in the lemon juice, coriander leaves and seasoning. Serve with cooked rice and Chapatis (page 253).
Variation: smaller portions of the chicken can be served hot or cold with salad as the first course of a meal.

Curries

I have headed this title in the plural for there are so many excellent and popular curries from various areas of the world that it is difficult to select just one. I have therefore chosen a great favourite of mine. Towards the end of the war my husband was appointed a relieving Commanding Officer to various R.A.F. staging posts in West Africa; this is the curry he enjoyed there. It was known as Chicken Chop and has a very hot taste.

The British have been associated with India, a home of splendid curries, since Queen Elizabeth created the charter for the English East India Company in 1600 and throughout the centuries Britishers living in that country enjoyed good curries made by native cooks. In the 1960's and onwards Indian restaurants opened in Britain; sadly the food in many of these was not good so we had to wait until the 1980's to learn from Madhur Jaffrey on television and from the books of other experts about authentic Indian food.

SERVES 4 TO 6

2 tablespoons groundnut or
   sunflower oil
1.8 kg/4 lb chicken, jointed
2 onions, chopped
1 large red chilli pepper, thinly sliced*
2 tablespoons grated root ginger
¼ teaspoon cayenne pepper
½ teaspoon turmeric
300 ml/½ pint chicken stock

300 ml/½ pint coconut milk, see below
5 cm/2 inch piece of cinnamon stick
1 teaspoon finely grated lemon zest
2 tablespoons lemon juice, or to taste
salt and freshly ground black pepper
115 g/4 oz fresh dates, weight when
   stoned

core and deseed before slicing for a less hot taste

Heat the oil, add the chicken and onions, stir over a low heat until both ingredients are a pale golden colour. Lift the chicken from the pan. Stir the chilli, ginger, cayenne and turmeric into the onions and heat gently for 1 minute. Pour in the stock and milk. Bring to the boil then return the chicken to the pan with the rest of the ingredients.

Cover tightly and then simmer very gently for 1½ to 2 hours or until the chicken is very tender. Remove the cinnamon stick. Serve with cooked rice, a sweet chutney and extra dates.

Note: to achieve a firmer textured chicken reduce the cooking time to 1¼ to 1½ hours.

To make coconut milk

In the 1970's this was not readily available in cans and the recommended method of obtaining the milk was as follows:

a) Halve a fresh coconut, remove the white flesh and grate it. Pour 300 ml/½ pint boiling water over the flesh, leave until cold. Strain through gauze then squeeze the gauze firmly to extract as much juice as possible.

b) Use 85 g/3 oz desiccated coconut and follow method a).

Chapatis

Chapatis are the thin unleavened breads that form an excellent accompaniment to various curried dishes. The salt is omitted in many Indian recipes but I find it makes the crisp bread more pleasant.

MAKES 9 TO 12

225 g/8 oz plain wholemeal flour
pinch salt
approximately 150 ml/¼ pint water

Sift the flour and salt into a bowl. Gradually mix in the water to give a pliable dough. Knead until smooth. Return to the bowl, cover with a cloth and leave for at least 45 minutes. Knead again and divide into small balls. Roll out each ball until very thin and an oval shape.

Preheat a griddle or a heavy frying pan. Add some of the Chapatis and cook for a few seconds (they brown quickly). Turn over and cook for the same time on the second side. Turn again and cook until firm. Lift out and continue to cook the rest of the Chapatis. Serve freshly made.

Variation: Granary flour makes interesting Chapatis.

Nut Roast

Many people were becoming vegetarian at this time, the younger generation particularly were inclined to become 'non-meat eaters', but in the 1970's there was not a range of interesting vegetarian dishes and there was far less of a selection of foods that fitted into their mode of life. Nut Roast recipes however became very plentiful.

SERVES 4

2 tablespoons sunflower oil

2 medium onions, chopped

1 or 2 garlic cloves, crushed

2 medium tomatoes, skinned
    and chopped

350 g/12 oz mixed nuts or use
    one type of nut such as cashews,
    coarsely chopped

2 tablespoons chopped parsley

1 teaspoon chopped sage or
    ½ teaspoon dried sage

50 g/2 oz soft breadcrumbs,
    preferably wholemeal

2 eggs

salt and freshly ground black pepper

Preheat the oven to 180°C/350°F/Gas Mark 4/170°C with a fan oven. Grease a 675 g/1½ lb loaf tin or baking dish.

Heat the oil and fry the onions for a few minutes, add the garlic and tomatoes and cook gently until a soft pulp. Remove from the heat and stir in all the remaining ingredients.

Spoon into the prepared tin or dish. Cover with greased foil and bake for 45 minutes or until firm. Turn out and serve with Mushroom Sauce (page 63) and a selection of vegetables.

Tofu with Water Chestnuts

We had been familiar with the name 'bean curd' for some time as this is an essential ingredient in many Oriental dishes, so when Tofu, a commercially prepared bean curd, came on the market the public were happy to try it. Tofu is an excellent source of vegetable protein, and as it can replace meat or fish in many recipes, it enables vegetarians to extend their range of dishes. It is somewhat lacking in natural flavour and therefore it is at its best when mixed with fairly highly flavoured ingredients.

SERVES 4

350 g/12 oz tofu

FOR THE MARINADE:

1 tablespoon groundnut or
   sunflower oil

2 teaspoons sesame oil

2 tablespoons rice vinegar

1 tablespoon soy sauce

1 tablespoon brown sugar

1 tablespoon tomato ketchup

1 teaspoon grated root ginger

pinch chilli powder or cayenne pepper

salt and freshly ground white pepper

FOR THE SAUCE:

1 tablespoon groundnut or
   sunflower oil

small bunch spring onions, trimmed

1 small can water chestnuts

1 tablespoon rice wine or dry sherry

1 tablespoon chopped coriander

5 tablespoons vegetable stock or water

Cut the tofu into neat dice. Put into the marinade and leave for 1 hour. Turn over several times so the white bean curd becomes flavoured and coloured.

Heat the oil for the sauce, add the onions and fry steadily for a few minutes, until they become golden. Meanwhile drain the water chestnuts, discard the liquid and slice the chestnuts. Put these into the pan with the onions and heat for 3 minutes. Tip in the tofu plus the marinade, add the rice wine or sherry, coriander and stock or water. Bring to the boil then simmer steadily for 10 minutes until the ingredients are well heated and the sauce has thickened. Taste and adjust the seasoning. Serve with cooked rice. Bean sprouts are another good accompaniment.

Variation: Quorn is another vegetarian product that came on the market after tofu. It can be used in the recipe above. Quorn is better if it stands for some time in the hot sauce so prepare the dish ahead, heat the ingredients as stated in the recipe. Allow the mixture to stand for several hours then reheat again before serving.

Pecan Pie

I am sure many people had read recipes for American Pecan Pie during the 1960's but found difficulty in making the pie until the 1970's, when pecan nuts became much more plentiful. In the past I had often suggested substituting walnuts for pecans, although I always pointed out that the flavour was very different. Pecan Pie has seemed to fade from popularity, giving rise to other sweet desserts, but it is always worth making.

SERVES 4 TO 6

Shortcrust Pastry made with
    175 g/6 oz flour, etc. as page 82
FOR THE FILLING;
175 g/6 oz pecan nuts,
    coarsely chopped
50 g/2 oz butter

3 medium eggs
115 g/4 oz soft brown sugar
$^{1}/_{4}$ to $^{1}/_{2}$ teaspoon vanilla extract
    or essence
5 level tablespoons golden syrup

Preheat the oven to 200°C/400°F/Gas Mark 6/190°C with a fan oven. Roll out the pastry and line a 20 to 23 cm/8 to 9 inch shallow flan tin or dish. Bake 'blind' (page 188) for 7 minutes only. The pastry will not be coloured at the end of that time. Lower the oven setting to 160°C/325°F/Gas Mark 3/150°C with a fan oven.

Mix all the ingredients for the filling together. Spoon into the lightly cooked pastry case. Bake for 30 minutes or until both the pastry and filling are firm. Serve warm or cold with crème fraîche, whipped cream or ice cream.

Bread and Butter Pudding

If someone had told me years ago that Bread and Butter Pudding would be featured on the menu of some of the most sophisticated restaurants I would have been amazed. I have always enjoyed the pudding but regarded it as plain family fare. Recipes vary enormously but this is my version.

SERVES 4

BASIC RECIPE:
2 large slices of white bread
40 g/1½ oz butter
50 to 115 g/2 to 4 oz sultanas
2 large eggs
2 egg yolks
40 to 50 g/1½ to 2 oz caster or
    light brown sugar

600 ml/1 pint full-cream milk
EXTRAS:
8 to 10 ratafias
85 g/3 oz tenderized dried apricots,
    cut into narrow strips

Preheat the oven to 150°C/300°F/Gas Mark 2/140°C with a fan oven. The crusts may be removed or left on the bread. I think they give a change of texture and colour to the pudding and leave them on.

Spread the bread with the butter and cut into small squares or triangles. Arrange neatly in a 1.2 litre/2 pint pie dish. Add the sultanas.

Beat the eggs and egg yolks with most of the sugar. Warm the milk and blend with the beaten eggs. If using ratafias and apricots add these to the bread and butter. Strain the custard into the dish and leave for 30 minutes before cooking; sprinkle with the last of the sugar. Bake for 1¼ hours or until just firm. Serve hot. Ice cream makes a good accompaniment.

Variations: use a small amount of single or double cream instead of the same amount of milk.

Flavour the custard with the finely grated zest of 1 or 2 oranges.

Top the pudding with grated or ground nutmeg as well as the sugar.

Osborne Pudding: spread marmalade over the bread and butter and flavour the eggs and milk with grated orange zest and 2 tablespoons brandy or rum.

Caramellised Oranges

Some cooks have always been nervous of making a caramel. This is not the easiest technique, for it means allowing the sugar mixture to reach a high temperature, which can so easily turn into a 'burnt offering'. However the fashion for this simple, but elegant, dish tempted the nervous to embark on making caramel.

SERVES 4

8 medium oranges
300 ml/½ pint water
85 g/3 oz caster sugar

TO DECORATE:
8 maraschino or glacé cherries
8 cocktail sticks

Using a very sharp small knife cut away the peel and bitter pith from all the oranges, do this over a basin so as to collect any juice. Leave the oranges whole at this stage.

Take the removed peel from 2 oranges and carefully cut away the pith, leaving just the golden zest, cut this into matchstick pieces. Put these into a saucepan with the water and any orange juice from the basin. If time permits allow the peel to soak for 30 minutes then cover the pan and simmer gently for 15 minutes or until the peel is tender. Save both peel and liquid.

Spoon out 3 tablespoons of the orange liquid into a saucepan, add the sugar and stir until this has dissolved. Boil steadily, without stirring until you have a pale golden caramel. Do not allow it to become too dark and bitter for this particular dish, see below. Add the peel and the rest of the liquid and boil for 2 or 3 minutes or until slightly syrupy then cool.

Cut the oranges into horizontal slices, take out any pips. Form into the whole orange shape again. Put the cherries on to the ends of the cocktail sticks and press into the tops of the oranges. Lift into a serving dish. Pour the caramel liquid and peel over the fruit. Chill and serve within a short time of preparation.

A modern touch: leave the oranges in slices and pour over the peel and sauce.

Note: it is a good idea to have a large **metal** container of cold water or water and ice cubes ready. When the caramel reaches the right stage plunge the saucepan into the container. This stops over-cooking. Never use a plastic container or plastic sink. Extra cold water can be added to the sauce too but this can alter the consistency.

Passion Cake

I first came across this cake when I was at an airport, it was being sold in the restaurant. I was not particularly hungry but purchased a slice to find out the ingredients. I subsequently experimented and this is my version of the celebrated Carrot, or Passion Cake. It freezes exceptionally well so can be made ahead.

SERVES 8

175 g/6 oz carrots, preferably young, weight when peeled

85 g/3 oz walnuts or pecan nuts

175 g/6 oz butter

175 g/6 oz caster sugar

3 large eggs

175 g/6 oz wholemeal self-raising flour or plain flour sifted with 1½ teaspoons baking powder

½ to 1 teaspoon mixed spice, optional

50 g/2 oz ground almonds

1 tablespoon milk

TO DECORATE:

300 to 350 g/10 to 12 oz Quark (German soft slightly acid cheese)

50 g/2 oz icing sugar, sifted

about 12 halved walnuts or pecan nuts

Preheat the oven to 180°C/350°F/Gas Mark 4/170°C with a fan oven. Grease and flour or line a 20 cm/8 inch cake tin. Finely grate the carrots, do not put them in water. Coarsely chop the nuts; this is important so they give real texture to the cake.

Cream the butter and sugar until soft and light; whisk the eggs and gradually beat into the creamed mixture. Sift the flour, or flour and baking powder, with the spice and ground almonds. Fold into the creamed ingredients together with the nuts, milk and grated carrots. Spoon into the cake tin. Bake for 1 hour or until firm to the touch. Cool in the tin for 5 minutes then turn out on to a wire cooling tray.

Blend the Quark with the icing sugar. Split the cold cake horizontally, fill with a generous layer of Quark. Top the cake with the remainder of the Quark and swirl this into a neat design. Add the nuts.

Variations: use white flour and omit the milk.

Use cream cheese with a little lemon juice instead of Quark.

Hazelnut Roulade

Savoury and sweet roulades have proved elegant ways of serving fairly simple ingredients. The following is a delicious dessert.

In classic recipes no baking powder is used, for the whisking of the eggs and sugar should aerate the mixture. If you have never made a sponge you may feel happier to include a small amount of baking powder.

SERVES 6

FOR THE ROULADE:
3 large eggs
115 g/4 oz caster sugar
25 g/1 oz plain flour
1/2 teaspoon baking powder, optional
65 g/2 1/2 oz hazelnuts, finely chopped
FOR THE COATING AND DECORATION:
40 g/1 1/2 oz caster sugar

300 ml/10 fl oz double cream
225 to 350 g/8 to 12 oz raspberries
few hazelnuts
FOR THE RASPBERRY COULIS:
150 ml/1/4 pint water
25 g/1 oz sugar
225 g/8 oz raspberries
2 tablespoons redcurrant jelly

Preheat the oven to 190°C/375°F/Gas Mark 5/180°C with a fan oven. Line a Swiss roll tin, measuring approximately 20 x 30 cm/8 x 12 inches with greaseproof paper or baking parchment.

Put the eggs and sugar into a bowl and whisk until thick and creamy, you should see the trail of the whisk. Sift the flour and baking powder, add to the nuts and very gently fold this mixture into the whisked eggs. Pour into the tin and bake for 12 minutes, or until firm to a gentle touch.

Use about a third of the sugar to sprinkle over a sheet of greaseproof paper or baking parchment. Turn the sponge on to this and remove the cooking paper or parchment. Place a fresh sheet of greaseproof or parchment on top of the sponge and roll firmly, then cool. Unroll the roulade to give a flat sponge once more.

Whip the cream, spread about three-quarters over the sponge; mash most of the raspberries with the remaining 25 g/1 oz sugar and spread over the cream. Roll the roulade again. Decorate the top of the roulade with cream, raspberries and hazelnuts.

Heat the water and sugar for the coulis, add the raspberries, cook gently for a few minutes. Stir in the jelly and heat until this dissolves. Sieve and serve cold with the roulade.

1980 to 1989

pasta, pasta, pasta

Millions faced famine in East Africa due to two years of drought and local wars. Crops failed and the world was asked to help.

In 1981 both American President Reagan and Pope John-Paul were shot. Fortunately both men recovered.

In April 1982 Argentinian forces invaded the Falkland Islands. They disregarded the appeal to withdraw by the United Nations. Britain sent forces to the Falklands. On June 14th there was an end to the hostilities.

There was sadness in 1982 when Princess Grace of Monaco (previously Grace Kelly the famous film actress), died in a car accident.

In 1986 the French and British leaders confirmed they had agreed to construct the Channel Tunnel in the future.

Space travel had begun to be accepted as a common event and to be safe but in January 1986 an American space ship exploded on lift-off.

In 1989 the Berlin Wall came down, so East and Wet Germany were united.

The most exciting royal occasion was in July 1981 when Lady Diana Spencer and Charles, Prince of Wales, were married. Enormous crowds lined the route to St. Paul's Cathedral to see the new Princess of Wales. This event was followed by a second royal wedding later in the decade. Prince Andrew, Duke of York, married Miss Sarah Ferguson.

The Princess gave birth of Prince William in 1982 and to Prince Henry in 1984.

Life in Britain from 1980 to 1989

By 1980 the number of unemployed in Britain had reached 3 million. Obviously these families faced financial difficulties but, thankfully, their plight was not that of those before the introduction of the Welfare State.

In November 1983 Queen Elizabeth awarded the Order of Merit to Mother Theresa of Calcutta, often known as 'The Angel of Mercy'.

On December 3rd 1988 Mrs. Edwina Currie, the Minister of Food, stated that a proportion of British eggs contained salmonella. The result of this was that the public bought less eggs and poultry farmers suffered. Mrs. Currie resigned from office later that month. Warnings were given to the public about eating eggs.

The Kitchens

By this decade the kitchen had become more and more elegant and well-fitted. The Aga cooker had always been held in esteem, but now many more models were being sold. Owners no longer needed to stoke the cooker with solid fuel.

Cooks were becoming confident about stir-frying. Due to seeing woks used on television during various cookery programmes, they had become desirable utensils. Microwaves had more sophisticated features and sales were rising rapidly.

The Foods of Britain

This was the era when grave warnings started about the British diet. It was stated that we were healthier during the years of rationing than at the present time. It sounded almost unbelievable when one considered the huge range of foods available in the 1980's but the comments were made repeatedly by various experts.

We were informed that there was too much fat in the diet of the average person and it should be reduced. We were urged to cut down on animal fats in particular. A great many articles dealt with the dangers of people having high cholesterol, which could contribute to heart trouble.

The sale of chickens and turkeys increased; these were recommended for being low in fat content. I have included turkey in the dishes of this decade for it became an 'all-the-year' round bird, rather than just a Christmas dish. Portions were on sale as well as whole birds. Cranberry Sauce far outstripped Bread Sauce as the accompaniment.

Low fat spreads and semi-skimmed and skimmed milk were sold. Over the years there was a reduction in the fat content of meat, due to different methods of breeding and rearing animals.

Less well-known fish appeared. Canned tuna had been a favourite for many years but fresh tuna was virtually unknown; now small supplies became available. Shark steaks were offered in some restaurants and fishmongers.

Dishes from the East were shown on television; Thai restaurants opened. The dishes in Indian and Chinese restaurants improved a great deal as the public learned more about authentic dishes from these countries.

Fruits and Vegetables

Strawberries were imported from various countries, so became available throughout the year. Nectarines were becoming more common than peaches.

Fresh herbs were sold in packs and pots by supermarkets - basil, coriander and flat-leaved parsley became the herbs of the day. There was a wide range of lettuces available. Mangetout peas were an everyday food.

Using shell eggs

After Mrs. Currie's announcement, attempts were made to clarify the egg situation. The Government were anxious there should be no undue panic but that the public should realise there could be a risk of serious illness if they ate a badly infected egg and so should take precautions. Cookery writers gave advice that fitted in with the Government's guidelines.

It was stressed that eggs should be used as fresh as possible, so there was less danger of salmonella developing. People should check the date stamp where given. It was wise to keep the eggs in the refrigerator. It was inadvisable to use raw eggs, unless one was absolutely certain of their source. This led to questions about classic mayonnaise, cold soufflées and mousses, etc. You will find a recipe for Hard-boiled Egg Mayonnaise on page 278.

After a time people were less inclined to worry, but most cookery writers still give a warning, similar to that printed below, if they included a raw egg in a recipe.

Warnings about using uncooked eggs

It is inadvisable to give dishes containing uncooked eggs to the most vulnerable, i.e. babies and young children, pregnant women, people who are unwell and the elderly.

Cooking eggs

It is advisable that boiled, fried, poached, scrambled eggs and omelettes are firmly set.

Convenience Foods

Within about two weeks of Mrs. Currie's remarks dried egg was on sale; some older people were delighted by the return of a much-liked food. Manufacturers of processed foods now printed times for heating or cooking in the microwave on the packs.

The variety of frozen foods for microwave and conventional cooking increased enormously. There were more ready-made sauces. These were in keeping with the flavours of the moment, such as 'Sweet and Sour'.

A diversity of chilled foods were sold.

Sun-dried tomatoes were the most 'fashionable' flavouring and, as the years passed, they were used more and more. The fondness for Italian dishes encouraged people to buy porcini (dried mushrooms), as well as newer varieties of mushrooms.

The end of the 1980's saw a vast increase in the selection and use of oils and an awareness of the variety of vinegars available. Cumin was a spice used in recipes of the era. Fresh as well as dried pasta was sold.

Favourite Drinks

Wines from a wide range of countries were available and the interest in learning more about wine increased.

Cartons and bottles of various soft drinks were popular.

There was a greater use of mineral waters, both still and sparkling. People ordered mineral water as well as wine when dining in restaurants. Sometimes this was because the establishment was not inclined to provide chilled tap water or diners were nervous about drinking it. There had been various complaints about the quality of our water during this decade.

Meals of 1980 to 1989

This was a decade of great change. On the one hand we were excited about the new foods and fascinating new dishes being shown on television and written about in magazines and papers. On the other hand one had to be aware that a number of people had to cater very economically.

In 1980 I had written a book on Entertaining. The first question one B.B.C. interviewer asked me was 'What is in your book for the unemployed and those made redundant?' This gave me much food for thought.

The diversity of eating habits and range of foods make it difficult to give special menus.

The dishes that follow sum up the wide choice in this decade.

Classic dishes, such as Moules Marinière, Beef Wellington (Boeuf en Crôute) and Crème Brûlée, which had been known for some time, were suddenly the dishes of the age.

Frozen and fresh pizzas were available, with a great variety of toppings, but a number of people started to make them at home.

We were advised to eat more fish and the public responded. There are more fish dishes in this section than in the others.

Vegetarians increased in number and even many meat-eaters decided they liked the new vegetable dishes.

Cookery Influences

Madhur Jaffrey demonstrated dishes from India and later from the Far East on television with beautifully produced books accompanying the series. This graceful and expert lady was much admired as she introduced viewers to real Indian dishes they could make in their own homes. Ken Hom was just as expert at showing the delights of true Chinese food on television.

Keith Floyd combined cookery with travel in this and the next decade and he brought a new style of relaxed light-hearted instruction to the television screen.

Cookery books, magazine and newspaper articles all gave a wide selection of excellent recipes. Many of these were written by members of the Guild of Food Writers.

1980 to 1989

The Recipes

Smoked Fish

Smoked salmon had been enjoyed throughout this century but in the early 1980's other smoked fish became extremely popular as an hors d'oeuvre. Smoked eel, trout and mackerel were served with horseradish cream or horseradish sauce.

All these fish, but particularly smoked eel, are excellent with scrambled eggs, see below. Smoked cod's roe is the main ingredient for Taramasalata.

Scrambled Eggs

SERVES 4

25 g/1 oz butter
1 tablespoon milk
4 eggs, beaten

salt and freshly ground black pepper
1 tablespoon chopped parsley, optional

Heat the butter and milk in a pan, add the eggs with a little seasoning. Cook slowly, stirring occasionally. Add the parsley towards the end of the cooking time. Serve with the smoked fish.

Taramasalata

SERVES 4 TO 6

350 g/12 oz smoked cod's roe,
    weight when skinned
1 garlic clove, crushed

85 g/3 oz butter, softened
1 tablespoon lemon juice or to taste
freshly ground black pepper

Mix all the ingredients together and beat until a smooth light mixture. The ingredients can be blended together in a food processor. Do **not** over-process for this gives a sticky consistency. Garnish with a little salad and serve with hot toast and butter. **Variations:** the recipe gives a strongly flavoured pâté. For a less strong flavour moisten 25 to 50 g/1 to 2 oz very fine soft breadcrumbs with a little cream or milk and blend with the ingredients above.
Another variation is to blend the smoked cod's roe with the garlic, lemon juice and parsley as above then gradually beat in enough extra virgin olive oil to make a soft consistency. Add pepper to taste.
A modern touch: serve Taramasalata with pitta bread.

Grilled Goat's Cheese Salad

The selection of cheeses available today in Britain is incredibly impressive. We import a number from many countries but our own dairy farmers are producing most interesting new varieties, as well as old favourites. Goat's cheese makes a splendid and simple start to a meal. The small round individual cheeses look the most appetising. Some of these are quite thick, so one cheese is sufficiently large to give two portions.

SERVES 4

FOR THE DRESSING:
1 tablespoon finely diced sun-dried
   tomatoes*
1 garlic clove, crushed
4 tablespoons extra virgin olive oil
2 tablespoons sherry vinegar
few drops balsamic vinegar, optional
1 teaspoon Dijon mustard
salt and freshly ground black pepper

4 small or 2 larger goat's cheeses,
   halved as suggested above
mixture of salad leaves

* if in olive oil drain and chop. If in a packet,
soak as directed then chop.

Mix the ingredients for the dressing together. Place the goat's cheeses on a piece of foil on the rack of the grill pan. Moisten each portion with a teaspoon of the dressing and leave until just before the meal.

Arrange the salad leaves on individual plates. Preheat the grill and heat the cheese until they show signs of melting. Top the salad with the dressing and place the hot cheeses in the centre of the salad. Serve at once with warm bread.

Variations: flavour the salad with 1 to 2 teaspoons crushed sesame or cumin seeds instead of garlic. Use slices of goat's cheese instead of the individual portions. Serve the hot goat's cheese with the salad and a small helping of hot Roasted Vegetables.

Roasted Vegetables: deseed a red, green and yellow pepper, cut into thick slices; thinly slice a medium aubergine and 1 or 2 courgettes. Peel several small onions or shallots and divide the bulbs into quarters. Arrange the vegetables in a flat layer in a dish. Season and drizzle over enough olive oil to moisten them. Preheat the oven to 160°C/325°F/Gas Mark 3°/150°C with a fan oven. Cover the dish with foil and bake for an hour or until all the vegetables are very soft.

271

Gulai Ikan

This Indonesian fish dish is made with fresh tuna, although other fish could be substituted, see under Variations. Nutritious canned tuna has been popular for many years but, until the late 1980's, fresh tuna had been far less well known, for it was not easy to obtain. Now there were good supplies available. The fish is very satisfying so fairly small amounts are required. Tamarind purée, which has a very acid taste, is a feature of some Indonesian dishes. It is obtainable from shops specialising in foods from the Far East.

SERVES 4

2 medium onions, chopped
2 garlic cloves, crushed
300 ml/½ pint canned coconut milk
2 teaspoons finely grated root ginger
½ teaspoon turmeric
pinch chilli powder
2 teaspoons chopped lemon grass or
    finely grated lemon zest

6 tablespoons tamarind or tomato
    purée, or to taste, see Variations
450 to 550 g/1 to 1¼ lb fresh tuna,
    cut into 4 portions
salt and freshly ground black pepper

Put the onions, garlic, half the coconut milk, ginger, spices and lemon grass or zest into a deep frying pan or wok. Cover tightly with a lid or with foil and simmer gently for 10 minutes or until the onions are tender. Add the tamarind or tomato purée and the fish with a little seasoning, simmer gently for 15 minutes, or until the fish is cooked. Do not allow the ingredients to boil for the acid tamarind or tomato would cause the milk to curdle.

When the fish is cooked pour in the rest of the coconut milk and add extra seasoning, if required. Heat gently for a minute. Serve with cooked rice.

Variations: salmon or salmon trout or mackerel make good alternatives to the tuna and so do portions of shark.

Instead of the tamarind purée make a thick purée of fresh tomatoes, which should be skinned and deseeded first. This purée can be given a sharper taste by adding a little lime or lemon juice. Tomato purée from a tube or can could be used.

Grilled Goat's Cheese Salad (page 271)

Sardines Provençal

Many people, used only to the canned variety, are surprised when they see the size of fresh sardines. These fresh fish, which can be really quite large, are excellent grilled or fried and the following recipe makes an interesting light main dish.

SERVES 4

FOR THE BASE:
1 tablespoon sunflower oil
1 onion, chopped
1 garlic clove, crushed
350 g/12 oz tomatoes, skinned,
    deseeded and chopped
2 tablespoons chopped parsley
salt and freshly ground black pepper
few black olives

TO COOK THE SARDINES:
3 teaspoons sunflower oil
2 teaspoons lemon juice
1 tablespoon chopped parsley
1 teaspoon chopped tarragon
8 sardines

Heat the oil in a pan, add the onion and cook for 5 minutes, then put in the garlic and tomatoes with the parsley and cook steadily for 10 minutes. Season well and add the olives.

Meanwhile mix 2 teaspoons of the oil for cooking the sardines with the lemon juice and herbs. Season to taste. Split and bone the sardines and fill with the herb mixture.

Preheat the grill, place the sardines over foil on the grid of the grill pan. Brush with the last of the oil and cook for 5 to 6 minutes. Serve the sardines over the tomato mixture.

Moules Marinière

By the 1980's this had become one of the favourite shellfish dishes; that fact is not surprising for the mussels and the cooking liquid are both full of flavour. The dish can be served as an hors d'oeuvre or a light main course. Mussels had been difficult to obtain in the past but from 1980 onwards fishmongers and supermarkets had plentiful supplies. Mussels are alive when you buy them and the method of preparation is given below.

SERVES 4 TO 6

2 litres/3½ pints mussels
150 ml/¼ pint dry white wine
150 ml/¼ pint water
1 medium onion, finely chopped
small bunch parsley

1 tablespoon lemon juice, optional
salt and freshly ground white pepper
150 ml/5 fl oz single cream
1 tablespoon finely chopped parsley

Wash the mussels in plenty of cold water, remove the small growth (the beard) that adheres to some shells. Discard any mussels that do not close when the shells are sharply tapped. Put the fish into a large saucepan with the wine, water, onion and parsley. Heat steadily for a few minutes until the shells open. Do not continue cooking. Strain the liquid and reserve this. Check the mussels, if any shells are still closed discard those fish.

For this dish the mussels can be served on both shells or one shell removed. Pour the cooking liquid into a pan, add the lemon juice, seasoning, cream and parsley. Return the mussels to the pan and heat for just a very few minutes then serve with plenty of sliced hot French bread.

Variation: the cream can be omitted and the mussels served in the clear liquid only.

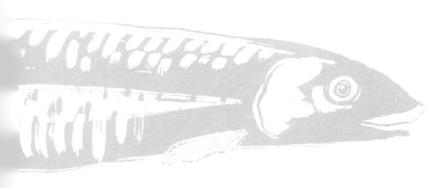

Chinese Stir-fry Fish

Stir-frying is a method of cooking that has become firmly established in this country. While a wok is not essential it does make the cooking process very simple and efficient. This particular dish has a sweet and sour taste but this can be changed, see under Variations.

SERVES 4 TO 6

2 teaspoons cornflour
salt and freshly ground white pepper
450 to 675 g/1 to 1 ½ lb monk fish or
    salmon, cut into neat strips
2 tablespoons sunflower or
    groundnut oil
8 spring onions, trimmed
1 red pepper, deseeded and cut into
    2.5 cm/1 inch strips
50 g/2 oz canned bamboo shoots, diced
50 g/2 oz water chestnuts, diced

FOR THE SAUCE:
1 ½ teaspoons cornflour
150 ml/ ¼ pint fish stock as page 16
2 tablespoons light soy sauce
1 tablespoon rice wine or white wine
1 tablespoon rice vinegar
1 tablespoon tomato ketchup
1 tablespoon caster sugar
1 or 2 teaspoons grated root ginger,
    optional

Mix the cornflour with a little seasoning. Place the fish on a flat board or platter and dust with the cornflour. Turn the fish around so all sides are lightly coated. Heat the oil in the wok or frying pan. Add the fish and stir-fry for about 5 minutes. Put in the onions, red pepper, bamboo shoots and water chestnuts. Continue to turn over and around until all the ingredients are tender.

Blend the 1 ½ teaspoons cornflour with the fish stock in a basin. Add all the other ingredients for the sauce. Pour over the ingredients in the wok or frying pan and stir over a low heat until the sauce thickens. Serve with cooked rice or noodles.

Variations: to avoid the slightly sweet and sour taste omit the vinegar, tomato ketchup and sugar.

Try stir-frying young sliced carrots, turnips, cauliflower florets, mangetout peas and tender beans instead of cooking them in water in a saucepan. You retain all the flavour and texture. Young spinach leaves, bok choy and Chinese cabbage are also excellent when stir-fried.

Pasta and Salmon Salad

Within a comparatively short period pasta dishes have become one of the best liked foods in Britain. Gradually the public are beginning to enjoy cold pasta in the form of salads. It is important that the dressing is well-flavoured and mixed with the hot pasta, so this absorbs the flavour well. One of the twisted pasta shapes, such as fusilli, is a good choice, it looks attractive and is pleasantly firm.

SERVES 4

2.4 litres/4 pints water
salt and freshly ground black pepper
225 g/8 oz fusilli
6 tablespoons mayonnaise*
1 tablespoon extra virgin olive oil
1 tablespoon sherry vinegar or
   lemon juice
1 tablespoon chopped fennel leaves
1 garlic clove, crushed

salad leaves
225 g/8 oz cooked or canned salmon
2 tablespoons finely chopped
   fennel bulb
115 g/4 oz cooked mangetout peas
4 to 6 cherry tomatoes, halved or
   quartered

* the Hard-boiled Egg Mayonnaise on page
278 is a good choice for this dish.

Bring the water to the boil, add a teaspoon of salt then put in the fusilli. Cook until **'al dente'**. Strain thoroughly. Mix the mayonnaise with the oil, vinegar or lemon juice, fennel, garlic and seasoning. Toss the pasta in this dressing. Cover and leave until cold.

Arrange the salad leaves on one large dish or several plates. Mix the pasta with the other ingredients and spoon over the salad leaves. Serve with extra mayonnaise or with an oil and vinegar dressing.

Variation: instead of salmon use cooked lentils. Puy lentils have the best flavour and are ideal for salads.

Hard-boiled Egg Mayonnaise

When the newspapers became full of warnings about salmonella in eggs and the advice not to use them uncooked, I was besieged with requests asking how to make a safe mayonnaise. I remembered that during the years of rationing I had experimented with using hard-boiled dried eggs for mayonnaise. This was necessary for uncooked dried eggs tasted extremely unpleasant and fresh eggs were severely rationed. In those days I had to use melted margarine instead of oil, which was very scarce.

Now, with shell eggs and plenty of oil available, it was time to experiment again and I was happy to find a very pleasant and safe dressing.

SERVES: DEPENDENT ON THE RECIPE

2 large eggs
1 teaspoon made English or
   Dijon mustard
salt and freshly ground white pepper
up to 300 ml/$\frac{1}{2}$ pint extra virgin olive

oil or alternative
1 to 3 teaspoons lemon juice or
   white wine vinegar or alternative
1 tablespoon very hot water, optional

Hard-boil the eggs, shell and remove the yolks. The whites can be added to a salad. If making the dressing by hand sieve the yolks and pound with the mustard until very smooth. Add a little seasoning then gradually whisk in the amount of oil required. When thickened and smooth stir in the lemon juice or vinegar. Lastly add the water. This is not essential but it does lighten the dressing.

If making the mayonnaise in a liquidizer or food processor put the egg yolks, mustard and seasoning into the goblet or bowl. With the motor running add the oil slowly at first then a little more rapidly. Lastly add the lemon juice or vinegar and hot water.

Variations: use different oils, i.e. a little sesame oil plus olive oil gives a very piquant flavour; corn or sunflower or safflower oils a lighter texture. The nut oils, such as walnut or almond are excellent too.

Use rice vinegar, balsamic vinegar or sherry vinegar.

Creamy Mayonnaise: blend 2 tablespoons single cream with the hard-boiled egg yolks.

Beef Wellington

This was considered **the** luxury dish of the era by lovers of prime beef, as it looks impressive and exciting and tastes delicious. The savoury mushroom stuffing and crisp puff pastry enhance the flavour of perfectly cooked steak; in order to prevent the puff pastry from being over-cooked it is essential to roast the beef for a short time, allow it to cool then enrobe it in stuffing and pastry.

By the 1980's few people made puff pastry for the frozen kind was considered reasonably good but there is a recipe for home-made puff pastry on page 178.

The other name by which this dish is known is 'Boeuf en Croute'.

SERVES 4 TO 6

675 g/1 ½ lb fillet steak, cut in one piece
25 g/1 oz butter

FOR THE MUSHROOM STUFFING:
25 g/1 oz butter
1 medium onion, finely chopped
300 g/10 oz mushrooms, finely chopped
1 tablespoon chopped parsley

2 teaspoons chopped coriander
salt and freshly ground black pepper

450 g/1 lb frozen puff pastry
TO GLAZE:
1 egg, beaten

Preheat the oven to 220°C/425°F/Gas Mark 7/200°C with a fan oven. Place the steak in a roasting tin and spread with the butter. Roast for 10 to 20 minutes, depending upon how well done you like beef. It should be partially, but not completely, cooked. Leave until quite cold.

Heat the butter, add the onion, cook for 5 minutes then mix in all the other stuffing ingredients.

Meanwhile defrost the pastry. Roll out most of this to make an oblong shape sufficiently large to cover the beef, put the rest of the pastry on one side for decoration.

Spread the stuffing over the pastry but leave a good 1.25 cm/^{1}/$_2$ inch uncovered on all sides. Put the beef in the centre of the pastry, brush all edges with water then fold the pastry neatly to cover the meat. Seal the ends and the centre join. Turn over so the join is underneath. Roll out the remaining pastry and make leaf and rose shapes. Press on top of the pastry. Make 2 or 3 slits to allow steam to escape.

Lift on to a baking sheet and brush with the egg. Bake for 35 to 40 minutes at the temperature given above but reduce the heat slightly after 25 minutes if the pastry is becoming too brown. A Madeira Sauce (page 321) is an excellent accompaniment to this dish.

Variations: the same principle could be used to cover individual portions of beef steak, lamb cutlets or large portions of salmon.

A modern touch: use filo pastry instead of the richer puff pasty.

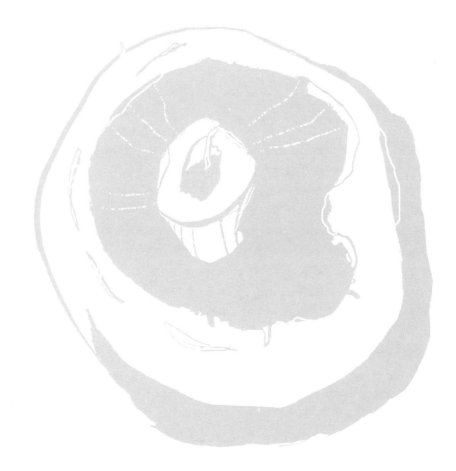

Barbecued Spare Ribs

These form an interesting part of an informal meal. As the method of preparation is fairly complicated, I find most people like to do this in the kitchen then serve the ribs out of doors. An alternative method of preparation is given under Variation.

SERVES 4 TO 6

2 kg/4½ lb pork ribs
1 tablespoon brown malt vinegar
1 onion, sliced
1 garlic clove, chopped
pinch ground ginger
salt and freshly ground black pepper
FOR THE SAUCE:
2 tablespoons sunflower oil
1 medium onion, finely chopped
1½ level teaspoons cornflour

150 ml/¼ pint stock, see method
good pinch ground ginger
1 tablespoon soy sauce
2 tablespoons tomato ketchup
1 tablespoon clear honey or
   brown sugar
2 tablespoons pineapple syrup
   or sweetened apple or orange juice
4 to 6 tablespoons brown malt vinegar

Preheat the oven to 220°C/425°F/Gas Mark 7/200°F with a fan oven.

Place the ribs into a large saucepan with just enough cold water to cover. Add the sliced onion, chopped garlic, ginger and seasoning. Bring the water to simmering point, cover the pan and simmer for 25 minutes. Strain the liquid, keep 150 ml/¼ pint for the sauce. Dry the ribs very well then put into a roasting tin, in as flat a layer as possible, and roast for 25 minutes or until the outsides are crisp.

Prepare the sauce. Heat the oil, add the onion and cook for 5 minutes. Blend the cornflour with the stock, pour over the onion then add the remainder of the sauce ingredients. Stir over a medium heat until thickened, season to taste.

Drain away all excess fat from the roasting tin. Lower the heat to 180°C/350°F/Gas Mark 4/170°C with a fan oven. Pour the sauce over the ribs and turn these around until completely coated with the mixture. Return the tin to the oven and cook for 10 to 15 minutes. As the ribs are very sticky provide plenty of paper napkins. If serving indoors provide finger bowls.

Variation: simmer the ribs in the water, drain and dry well, make the sauce as above. Cook the ribs over the hot barbecue fire until very crisp, basting with the sauce.

Roast Turkey with Cranberry Sauce

Over the past decades roast turkey had become the dish for Christmas Day. People could choose an economical frozen turkey, and buy this some time before Christmas and store it in their freezer, or the more expensive fresh turkey.

Turkey is a lean poultry and care should be taken to keep it moist in cooking so it is advisable to cook it with the breast downwards for the first half of the roasting time; then turn it with the breast uppermost.

SERVES 8 TO 10

4.5 kg/10 lb turkey, weight when
   trussed and oven-ready
85 g/3 oz butter
salt and freshly ground black pepper

FOR THE CHESTNUT STUFFING:
450 g/1 lb chestnuts
150 ml/¼ pint turkey stock*

50 g/2 oz butter, melted
115 g/4 oz bacon, derinded
   and chopped
2 tablespoons chopped parsley
1 teaspoon finely grated lemon zest
50 g/2 oz walnuts, coarsely chopped

* from cooking the giblets. If not available use chicken stock.

To prepare the turkey: wipe the turkey well inside and out. Spread with the softened butter and lightly season.

For the stuffing: slit the chestnuts in the shape of a cross at one end; simmer in water to cover for 10 minutes. Remove from the water and discard this. Cool the nuts slightly then remove the outer shells and brown skins.

Put the peeled chestnuts into a saucepan with the stock. Cover the pan and simmer for 15 minutes. At the end of this time most of the stock will have been absorbed but save whatever remains. Sieve or liquidize the chestnuts and blend with the butter, the uncooked bacon and the rest of the ingredients. Add just enough stock to make a soft mixture. Season well.

To cook the turkey: by the end of the 1980's it had been established that it was unwise to put stuffing into the body of poultry, so spoon this into the neck end only and pull the skin over it. Any stuffing left can be put into an ovenproof dish, covered and baked for 40 to 50 minutes.

Weigh the turkey after inserting the stuffing as described above.

A fresh turkey: preheat the oven to 220°C/425°F/Gas Mark 7/190 to 200°C with a fan oven.

Allow 15 minutes per 450 g/1 lb and 15 minutes over. After 1½ hours the oven can be reduced to 190°C/375°F/Gas Mark 5/180°C with a fan oven.

A defrosted turkey: it is advisable to cook this more slowly.

Preheat the oven to 180°C/350°F/Gas Mark 4/170°C with a fan oven.

Allow 22 to 25 minutes per 450 g/1 lb and 22 to 25 minutes over.

Always test the turkey just ahead of the end of the cooking time, for the tenderness and quality of birds vary.

Insert the tip of a sharp knife in the bird where the leg joins the body. If the juice that flows is clear the bird is cooked. If pink it needs longer cooking.

Allow the turkey to stand for 10 to 15 minutes before carving. Cover with foil to retain the heat of the bird.

Note: if you place foil lightly over the bird during cooking there is no need to increase the cooking time. If you are wrapping the turkey in foil, allow an extra 10 minutes cooking time.

Cranberry sauce

150 ml/¼ pint water	450 g/1 lb cranberries
150 g/5 oz caster sugar	3 tablespoons redcurrant jelly

Put the water and sugar in a saucepan, stir over a low heat until the sugar dissolves. Add the cranberries, cover the pan tightly, for cranberries tend to explode in cooking. Simmer for 6 minutes or until the cranberries no longer 'pop'. Add the jelly and heat very gently until the jelly dissolves. This gives added sweetness and a glaze to the sauce.

Variations: use orange juice instead of water.

Use less water and a little port wine.

A modern touch: use canned chestnut purée or vacuum-packed whole chestnuts instead of cooking the chestnuts.

Frozen cranberries are available all the year.

Roast Duck

Roast ducks are much more popular than they were several decades ago. People have slowly realised that modern ducklings are very young and tender and, while they do contain much more fat than turkeys or chickens, this is not a problem if dealt with properly.

To cook duck: follow the cooking times and temperatures given for fresh or defrosted frozen turkey on this page. Stand the bird(s) on a trivet in the roasting tin. Do not cover. Prick lightly after each 30 to 40 minutes cooking time. The fat under the skin will spurt out, leaving lean meat and a crisp skin. The skin can be given more flavour if brushed with a little honey blended with orange juice. Traditional accompaniments are as given for pork on page 206.

Roast Goose

This was the favourite bird for special occasions in the last century but now turkey has taken its place. However goose farmers say they are rearing more birds as there is now more interest in them.

To cook goose: follow the timing for fresh or defrosted frozen turkeys on this page but stand the bird on a rack and prick as detailed for duck.

Traditional accompaniments are those given for pork on page 206.

A stuffing of cooked prunes and diced apples, moistened with a little port wine, is very delicious with goose.

Venison in Calvados

For centuries many people living in the country had the opportunity to cook venison. Though in towns and cities the game was virtually unknown. The late 1980's changed this situation as both wild and farmed venison came into supermarkets.

SERVES 4

4 unsmoked bacon rashers, derinded
2 dessert apples, peeled and cored
50 g/2 oz butter
1 tablespoon olive oil
1 tablespoon soft brown sugar
salt and freshly ground black pepper
4 portions venison fillet
5 tablespoons Calvados
25 g/1 oz plain flour

150 ml/¼ pint game or
  beef stock (page 16)
225 m/7 ½ fl oz red wine
1 teaspoon juniper berries, crushed
1 teaspoon rosemary leaves or
  ½ teaspoon dried rosemary
3 tablespoons double cream

Preheat the oven to 180°C/350°F/Gas Mark 4/170°C with a fan oven. Cut the bacon into 2.5 cm/1 inch pieces and each apple into 8 slices. Cook the bacon in a frying pan for 5 minutes, remove with a slotted spoon. Add half the butter and half the oil, put in the apple slices and cook gently until golden brown on both sides. Sprinkle with the sugar as they brown, so they become slightly caramellized. Lift out of the pan. Heat the remaining butter and oil in the frying pan, season the venison and place in the hot fat. Cook steadily for 2 minutes on either side, moistening with 2 tablespoons of the Calvados. Lift into a casserole; add the bacon and apple.

Stir the flour into the fat and juices remaining in the pan; gradually add the stock and wine. Stir over a moderate heat until thickened then stir in the juniper berries, rosemary, remaining Calvados and any extra seasoning required. Pour into the casserole. Cover and cook for 35 minutes or until the meat is tender.

Top with the cream and serve with seasonal vegetables.

Variations: if choosing less tender venison marinate the portions in 8 tablespoons red wine, 2 tablespoons olive oil, 1 crushed garlic clove and a little seasoning for 3 hours. Turn over several times. Drain well and cook as above but allow 1 ¼ hours in a preheated oven set to 160°C/325°F/Gas Mark 3/150°C with a fan oven.

Rösti

It was fascinating how Rösti, that simple but very pleasing Swiss potato dish, suddenly became the way of cooking potatoes. One minute it was almost unknown then within weeks every menu seemed to include it. There are two ways of preparing the dish, in the first the potatoes are raw and in the second partially cooked. When using cooked potatoes it is essential that the potatoes are coarsely grated and not allowed to become mushy. It is best to prepare them just before cooking.

SERVES 4

450 g/1 lb potatoes, peeled and
   coarsely grated old or new
salt and freshly ground black pepper

FOR FRYING:

4 tablespoons sunflower or
   olive or groundnut oil or use half
   oil and half butter

Allow the grated potatoes to drop into a basin, season well and make into 4 portions, form into round cakes with your hands. You can exert some pressure to do this and, as you handle them, you squeeze out some of the potato liquid.

Heat the oil, or oil and butter, in a frying pan, put in the potato cakes. Press down firmly with a spatula or palette knife and fry steadily for 2 minutes or until golden on the under side. Turn over and fry on the second side for the same time. Lower the heat and cook for a further 5 minutes or until the potatoes are tender. Serve as soon as possible after cooking.

Variations: flavour the potatoes with finely chopped spring onions or chopped fried onions or shredded leek, crushed or chopped garlic and other herbs. Grated cheese, chopped cooked bacon or ham are other good additions.

Grated carrots, celeriac, young turnips and parsnips make excellent Rösti, either mixed with potatoes or cooked by themselves in the same way.

Instead of making several small potato cakes cook the grated potato as one large cake. Fry steadily in the oil for 5 minutes then turn over with the help of a large fish slice or invert the frying pan over a plate so the potato cake drops out with the browned side uppermost. Slide back into the pan and continue cooking for a further 5 to 7 minutes. Cut into neat slices.

Rösti with partially cooked potatoes: Wash about 450 g/1 lb potatoes, do not peel. Boil steadily for 10 to 15 minutes or until nearly cooked in salted water, drain and cool then remove the skin. Shred coarsely, season then cook as above.

Venison in Calvados (page 285)

Lentil and Cashew Nut Terrine

In the past the most popular use of lentils was in satisfying and economical soups but with the increasing interest in non-meat dishes, cooks have found many other ways to use this dried vegetable. Lentils make delicious curries and salads.

SERVES 4 TO 6

FOR THE TERRINE:
225 g/8 oz red split lentils
3 medium onions, chopped
salt and freshly ground black pepper
2 tablespoons olive oil
2 medium tomatoes, skinned
    and chopped
1 small dessert apple, grated
2 teaspoons chopped basil
50 g/2 oz cashew nuts,
    coarsely chopped
50 g/2 oz soft breadcrumbs
2 small eggs, beaten

FOR THE FILLING:
2 teaspoons sesame oil
25 g/1 oz soft breadcrumbs
1 tablespoon chopped parsley
1 teaspoon sesame seeds
2 tablespoons sliced spring onions
50 g/2 oz cashew nuts,
    coarsely chopped
FOR THE TOPPING:
50 g/2 oz cashew nuts
2 teaspoons sesame seeds

Split red lentils do not need soaking so wash them in cold water then put into a saucepan with enough cold water to cover, 1 of the onions and seasoning. Cook steadily for approximately 20 minutes or until soft, but unbroken. Drain thoroughly.

Meanwhile preheat the oven to 180°C/350°F/Gas Mark 4/170°C with a fan oven and line a 1.2 to 1.3 kg/2½ to 3 lb loaf tin with greaseproof paper or baking parchment. Heat the oil and cook the 2 onions for 5 minutes, add the tomatoes and apple and continue cooking for a further 5 minutes. Add the cooked lentils and the rest of the ingredients for the terrine. Mix all the ingredients for the filling.

Spoon half the terrine mixture into the tin, add the filling then the rest of the terrine mixture. Cover the top of the tin with foil and bake for 55 minutes, or until firm. Remove from the oven, add the whole cashew nuts and sesame seeds and return to the oven for a further 5 to 10 minutes. Remove from the tin and serve.

Stuffed Aubergines

One attractive name for stuffed aubergines is 'little slippers' and I have adapted the meat filling I have used for years to make these 'slippers' into a very inviting vegetarian dish. Chick peas have not been used a great deal in Britain in the past but they are now becoming both well-known and popular. You will find more comments about the flavour of aubergines on page 292.

SERVES 4

2 large or 4 small aubergines
salt and freshly ground black pepper
2 teaspoons olive oil
FOR THE FILLING:
2 tablespoons olive oil
2 medium onions, chopped
2 garlic cloves, chopped
3 large tomatoes, skinned and chopped

225 g/8 oz canned or
    cooked chick peas
pinch cayenne pepper
pinch ground cumin
2 tablespoons chopped coriander
FOR THE TOPPING:
1 tablespoon olive oil
50 g/2 oz soft breadcrumbs

Preheat the oven to 200°C/400°F/Gas Mark 6/190°C with a fan oven. If you want to be certain there is no bitter taste from the aubergines score the outside of the vegetables lightly with a knife, sprinkle with salt then leave for 30 minutes. Drain away the liquid, rinse in cold water and dry well.

Halve the vegetables lengthways, brush the cut surfaces with the oil and put into a greased dish. Cover with foil and bake for 20 minutes or until the centres are softened. Scoop out the centre pulp and chop this finely.

Heat the oil in a pan, add the onions and cook steadily until nearly soft. Add the garlic and the tomatoes and continue cooking for 10 minutes. Stir in the rest of the filling ingredients and the softened aubergine pulp. Spoon into the aubergine skins.

Blend the oil with the breadcrumbs, sprinkle over the filling and return to the oven for a further 15 minutes.

Variation: instead of the chick peas use cooked green peas or chopped cooked beans or coarsely chopped walnuts or pecan nuts.

Pizza

Pizzas were enjoyed in restaurants and sold in supermarkets well before the 1980's but relatively few people made a pizza at home. They seemed to find the thought of making a yeast dough daunting. When the quick acting dried yeasts came onto the market these proved an encouragement. Of course a home-made pizza is never quite the same as a very good one cooked in a pizza oven as domestic ovens are not heated in the same way but by preheating a metal baking sheet in the oven you encourage the base of the pizza to brown and become crisp.

SERVES 4

FOR THE TOMATO MIXTURE:
1 tablespoon olive oil
2 medium onions, finely chopped
1 to 2 garlic cloves, crushed
675 g/1 1/2 lb tomatoes, skinned and
    chopped or a 425 g can chopped
    plum tomatoes
1 to 2 teaspoons chopped oregano
    or 1/2 to 1 teaspoon dried oregano
salt and freshly ground black pepper
FOR THE DOUGH:
225 g/8 oz strong flour*
good pinch salt

1/2 level teaspoon easy blend yeast
150 ml/1/4 pint water
1 tablespoon olive oil plus a little extra
FOR THE TOPPING:
few drops olive oil
85 to 115 g/3 to 4 oz mozzarella
    cheese, grated or shredded
few canned anchovy fillets, optional
few black olives, optional

type sold for bread-making. Plain flour could be substituted.

For the tomato mixture: heat the oil in a pan, add the onions and cook gently for 5 minutes. Put in the garlic, tomatoes, oregano and a little seasoning. Simmer steadily until a thick purée. Allow to cool.

For the dough: sift the flour and salt into a bowl, add the yeast. Heat the water until comfortably warm, add to the flour with 1 tablespoon of the oil. Mix well, then turn on to a floured board and knead until smooth. To test if sufficiently kneaded press with a floured finger; if ready the impression will spring back out. Put the dough back in the bowl and brush with the remaining oil. Cover and leave for about 45 minutes, or until well-risen, at room temperature.

Preheat the oven to 220°C/425°F/Gas Mark 7/190 to 200°C with a fan oven. Place a strong metal baking sheet in the oven at the same time. Lightly oil a second baking sheet. Roll out the dough until 25 to 28 cm/10 to 11 inches in diameter. Place on the oiled sheet, top with the tomato mixture and the cheese. If using the anchovy fillets and olives arrange over some of the cheese topping then cover with the remainder of the cheese. Place the pizza on its baking sheet over the hot sheet. Bake for 15 to 20 minutes, or until the base is firm.

Variations: use cooked peppers or mushrooms or a selection of vegetables over the tomato mixture and cover with the cheese.

Grated Parmesan can be used, in which case reduce the amount to half, as it is so strongly flavoured. Cheddar and other good cooking cheeses are excellent.

Chopped bacon, salami, or cooked thinly sliced chicken or ham make good toppings.

Omit the tomato layer, place chosen toppings over the oiled dough.

A modern touch: it is possible to buy ready-prepared pizza bases. Pizza stones for cooking are available.

Ratatouille

This interesting mixture of vegetables comes from Provence but it has become an important part of British cuisine, which is not surprising as Ratatouille is an excellent vegetarian dish, topped with cheese, or it can be served as an accompaniment to meat, fish or poultry. It also makes a good hot or cold hors d'oeuvre. An added advantage is that it freezes well.

SERVES 6 TO 8

1 large or 2 medium aubergines
450 g/1 lb courgettes
salt and freshly ground black pepper
3 tablespoons olive oil
3 medium onions, chopped
2 garlic cloves, chopped
1 kg/2¼ lb tomatoes, concassed*
1 red pepper, deseeded and diced

1 green pepper, deseeded and diced
1 yellow pepper, deseeded and diced
2 tablespoons chopped parsley
TO GARNISH:
chopped parsley

this means skin, halve, remove the seeds and use the chopped pulp, use plum type if possible

When aubergines first became plentiful advice was given to score the skin with a knife, sprinkle with salt and leave for 30 minutes. The salt drew out the bitter tasting juices from the skin. As the years went on aubergines tended to lose this bitter taste, so the process described above was no longer essential. By drawing out the juices though you avoid using too much oil when frying aubergines; the same applies to courgettes.

Slice or dice both the aubergine(s) and courgettes. Sprinkle with salt, if desired, leave for 30 minutes, rinse in cold water and dry well.

Heat the oil in a large saucepan, add the onions and cook for 5 minutes, stir in the garlic and tomatoes, heat for 5 minutes, or until the tomato juice begins to flow. Add the aubergine(s), courgettes, peppers, parsley and seasoning to taste. Cover the pan, lower the heat and cook the vegetables until just tender. Stir several times during the cooking period. This will vary according to how soft you like the vegetables but it should be between 35 and 45 minutes. Top with parsley before serving.

Peperonata

Throughout the 1980's Ratatouille became such a favourite that people were ready to experiment with other vegetable stews. The obvious choice was to use peppers, for there was an excellent selection on sale. This classic Italian dish is both colourful and delicious.

SERVES 4 TO 6

2 small red peppers
1 small green pepper
1 small yellow pepper
1 small orange pepper
3 tablespoons olive oil
2 medium onions, finely chopped

2 garlic cloves, crushed
4 medium plum tomatoes, skinned
  and chopped
1 tablespoon chopped parsley
2 teaspoons chopped oregano
salt and freshly ground black pepper

Halve the peppers lengthwise and remove the cores and seeds. Place under a preheated grill until the skins turn black. Place the hot peppers into a large plastic bag, leave until cool then strip away the skins. Cut the peppers into thin strips. Heat the oil in a large saucepan, add the onions and cook gently for 5 minutes, put in the garlic and tomatoes. Continue cooking for a further 10 minutes. Add the peppers, herbs and seasoning and cover the pan. Cook gently until the peppers are tender, this takes about 20 minutes. Shake the pan from time to time to make sure the food does not stick and burn. Serve hot or cold.

Variations: roast the peppers in oil then add, without slicing, to the softened onions, garlic and tomatoes. Heat for 5 minutes. In this case use only 1 tablespoon oil in which to cook the onions, garlic and tomatoes.

Use a small can of chopped plum tomatoes instead of the fresh ones.

Risotto alla Milanese

Risottos had been served in Britain since the 19th century but without any particular recommendations as to the kind of rice that should be used. It was when I was asked to give some demonstrations on behalf of the Italian Trade Centre that I realised the importance of using what they termed 'medium grain' or 'Italian' rice and appreciated the difference this could make. Some years later 'arborio' rice (one name for Italian rice) was readily available. It is larger-grained and it gives a wonderfully creamy texture to the cooked dish.

SERVES 4

2 tablespoons olive oil
25 to 50 g/1 to 2 oz butter
1 medium onion, chopped
225 g/8 oz Italian (arborio) rice
900 ml/1 ½ pints chicken or beef or
  vegetable stock

pinch saffron powder or
  few saffron strands
salt and freshly ground black pepper
FOR THE TOPPING:
50 to 85 g/2 to 3 oz Parmesan cheese,
  grated

Heat the oil in a good-sized pan with half the butter. It is not essential to use butter at this stage but it does give a richer flavour to the dish. It is however important that 25 g/1 oz butter should be stirred into the cooked rice.

Add the onion and cook gently until nearly tender then tip in the rice and mix with the onion and oil, or oil and butter. Meanwhile bring the stock to boiling point in another pan with the saffron powder or strands. If you dislike seeing strands in the finished dish simply let these infuse in the hot stock for a short time, strain and reheat the liquid. Pour sufficient hot stock over the rice to cover, season, then stir and continue to cook until the liquid is absorbed. Continue adding the stock and stiring like this until the rice is tender. A good risotto should be moist but not over-wet.

Stir the butter into the rice. Serve topped with the Parmesan cheese.

Variations: one vegetable, such as fresh or prepared dried mushrooms could be cooked with the rice. In 1999 the favourite risotto is made by cooking wild mushrooms with the rice and flavouring the dish with truffle oil.

Crème Brûlée (page 296)

Crème Brûlée

It may seem strange to put this recipe into a fairly recent decade when it is similar to an old traditional British dessert known as Burnt Cream. It was however in the 1980's that it began to appear on many sophisticated menus. The recipe for Custard Sauce as page 96 can be used but the following is just a little richer. Vanilla pods are easily obtained and they do give the best flavour. Nowadays it is 'fashionable' to scrape the seeds from the pod, so the custard is studded with little specks.

Do use strong flameproof dishes to place under the grill. Chefs, of course, use a blow torch to brown and crisp the sugar topping. The first method of cooking is considered to be correct but baking in the oven is a pleasing alternative.

SERVES 4

300 ml/½ pint milk
300 m/10 fl oz double cream
3 large eggs
2 egg yolks
40 to 50 g/1½ to 2 oz caster sugar
1 vanilla pod or ¼ teaspoon vanilla
    extract*

FOR THE TOPPING:
50 to 85 g/2 to 3 oz sugar **

*vanilla extract has a truer flavour than most essences

** this can be caster or Demerara but a molasses sugar gives a treacly taste which many people like

Warm the milk and cream. Beat the eggs, egg yolks and sugar until well blended. Add the warm milk, cream and vanilla pod or extract. If you want to use the seeds split the pod and scrape out the seeds. Add to the custard as well as the pod.

Pour into the top of a double saucepan or basin over hot, but not boiling, water. Stir briskly or whisk over a low heat until the custard gives a fairly thick coating on the back of a wooden spoon. Remove the pod. Pour the custard into 4 individual dishes and allow to become cold.

Preheat the grill. Spoon the sugar over the custard, cook under the grill until the topping is crisp and brown. Serve soon after preparing this final stage.

Variations: preheat the oven to 140°C/275°F/Gas Mark 1/130°C with a fan oven. Pour the custard into individual ovenproof dishes. Stand in a 'bain-marie' containing hot water. Bake for approximately 45 minutes or until set. Cool then add the topping.

Fruit Brûlée: blend thick fruit purée and custard, top with sugar and crisp.

Banoffee Pie

It took some little time for printed recipes for Banoffee Pie to become available and I think it was a dessert that people first ate in a restaurant or at a friend's house without knowing just how it was made. If they liked it, and most people did, they either begged for the recipe or created their own version.

As it became more and more popular recipes were published; these varied a little but the two essentials in every case were the fudge layer and bananas. The fudge is created by boiling an unopened can of sweetened condensed milk. **It is essential to ensure this is covered with water throughout the heating process**, otherwise there is a possibility of the can exploding.

SERVES 6

FOR THE FUDGE:
410 g can full cream sweetened
  condensed milk

FOR THE FLAN:
65 g/2 ½ oz butter, melted
50 /2 oz caster sugar
2 teaspoons thin honey
175 g/6 oz digestive biscuits, crushed

FOR THE FILLING:
450 g/1 lb ripe bananas
2 teaspoons lemon juice
150 ml/5 fl oz double or
  whipping cream
1 to 2 teaspoons instant coffee powder
little sugar, see method
25 to 50 g/1 to 2 oz plain chocolate,
  coarsely grated

Put the unopened can of milk into a saucepan of cold water, bring this to the boil and allow the water to boil steadily for 2 hours or 3 hours for a darker caramel. Cool, remove the caramel and beat to a spreading consistency.

Mix the ingredients for the flan together, press into a 20 to 23 cm/8 to 9 inch flan ring on an upturned baking tray or a flan dish. Either chill in the refrigerator or, for greater crispness, preheat the oven to 160°C/325°F/Gas Mark 3/150°C with a fan oven and bake for 10 minutes. If using a flan ring slide the shape on to a serving plate and remove the ring.

When the flan is cold spread with the caramel. Peel and mash the bananas with the lemon juice, spread over the caramel. Whip the cream, add the coffee powder and sugar to taste. Spoon over the bananas and top with the grated chocolate.

Tiramisu

The word Tiramisu means 'pick me up' and the dessert has a sufficiently appealing taste to do just that. When Italian food became fashionable in the 1960's and early 1970's this dessert was little known but it has now become a great favourite. The classic version uses uncooked eggs so I give an alternative under Variation. Savoiardi are Italian sponge fingers but the better known boudoir biscuits make an excellent alternative. It is essential that the cheese is very fresh; it should be soft and creamy.

SERVES 4 TO 6

12 to 14 savoiardi or boudoir biscuits
approximately 300 g/10 oz canned,
    cooked or soft fruit, optional
3 tablespoons brandy
6 to 8 tablespoons strong coffee

2 large eggs
50 g/2 oz caster sugar
300 g/10 oz mascarpone cheese
50 to 100 g/2 to 4 oz bitter or
    plain chocolate, coarsely grated

Arrange the sponge fingers or biscuits at the bottom of a serving dish. If you decide to have a fruit layer then drain the canned or cooked fruit well or mash soft fruit. Spread over the bottom layer. Blend the brandy and coffee and spoon over the ingredients in the dish, make sure the sponges or biscuits are evenly moistened.

Separate the eggs, beat the yolks and sugar until thick and creamy then add to the mascarpone cheese. Whisk the whites until stiff, fold into the cheese then spoon into the dish. Spread flat and top with a thick layer of chocolate. Chill well and serve.

Variation: omit the eggs and mix 150 ml/5 fl oz whipping or double cream or crème fraîche or thick yoghurt with the mascarpone cheese. Sweeten with the sugar. A squeeze of lemon juice can be added.

1990 to 2000

the world's larder

There was rejoicing when much of the world watched the release of Nelson Mandela from prison in South Africa in 1990. Television cameras recorded the proceedings. In 1994 he was elected President of the country.

In 1990 Iraq invaded Kuwait, which led to the Gulf War.

The situation in Russia changed. In 1990 Lithuania and Uzbekistan declared their independence from the U.S.S.R. In the following year, Estonia, Latvia and Azerbaijan did the same.

In 1993 Czechoslovakia split into the Czech Republic and Slovakia.

The Channel Tunnel between Britain and France opened in 1994.

Hong Kong was returned to China with due ceremony in 1997.

Throughout much of the decade there had been floods, hurricanes and earthquakes in various parts of the world. There were particularly devastating floods in Bangladesh in 1998.

This was an unhappy decade for the royal family. In 1992 Princess Anne and Captain Mark Phillips were divorced. This was followed in May 1994 by the divorce of the Duke and Duchess of York and in August of the same year by that of the Prince and Princess of Wales.

It is no wonder that in one of her Christmas broadcasts the Queen declared it had been an 'Annus Horribilis'.

1997 brought a terrible tragedy. Princess Diana was killed in a car crash in Paris. The grief at her death showed the affection in which she was held by a vast number of the British people.

that follow. These make an excellent start to a meal, or a light main course. They provide essential nutrients and show how newer ingredients have become part of our cuisine.

The great diversity of dishes and flavours that are popular today make it difficult to define what is the menu of 1999. You can have a most enjoyable time planning meals from a wide range of dishes that typify the last decade of the twentieth century.

Cookery Influences

During this decade there has been an 'explosion' of cookery programmes on television. Many of these, such as 'Ready Steady Cook' combine cookery and entertainment. Professional chefs have come from their kitchens to share their expertise with the public. On the other hand there has been an enormous increase in the number of convenience foods on the market and these demand little skill in heating.

There are so many gifted people in the world of cookery that it is difficult to mention all the names but Ainsley Harriott has more than once been voted the most popular television chef with Brian Turner and Antony Worrall Thompson also mentioned. Sophie Grigson is repeating the expertise of her mother with her exciting television programmes and books. This decade, like others of the past, produced a completely new approach to cookery instruction in the TV. Series - 'Two Fat Ladies'.

Prue Leith, O.B.E. has shown great initiative in organising a Cookery Bus which is travelling around the country enabling children to take part in cookery sessions. Books and articles are being continually published and so everyone should be learning to cook well but the most worrying aspect of this decade is the removal of Home Economics from the core curriculum in schools.

What lies ahead for 2000 onwards?

I am confident that many of the dishes given in the past decades of the twentieth century will continue into the future. They have proved their popularity, in fact they have become culinary classics. At the same time I have no doubt we shall seek out new ideas - new ingredients - new methods of cooking. Undoubtedly like all keen explorers, we will continue to search for previously unknown dishes. If we enjoy them sufficiently we will pass them on and they may well become part of our way of life.

It is interesting how, during the past years, we in Britain have become the most cosmopolitan of nations. We welcome new restaurants, we embrace new ingredients but in many ways we are returning to our past. In the days of Queen Elizabeth I we were known, with the Arabs, as providing the finest cuisine in the world. Let us return to that happy state in the century ahead.

I hope the encouragement given to organic farming at the moment will continue. This will enable us to discover the true flavours and health-giving priorities of many of the foods we eat. Like most people I think we must question genetic engineering of foods.

We have been told in the government paper, The Health of the Nation, that some people in this country do not eat as wisely as they should. Let those of us who write and talk about cookery continue to play our part in suggesting wise changes but please never allow our advice to suggest that healthy food is not enjoyable food. That belief is quite wrong, some of the most delicious dishes are the healthiest.

There is excitement about entering into a new century. It may well have new challenges and new discoveries. Let us hope that we in Britain continue to enjoy our interesting foods. It would be wonderful if we could succeed in ensuring that people from those parts of the world, where food is so scarce, will become well-fed too.

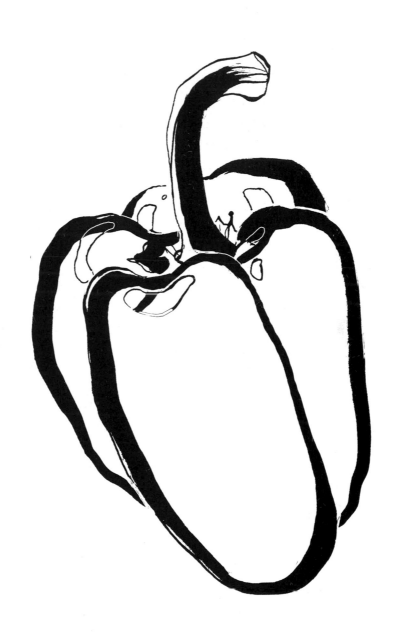

1990 to 2000

The Recipes

Twice Baked Cheese Soufflé

I cannot help wondering what Escoffier would have thought of our modern idea of reheating cooked cheese soufflés. The great advantage is that there is no panic about serving them the moment they come from the oven. The disadvantage, in my opinion, is that the mixture is never quite as light and delicate as when cooked just once.

We have grown used to dishes with more pronounced flavours these days and I suggest that the milk for the soufflé is given a more interesting taste by the use of herbs. Parmesan cheese can be used for the soufflé but I prefer a less dry cheese for the topping.

SERVES 4 TO 6

ingredients as Parmesan Soufflé (page 60) with a few coriander leaves, snipped chives and 1 garlic clove, chopped plus a little extra milk, see method

FOR THE TOPPING:
4 to 6 tablespoons grated Gruyère or mature Cheddar cheese
4 tablespoons single cream

TO GARNISH:
little finely chopped coriander or chives

Preheat the oven to 190°C/375°F/Gas Mark 5/180°C with a fan oven. It is easier to turn out several small soufflés, rather than one large one, so lightly grease 4 to 6 individual soufflé dishes. Place a sheet of greased greaseproof paper or baking parchment on a baking sheet.

To introduce more flavour into the milk bring this to boiling point with the coriander, chives and garlic. Remove from the heat and leave until cold then strain and add more cold milk to make 150 ml/¼ pint again.

Make the soufflé as page 60. Divide between the individual dishes and bake for about 15 minutes, or until well-risen and set. Leave in the dishes until almost cold, then carefully loosen with the tip of a knife. Turn out and immediately invert, so the top side is uppermost again. Place on the lined baking sheet.

At this stage lightly cover the soufflés with clingfilm and keep in the refrigerator until just before they are required.

Preheat the oven at the temperature given above. Sprinkle the grated cheese over the top of the soufflés and spoon on half the cream. Bake for about 15 minutes or until well-risen again and piping hot.

Top with the rest of the cream and the herbs and serve.

Variations: use a smooth spinach purée instead of milk. Flavour this with finely grated nutmeg or use fresh tomato purée with a little finely chopped basil.

Note: I have tried this double heating with sweet soufflés but they are not as successful as I would wish.

Hummus

If you enjoy chick peas this is an ideal appetizer to serve. Recipes vary slightly but this is my favourite. It is very simple, with easily obtainable ingredients.

SERVES 4

427 g can chick peas
1 tablespoon sesame seeds
1 garlic clove, chopped
1 tablespoon lemon juice, or to taste
1 tablespoon olive oil
few drops Tabasco sauce or pinch
   cayenne pepper

salt and freshly ground black pepper
1 to 2 tablespoons thick Greek
   yoghurt, optional
TO SERVE:
pitta bread
crudités

Thoroughly drain the chick peas, put into a food processor with the sesame seeds, garlic, lemon juice and olive oil. Switch on until a smooth purée.

Gradually add the Tabasco or cayenne, seasoning and yoghurt to give the desired consistency. Spoon into a bowl. Serve with the pitta bread and crudités, (strips of young carrot, celery, red and green peppers).

Variations: the pitta bread can be heated until very crisp.

Instead of sesame seeds add 1 to 2 tablespoons tahini paste and/or a few cumin seeds.

Piquant Scallop Salad

During the 1990's the combination of hot and cold food in a salad became increasingly popular. It is important that this salad is tossed in the dressing beforehand and the hot ingredients added immediately before serving, so that the salad retains its crisp texture. Bags of assorted salad ingredients, including rocket and mâche are easily obtainable in supermarkets. The knowledge of oils has increased during the decade and the public are buying a wide selection of oils and vinegars.

SERVES 4

mixed green salad ingredients

FOR THE TOMATO-LEMON GRASS DRESSING:

3 tablespoons extra virgin olive oil

1 tablespoon rice vinegar

1/2 tablespoon balsamic or sherry
   vinegar or more rice vinegar

1 teaspoon sugar

salt and freshly ground black pepper

2 tablespoons chopped sun-dried
   tomatoes

2 tablespoons chopped lemon grass

FOR THE HOT SCALLOPS:

25 g/1 oz butter

1 teaspoon extra virgin olive oil

4 king scallops or 12 queen scallops

pinch Thai red curry powder

1 teaspoon tomato purée

4 tablespoons crème fraîche

2 teaspoons chopped coriander or
   1/2 teaspoon dried coriander

Prepare the salad ingredients. Mix the dressing. Toss the salad in the dressing just before the meal and arrange on 4 serving plates.

Heat the butter and oil in a pan. Cut the large king scallops into 3 or 4 slices. Put the scallops into the hot fat and cook for 2 minutes only. Add the rest of the ingredients. Heat for 1 minute then spoon the hot fish mixture on to the salad and serve at once.

Twice Baked Cheese Soufflé (page 308)

Prawns in Lime and Coconut

This dish cannot be attributed to any one country but it does reflect the way we have absorbed the ingredients of so many cultures. I am a lover of coconut in various forms. Often I serve this dish for a light luncheon but it is also a good hors d'oeuvre, when it would serve more people. Fresh, rather than frozen prawns, are best. If they have been frozen defrost completely and dry very well.

To emphasise the coconut flavour a little of the coconut milk can be used with the water when cooking the rice (page 253).

SERVES 4

2 teaspoons finely grated lime zest

2 tablespoons lime juice

450 g/1 lb prawns, peeled weight

1 tablespoon sunflower oil

1 teaspoon sesame oil

225 ml/7 1/2 fl oz canned coconut milk

2 teaspoons light soy sauce

salt and freshly ground black pepper

2 teaspoons chopped lemon grass

TO GARNISH:

chopped lemon grass

2 teaspoons sesame seeds

coriander leaves

Put the lime zest and juice into a dish then add the prawns. Cover the dish and leave for 1 hour in the refrigerator. Turn over once or twice.

Heat the oils in a frying pan or wok, add the prawns and cook for 2 minutes. Pour in the milk and soy sauce and heat for 1 minute then stir in the seasoning and lemon grass.

Serve in a border of cooked rice and top with the lemon grass, sesame seeds and coriander.

Variation: up to 300 ml/10 fl oz coconut milk can be used to give a more liquid mixture.

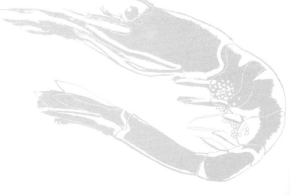

Soto Ajam

This is a chicken soup with a difference. Although it is an Indonesian soup I have made for years, recently I have changed the ingredients to include some we associate with Thai cooking. It does therefore sum up our 1999 attitude to cooking - take the ingredients you like from various cuisines and create interesting dishes. Galangal is similar to root ginger but it has a milder flavour. If unobtainable use slightly less root ginger.

SERVES 4

2 tablespoons groundnut or
    sunflower oil
2 medium onions, finely diced
2 garlic cloves, finely chopped
1½ tablespoons grated galangal
1 chicken breast, minced or finely diced
1.2 litres/2 pints chicken stock
    as page 16
1 tablespoon thinly sliced lemon grass

150 ml/5 fl oz coconut milk
salt and freshly ground black pepper
50 g/2 oz bean sprouts
1 tablespoon lime or lemon juice
1 tablespoon chopped coriander
TO GARNISH:
2 eggs, hard-boiled and chopped
2 teaspoons chopped coriander

Heat the oil, add the onions and cook gently for 5 minutes, stir in the garlic, galangal and chicken. Cook for another 5 minutes or until the chicken becomes pale golden brown. Pour the stock into the pan, bring to the boil, add the lemon grass. Cover the pan and simmer for 10 minutes. Stir in the coconut milk, seasoning to taste and the bean sprouts. Cook for a further 3 to 4 minutes. Stir in the juice and coriander. Spoon into soup bowls and top with the egg and a light sprinkling of coriander.

Variation: to make a more sustaining dish heat finely diced cooked potatoes and carrots in a little oil. Put into the soup bowls before adding the soup.

Fish and Vegetable Tempura

Tempura is the Japanese method of frying various foods so they become golden and beautifully crisp. While you can make Tempura with just one ingredient, such as prawns, it becomes a more interesting and delicious dish if a selection of foods are chosen. Recipes for Tempura batter vary but I like a combination of flour and cornflour.

SERVES 4

FOR THE BATTER:
50 g/2 oz plain flour
50 g/2 oz cornflour
1 teaspoon baking powder
1 egg, whisked lightly
200 ml/7 fl oz cold water
FOR THE DIPPING SAUCE:
3 tablespoons sake or dry sherry
2 tablespoons soy sauce
225 ml/7 ½ fl oz dashi or
   fish stock as page 16

1 tablespoon finely grated root ginger
3 tablespoons finely grated white radish
   or ordinary radishes
FOR THE TEMPURA:
300 g/10 oz monk fish or other firm
   fish or scallops
8 to 12 large prawns, preferably
   uncooked
selection of vegetables,
   such as mangetout peas, small
   mushrooms, small green beans
groundnut or sunflower oil

Mix all the ingredients for the batter together. Pour the wine or sherry, soy sauce and stock into a saucepan. Bring just to boiling point. Keep hot and add the grated ginger and radish just before serving.

Cut the fish into neat dice; peel the prawns, although it is considered correct to leave on the tails. Wash and dry the vegetables, trim away any tough ends. Preheat the oil to 185°C/365°F (or when a cube of 24-hour bread turns golden in under ¾ minute).

Dip the foods into the batter, make sure they are coated with a thin layer but have no excess batter falling off; this could burn in the oil. Drop small amounts of the coated foods into the oil and cook steadily until crisp and golden. Lift out on to absorbent paper then either keep hot or serve immediately. The hot dipping sauce should be poured into small bowls and served with the food.

Pork Satay

The pork that is on sale today is much leaner than the meat of days past and therefore ideal for this dish. As the sauce is based upon peanut butter and peanuts it is essential to check that no-one is allergic to these nuts.

Always soak new bamboo skewers in hot water before using as this stops them scorching.

SERVES 4 TO 6

FOR THE MARINADE:

2 small onions, chopped
2 garlic cloves, crushed
2 teaspoons lemon grass or lemon zest
1 tablespoon sunflower oil
1 tablespoon soy sauce
½ teaspoon ground coriander
pinch chilli powder

550 to 675 g/1¼ to 1½ lb lean pork

FOR THE SATAY SAUCE:

2 to 3 tablespoons peanut butter
175 g/6 oz roasted peanuts
150 ml/5 fl oz canned coconut milk
1 tablespoon lime or lemon juice
1 tablespoon brown sugar
1 tablespoon soy sauce
salt and freshly ground black pepper

12 to 18 bamboo skewers

Mix all the ingredients for the marinade in a large container. Cut the pork into 2.5 to 3.75 cm/1 to 1½ inch dice. Put into the marinade and leave for 1 hour, so the meat absorbs the flavours. Turn over several times. Meanwhile prepare the sauce. Put all the ingredients into a liquidizer or food processor and make a smooth thick mixture.

Lift the pork from the marinade, drain well and thread on the bamboo skewers. Cook over a hot barbecue or under the preheated grill until tender. Baste once with the marinade during cooking. Always turn over with the help of tongs when using the barbecue. Serve with the cold sauce and hot saffron flavoured cooked rice.
Variations: if the sauce is a little too thick dilute with more coconut milk.

If roasted peanuts are not available then put fresh peanuts on a metal tray and cook under a preheated grill or for about 10 minutes in a preheated oven set to 180°C/350°F/ Gas Mark 4/170°C with a fan oven. Turn the nuts over during grilling or baking so they are evenly browned.

Roast Game

Few foods can be more traditional to Britain than game, for it has been a familiar food for country people for centuries. Now it has become more widely available to town dwellers, for supermarkets, good butchers and game dealers sell fresh game when in season or frozen birds. However game birds are like chicken and turkey, they contain little fat, so care must be taken that they do not become dry in cooking.

THE MOST EASILY AVAILABLE GAME BIRDS ARE:
grouse, partridge, pigeon, pheasant, wild duck (mallard and teal),
woodcock (this is not trussed but roasted on slices of toast).
Guinea fowl is often classed as game too.
Other game: hare, rabbit and venison.

In order to help game birds keep moist put a small piece of butter (15 to 25 g/ ½ to 1 oz) inside each bird before cooking. If you are anxious to avoid adding fat to your diet use a small peeled potato and/or sliced onion instead. Cream cheese, mixed with chopped herbs or grapes, is another excellent filling. You can add chopped herbs, such as tarragon or rosemary, or spices, like ground cinnamon or cumin to the butter inside the bird or the coating on the breast. Inserting wafer-thin slivers of garlic or galangal at regular intervals into the skin produces a new taste.

Wild duck can be flavoured with sage leaves and slices of apple inside the body.

Cover the breast of the birds with softened butter or bacon rashers.

The back (saddle) of hare and a whole young rabbit are excellent roasted.

To cook: weigh and cook as chicken on page 111. The birds can be roasted with the breast downwards for the first half of the cooking period. Prime venison is roasted as beef (page 205).

Accompaniments to Roast Game:
Game Sauce, game chips and fried crumbs, redcurrant or rowan jelly and a green vegetable. A mixture of Brussels sprouts and cooked chestnuts.

To make game chips: peel and cut potatoes into wafer-thin slices by hand or with a food processor attachment. Heat oil to 190°C/375°F. Fry for 2 minutes, drain on absorbent paper and serve.

Fried Crumbs: traditionally fine breadcrumbs are used, but I like fairly coarse crumbs. Fry in a little hot butter, or butter and oil, until golden, drain on absorbent paper and serve. These freeze well. Open freeze to stop them sticking together then pack.

Fish and Vegetable Tempura (page 314)

Game Sauce

Perfectly cooked game demands really first class accompaniments and the recipe that follows produces a very delicious sauce that blends well with all types of game. The flavour depends upon really good stock plus a subtle mixture of savoury and sweet ingredients. If you want to prepare the sauce ahead and freeze it, omit the wine and vinegar then add these when reheating the defrosted sauce. In this way you gain the maximum flavour from these two ingredients.

SERVES 4 TO 6

TO FLAVOUR THE STOCK:
600 ml/1 pint game stock or
 brown stock as page 16
1 onion
1 carrot
2 celery sticks, chopped
FOR THE SAUCE:
50 g/2 oz butter or use half olive oil
 and half butter
1 medium onion, chopped
2 medium tomatoes, skinned

and deseeded
115 g/4 oz mushrooms, chopped
25 g/1 oz plain flour
300 ml/½ pint stock, see method
250 ml/8 fl oz red or port wine
2 tablespoons rowan or redcurrant or
 crab-apple jelly
2 teaspoons red wine or
 balsamic vinegar
salt and freshly ground black pepper
1 to 2 teaspoons sugar, or to taste

Bring the stock to the boil, add the vegetables and boil briskly for 5 minutes. Remove from the heat, cover the pan and stand for 1 hour. Remove the vegetables and boil the stock until reduced to 300 ml/½ pint.

Heat the butter or oil and butter in a saucepan, add the chopped onion and cook gently for 5 minutes. Put in the tomatoes and mushrooms and cook for a further 5 minutes. Stir in the flour, blend with the vegetables and then gradually add the 300 ml/½ pint stock. Bring to the boil, lower the heat and simmer for 5 minutes. Sieve or liquidize the mixture, return to the pan with the remaining ingredients. Stir over a low heat until the jelly has melted. Taste and adjust the amount of seasoning, sugar and consistency of the sauce.

Variations: instead of vinegar add a little soy sauce to give a 'bite' to the sauce.

Wood Pigeons in Madeira Sauce

Suddenly at the end of this century there seem many more pigeons on sale. I am delighted, for I think these birds are both economical and delicious, and I am sure they will become popular. Unlike many game birds they are in season throughout the year. In the early 1950's I cooked them in several ways on television. Farmers wanted to get rid of as many as possible, since they were eating their precious and much-needed grain.

After being 'in the doldrums' for some time, Madeira wines are becoming popular once more. I used Duke of Clarence for the sauce, but other kinds can be chosen.

SERVES 4

4 young tender wood pigeons (squabs)

FOR THE MARINADE:

300 ml/½ pint Duke of Clarence Madeira

2 tablespoons finely chopped spring onions or shallots

1 garlic clove, sliced

1 fresh or ½ dried bay leaf

1 level tablespoon tomato purée

FOR THE CARAMELLED ONIONS:

3 medium onions, thinly sliced

1 tablespoon olive oil

1 tablespoon caster sugar

FOR THE SAUCE:

25 g/1 oz butter

1 tablespoon olive oil

40 g/1½ oz plain flour

strained marinade

300 ml/½ pint game or chicken stock as page 16

5 tablespoons Duke of Clarence Madeira

2 tablespoons redcurrant jelly

8 glacé cherries, halved

8 small stoned green olives, halved

salt and freshly ground black pepper

1 or 2 teaspoons Dijon mustard

Split the pigeons down the back and breast to make 8 halves; flatten these joints with gentle pressure. Mix the marinade ingredients in a large container, add the pigeons and leave for at least 1 hour. At the end of this time preheat the oven to 180°C/350°F/Gas Mark 4/160°C with a fan oven.

While the pigeons are marinating prepare the onions. Cut the slices into smaller pieces. Heat the oil in a large frying pan, add the onions and the sugar. Stir well so the onions absorb the sugar. Cook very slowly until the onions turn a darkish golden; stir frequently so they do not burn. Spoon from the pan on to a plate. Lift the pigeons from the marinade, strain this and put on one side.

For the sauce: heat the butter and oil in the same pan in which the onions were cooked, add the pigeon halves and cook gently for 5 to 7 minutes or until slightly brown on the breast sides. You may have to do this in batches. Lift into a large roasting tin or casserole.

Stir the flour into the fat and juices remaining in the pan, continue stirring over a low heat until the flour darkens slightly. Add the strained marinade, stock and half the caramelled onions (the rest are for the Salsa). Stir as the sauce comes to the boil and thickens. Add the extra Madeira, jelly, cherries and olives. Bring to the boil and then simmer until the jelly melts. Season to taste, add the mustard and pour over the pigeons. Cover the tin or dish tightly and cook for 1 hour. Serve with the dishes below.

Variations: other game birds, such as pheasant can be cooked in the same way. This is also an excellent way to cook thick venison slices.

Mango and Sweet Onion Salsa
Mix the cold caramelled onions, prepared above, with the finely diced flesh of a ripe mango, 1 tablespoon chopped parsley, 1 tablespoon chopped olives, 1 to 2 teaspoons soft brown sugar and 2 teaspoons rice vinegar.

Celeriac and Potato Rösti
Partially cook 1 small celeriac root and 1 large or 2 medium potatoes as outlined on page 286 then proceed as that recipe.

Polenta au Gratin

Now that quick cooking polenta (cornmeal) is readily available this dish is made without much effort. It can be served by itself or as an accompaniment to meat, fish or vegetarian dishes. It can be prepared then served with any sauce you would normally serve with pasta.

SERVES 4 TO 6

300 to 350 g/10 to 12 oz polenta
water, as directed on packet
salt and freshly ground black pepper
115 g/4 oz Parmesan cheese, grated
2 teaspoons chopped basil
FOR THE TOPPING:
175 g/6 oz ricotta cheese

175 g/6 oz fontina cheese, thinly sliced
40 g/1½ oz butter, melted
2 tablespoons pine nuts
TO GARNISH:
basil leaves

Put the polenta in the amount of water indicated on the packet, season and cook as directed. Season well as it cooks. When ready stir in the Parmesan cheese and basil. Allow to cool then turn out of the pan and leave until cold. Cut into about 12 even sized slices with a very sharp knife.

Place in a flameproof dish (one that is safe under the grill). Top with the ricotta cheese and the sliced fontina. Spoon the melted butter over the slices. Top with the pine nuts. Preheat the grill and cook until the cheese is melted and the polenta is very hot. Garnish and serve.

Variations: preheat the oven to 200°C/400°F/Gas Mark 6/190°C with a fan oven. Place the prepared slices in an ovenproof dish and bake for about 15 minutes.

Cooked polenta, ready for slicing, can be used.

Penne with Three Cheeses and Beans

This dish can be prepared within a very short time. The quantities given in this recipe and those for spaghetti on page 214 refer to dried pasta. If buying fresh pasta allow almost three times as much in weight. Always check the cooking times on packets, for pasta varies in thickness; fresh pasta cooks more rapidly than dried but it requires the same proportion of liquid, i.e. a minimum of 1.2 litres/2 pints to each 115 g/4 oz.

I have used Greek feta cheese with two Italian types, for, apart from having a good flavour, the white cubes look attractive as a topping. For the finest Parmesan choose Parmigiano Reggiano.

SERVES 4

2.4 litres/4 pints water	1 tablespoon olive oil
salt and freshly ground black pepper	2 teaspoons chopped oregano
225 g/8 oz penne	50 g/2 oz Parmesan cheese, grated
225 g/8 oz green beans	50 g/2 oz fontina cheese, grated
225 g can red kidney beans	115 g/4 oz feta cheese, cubed

Bring the water to the boil, add 1 level teaspoon salt and then the penne. Cook until 'al dente' then strain.

While the pasta is cooking heat a little more salted water, add the green beans and cook until nearly tender. Drain the canned kidney beans, add to the green beans and heat for 2 minutes then strain.

Return the pasta to the pan with the oil, beans, oregano, half the Parmesan, all the fontina and any seasoning required. Stir over a low heat for 1 or 2 minutes. Serve topped with the feta cheese and remaining Parmesan.

Variation: cook the penne and serve with Pesto (page 325) and the cheeses in the recipe above.

Pesto

Although Pesto has been known to lovers of pasta and Italian food well before the 1990's it was at the beginning of this decade that various recipes for the sauce appeared with great regularity and Pesto became part of every cook's repertoire. It was found to be an excellent accompaniment to many foods, such as fish, vegetables, salads and even as a topping on some soups. But best of all it could turn cooked pasta into a gourmet's delight.

What is classic Pesto? Really a combination of pine nuts, Parmesan cheese, basil and olive oil. Over the years I have found, like many other cooks, that several of the ingredients can be changed. Most nuts can take the place of pine nuts, different cheeses can be added and other herbs used with, or instead of the basil - should you dislike its very definite flavour. The following is a version I developed, which I christened Green Pesto.

The herbs should be young and tender and the cheese freshly grated.

SERVES 4 TO 6 BUT DEPENDS ON THE DISH

about 24 basil leaves
4 small parsley sprigs
1 small marjoram sprig
2 garlic cloves, crushed
50 g/2 oz butter, optional, melted
85 g/3 oz Parmesan cheese, grated

50 to 85 g/2 to 3 oz Pecorino
   cheese*, grated
6 tablespoons extra virgin olive oil
115 g/4 oz pine nuts
salt and freshly ground black pepper

an optional extra but balances the flavour well

Shred the herb leaves by hand to save undue time in the liquidizer or food processor. Process the herbs and garlic for a few seconds, add the butter then the cheeses and process for another few seconds. Add the oil gradually with the motor running. Finally add the pine nuts and a little seasoning; process until smooth. Serve cold or warm gently. Do not over-heat.

Variations: use 2 tablespoons double cream instead of the butter.

Use a few uncooked young spinach leaves instead of basil.

Use fresh walnuts instead of pine nuts, they give a wonderful flavour.

Red Pesto: add 3 to 4 medium skinned and deseeded chopped plum tomatoes to the mixture **before** the oil. Tomato purée or sun-dried tomatoes could be used.

Passion Fruit and Kiwi Sorbet

This is a delightful combination of two fruits that have become great favourites. It is advisable to sieve the passion fruit pulp, for the seeds become very hard in freezing. The number of passion fruit refer to the small oval type; larger round ones have appeared on the market. In this case you can use 4 instead of 6.

SERVES 4 TO 6

6 passion fruit

300 ml/½ pint water

1 tablespoon lemon juice

50 to 85 g/2 to 3 oz caster sugar

6 kiwi fruit

TO DECORATE:

mint leaves

1 or 2 passion fruit

Halve the passion fruit, sieve and put the seeds with the water, lemon juice and sugar into a saucepan. The amount of sugar is a matter of personal taste. Stir until the sugar has dissolved then boil briskly for 3 minutes, or until a light syrup. Strain again and cool.

Halve the kiwi fruits and scoop out the pulp, sieve or liquidize this. Add the passion fruit and kiwi purée to the syrup. Pour into an ice cream maker, switch on until frozen. Spoon into a container and place in the freezer or freezing compartment of the refrigerator. Remove about 15 minutes before serving, so the mixture is not too hard. Top each portion with mint leaves and passion fruit pulp.

Variation: to make this sorbet without an ice cream maker, soften 1 teaspoon gelatine in 2 tablespoons cold water, add to the hot liquid and heat until dissolved. Cool then stir in the fruit purée, as above. Put into a container and freeze until mushy. Remove and whisk well. To lighten the mixture you can fold in 1 or 2 stiffly whisked egg whites but you will be using uncooked eggs, so read the comments on pages 265 - 6. Return the mixture to the freezer until required.

Pistachio and Pineapple Ice Cream (page 328)

Pistachio and Pineapple Ice Cream

This particular recipe contains a mixture of marshmallows, pineapple and nuts and these produce a dessert that typifies the interesting ice creams of the 1990's. I first learned the value of marshmallows as a basis for certain ice creams in 1938, when I started working for Frigidaire as their home economist. As Frigidaire's parent company was American I was introduced to many unusual and delicious ice cream recipes from that country. Marshmallows help to produce a smooth texture to ice cream for they contain gelatine; they also include egg whites, which lighten the mixture. Small white marshmallows, that dissolve quickly, are readily available today.

SERVES 4 TO 6

175 g/6 oz white marshmallows
227 g can pineapple rings in
    natural juice
115 g/4 oz pistachio nuts, skinned
    and coarsely chopped*
25 g/1 oz vanilla sugar, or to taste**
300 ml/10 fl oz double cream

*to skin the nuts put into boiling water for about 1 minute then pull away the skins

**Vanilla Sugar: place 1 or 2 vanilla pods into jars of caster and icing sugar. The pods give a true vanilla flavour to the sugar. Spoon out amount required then fill up with more sugar.

Put the marshmallows into a basin. Strain the pineapple, measure out up to 150 ml/¼ pint of juice, add to the marshmallows. Stand basin over a saucepan of hot, but not boiling, water and leave until just dissolved. This can be done on the defrost setting in a microwave. Allow the mixture to cool.

Finely chop the pineapple rings, add to the marshmallows with the nuts and sugar. Whip the cream until it stands in soft peaks, do not over-whip Whipping is not necessary with an ice cream maker. Fold into the other ingredients. Either spoon into the ice cream maker and freeze or put into a dish and place in the freezer.

Variations: other fruits and nuts can be used.

The marshmallows can be dissolved in vermouth, instead of fruit juice.

Raspberry Ice Cream: dissolve the marshmallows in 225 ml/7 ½ fl oz fresh raspberry purée, add the sugar and cream as above. Other soft fruits can be used in the same way.

Sticky Toffee Pudding

At the end of the 20th century, when we are enjoying exotic dishes from around the world, a typically hot British pudding is deservedly a favourite way to end a meal. Sticky Toffee Pudding combines a delicious fruit sponge with a mouth-watering sauce.

SERVES 6 TO 8

150 g/5 oz dates, weight when stoned and finely chopped

120 ml/4 fl oz boiling water

85 g/3 oz butter

150 g/5 oz soft dark brown sugar

½ teaspoon natural almond essence, optional

2 large eggs

175 g/6 oz self-raising flour or

plain flour with 1½ teaspoons baking powder

FOR THE SAUCE:

85 g/3 oz butter

150 g/5 oz soft dark brown sugar

120 ml/4 fl oz double cream

TO DECORATE:

3 level tablespoons chopped blanched almonds, pecan nuts or walnuts

Preheat the oven to 180°C/350°F/Gas Mark 4/170°C with a fan oven. It is possible to cook the pudding in 6 to 8 individual soufflé dishes or 12 to 16 dariole moulds (castle pudding tins) or one 900 g/2 lb loaf tin, measuring 18 × 15 cm/7 × 6 inches (to give a good depth). Grease and flour the container(s).

Put the dates into a basin, add the boiling water and leave until cold. Cream the butter, sugar and essence. Whisk the eggs and gradually beat into the creamed mixture. Sift the flour, or flour and baking powder, add to the other ingredients with the dates and liquid. Spoon into the container(s). Add enough mixture to three-quarter fill soufflé dishes and dariole moulds (tap these firmly as the mixture is added).

Bake soufflés for 22 to 25 minutes, darioles for 15 to 18 minutes and the loaf for 35 to 40 minutes. Test by pressing firmly on top. Cool for 5 minutes before turning out.

Meanwhile make the sauce. Put the butter into a saucepan, melt over a low heat, add the sugar and stir until dissolved; pour in the cream and simmer for 3 minutes.

Cut the large pudding into portions then place these or the individual puddings into an ovenproof serving dish and coat with the hot sauce, return to the oven for 3 minutes, top with nuts and serve.

Variations: use light instead of dark brown sugar and sultanas instead of dates, moisten these with the boiling water. Omit the dates but use the same amount of water, which can be cold.

Steam the pudding(s) instead of baking them; allow 10 to 15 minutes longer cooking time for individual puddings and 25 to 30 minutes extra for a large pudding or cook in suitable containers in a microwave - check timing with manufacturer's manual.

Coffee Sticky Pudding: omit the essence; moisten the dates with moderately strong coffee instead of water.

Orange Sticky Pudding: omit the essence; add 1 teaspoon grated orange zest to the dates and moisten with boiling orange juice instead of water.

Page 8 - Queen Victoria (1819 - 1901) holds a garden party with members of her family in the grounds of Osborne House on the Isle of Wight, Hulton Getty Picture Library.

Page 9 - © Tab Anstice courtesy of Heligan Gardens Ltd.

Page 11 Breakfast Maid, 1900, Hulton Getty Picture Libarary.

Page 12 - National Gas Archive, BG Plc.

Page 13 - Automatic Tea Maker, 1904, Science Museum/ Science & Society Picture Library/ DOM/ B670104.

Page 44 (left) - Exotic Fruit - Due to potential potato famine, a market trader sells pineapples at a cheaper price than potatoes, 1917, Hulton Getty Picture Library.

Page 44 (right) - Greengrocer, Soho, 1907, Hulton Getty Picture Library.

Page 45 - Turkeys hanging in butchers shop ready for sale at Christmas, 1919, Hulton Getty Picture Library.

Page 46 - Beer Ration Card, 1918, Hulton Getty Picture Library.

Page 74 (left) - Christmas Dinner, 1919, Hulton Getty Picture Library.

Page 74 (right) - A meal of bread for a poverty stricken family in Shadwell in East London, 1920, Hulton Getty Picture Library.

Page 75 - The cocktail lounge. The epitome of sophistication - where one could get exotic mixtures such as a Gimlet, a Screwdriver, a White Lady, a Tom Collins, or even the humble Gin and It(alian), Hulton Getty Picture Library.

Page 76 - *Be-Ro Home Recipes Cookbook*, 6th Ed., published c.1928. First produced in 1923, the *Be-Ro Home Recipes Cookbook* has sold over 38 million copies to date. It is now in its 40th edition.

Page 102 - Waitresses, or 'nippies', at a Lyon's Corner House, London, on the first day of opening, 1939,

Hulton Getty Picture Library.

Page 103 (top) - A women working behind the bar of an English pub drinks a glass of beer, 1938, Hulton Getty Picture Library.

Page 103 (bottom left) - Page of a booklet advertising gifts for the kitchen, Science Museum/ Science & Society Picture Library/ DOM/ C200037.

Page 103 (bottom right) - ATORA Book of Olde Time Christmas Customs, Games and Recipes, published 1933.

Page 128 (left) - Jam Jar Tea - Service men and women being served tea in jam jars by the local WVS. The forces are passing through southern England on their way to camp, 1944, Hulton Getty Picture Library.

Page 128 (right) - Cake Rations - Hungry housewives bring their ration books to London's Petticoat Lane Market during World War II on the first day of bread rationing, 1946, Hulton Getty Picture Library.

Page 129 - War Food - People look at a basic menu while queuing to get into a makeshift canteen, 1940, Hulton Getty Picture Library.

Page 130 - 'The Housewife's Dream' market, 1941, Daily Herald Archive/ National Museum of Photography, Film & Television/SSPL/ WW2/ A006291.

Page 131 - Off Ration bread - A young girl leaving a bakers shop in Hornsey, London, after bread was sold off ration due to a strike by roundsmen, 1946, Hulton Getty Picture Library.

Page 156 (left) - Coffee Bar, Alex Dellow, 1955, Hulton Getty Picture Library.

Page 156 (right) - Milk Bar, 1950, Hulton Getty Picture Library.

Page 157 - Sunbeam 'Mixmaster' foodmixer, Science Museum/ Science & Society Picture Library/ DOM/ C100210.

Page 158 (left) - Formica Kitchen,

1954, Hulton Getty Picture Library.

Page 158 (right) - Electric Fridge, 1951, Hulton Getty Picture Library.

Page 192 - Comfort in the Home Exhibition, 1961, Hulton Getty Picture Library.

Page 193 - Automatic electric 'pop-up' toaster, Science Museum/ Science & Society Picture Library/ DOM/ C100205.

Page 194 - Spaghetti House, London, 1969, Hulton Getty Picture Library.

Page 195 - Safeway supermarket at East Ham, London, 1960, Jackson, Hulton Getty Picture Library.

Page 228 - Jenny Webb/ Microwave Association Archive.

Page 229 - The Aetherius Society Health Foods shop in Fulham, south west London, 1975, Hulton Getty Picture Library.

Page 231 - Delia Smith's Cookery Course Part One, BBC Publications.

Page 264 - Smallbone Kitchens.

Page 265 - Bibendum Restaurant, by kind permission of Conran Restaurants Ltd.

Page 266 - Oyster Bar, Bibendum Restaurant, by kind permission of Conran Restaurants Ltd.

Page 300 - © 1999 Stephen Hird, Old Spitalfields market.

Page 301 (left) - Planet Organic.

Page 301 (right) - Pret a Manger, by kind permission of Pret a Manger Ltd.

Page 303 - Quaglino's, by kind permission of Conran Restaurants Ltd.

Page 304 - Moshi Moshi Sushi, Tim MacPherson, The Anthony Blake Photography Library.